Michael Waddell

"SPEAK THAT I MAY SEE THEE!"

"SPEAK THAT I MAY SEE THEE!"

The Religious Significance of Language

By

Harold Stahmer

The Macmillan Company

NEW YORK

Library of Congress Catalog Card Number: 68-21305

FIRST PRINTING

The Macmillan Company, New York
Collier-Macmillan Canada Ltd., Toronto, Ontario

Printed in the United States of America

To
EUGEN,
Teacher and Friend,
in honor of his
eightieth birthday

Contents

Foreword

THE FOLLOWING MATERIAL deals with the religious significance of language, especially with the *spoken word*, as revealed in the writings of J. G. Hamann, Eugen Rosenstock-Huessy, Franz Rosenzweig, Martin Buber, and Ferdinand Ebner. With the exception of Hamann, all of those discussed began to occupy themselves with the problem of speech and communication either just prior to, during, or immediately after World War I. The last four men whose writings are discussed were either in constant touch with one another about the problem of language or, as in the case of Ebner, were familiar with one another's writings. In addition to the *Patmos Verlag*, periodicals such as the German publication *Die Kreatur* and the Austrian journal *Der Brenner* were frequently vehicles for publicizing their respective efforts. From one perspective these studies may be of interest to students of cultural history of this period. From another perspective, these studies may be of value to those interested in the thought of one or more of those whose writings are discussed, since it should soon become apparent that religious concern for language and dialogue was not an isolated phenomenon but rather a response to the cultural crises many experienced in Europe around the time of World War I. It is suggested that continued interest in these themes is due to similar problems in communication and spirituality cast in our contemporary idiom.

With the exception of the excellent historical and interpretative statements of men like Alexander Altmann, Arthur A. Cohen, Maurice Friedman, James O'Flaherty, Ronald Gregor Smith, and Georg Müller, most discussions of these themes and personalities have been by Europeans whose interests are either primarily doctrinal and theological, *e.g.*, the power and significance of *The*

[ix]

Word; or philosophical, *e.g.*, with *ontological* problems reflecting, for example, Martin Heidegger's influence. Although the format of this book betrays an indebtedness to elements from these traditions, it is hoped that the approach employed here has avoided focusing upon concerns associated with what Hamann long ago referred to as the Scylla and Charybdis of *theological* and *philosophical* approaches to language. Thus, Chapter 1 is an attempt to provide an alternate setting for considering the contributions of these men, and Chapter 7 is an attempt to evaluate their writings in the light of concerns that are decidedly more American than European in character. Some of the distinctiveness of this approach is reflected in the contributions of men like Amos Wilder, Eric Havelock, George Kennedy, Albert Lord, Cedric Whitman, and above all, Walter J. Ong, S.J. If in any sense this is a timely work, it is due to recent interest on the one hand by Marshall McLuhan, Buckminster Fuller, and others in communication in an electronic age, and on the other, in those theological writings devoted to dialogue, religionless Christianity, radical religion, and death-of-God themes. Although not written for theologians or even a necessarily religious audience, much that is discussed speaks to the issues raised by Dietrich Bonhoeffer, Amos Wilder, European hermeneutists, Bishop J. A. T. Robinson, Pierre Teilhard de Chardin, Ortega y Gasset, Harvey Cox, and William Hamilton. Hopefully, this book will be read by poets, speech teachers, and social workers; by those interested in literature and communication, as well as by those interested in religious, phenomenological, and existentialist themes.

For students of the thought of any one of these men, this book may serve to suggest unnoticed relationships between one man, his contemporaries, and their culture. Thus far a number of books and essays have been written about one or two of these personalities, but none, to the best of my knowledge, has attempted to deal with all of these men, much less from the perspective of a sacramental concern for speech and language.

The particular approach adopted here reflects the author's own biographical development, which began at Dartmouth College in 1948 as one of Eugen Rosenstock-Huessy's students. Of all those mentioned, Rosenstock-Huessy's influence was undoubtedly the most decisive in the adoption, shaping, and presentation of these themes. Not only through Rosenstock-Huessy, but through the in-

fluence of P. Caesarius Lauer, O.S.B., monk of the German Benedictine Abbey of Maria Laach, did I actually begin in 1951 to read
the writings of Hamann, Rosenzweig, Buber, and Ebner. While at
Union Theological Seminary, Wilhelm Pauck and Reinhold Niebuhr assisted in this development by supervising a B.D. thesis on the
Correspondence between Rosenstock-Huessy and Franz Rosenzweig. At Cambridge University, H. H. Farmer and J. A. T. Robinson made it possible for me to examine in detail the role of language
in Buber's writings. By way of an expression of indebtedness and
appreciation, may I say that this book would never have progressed
to this stage without the assistance, kind criticism, and counsel of
Eugen Rosenstock-Huessy, P. Caesarius Lauer, O.S.B., Wilhelm
Pauck, Martin Buber, Maurice Friedman, Walter J. Ong, S.J.,
Barry Ulanov, and many others. In different, but related and equally
important ways, had it not been for my father, my students, and
especially my wife's patience and tolerance, this book could never
have been completed.

One hopes that these studies will contribute to an understanding
and appreciation of the significance of the writings of these men,
and perhaps inspire others to add to and correct, where necessary,
those themes and issues treated here. Lastly, it is hoped that these
studies will enable people from all walks of life, especially those
outside the framework of institutional religion, to enhance their
respect for and confidence in the potentially sacred character of
human speech.

Pomona, New York
June 1967

"SPEAK THAT I MAY SEE THEE!"

The Power of Speech
in Oral and Aural Settings

Today we appear to be poised between two ages—one of detribalization and one of retribalization.

—MARSHALL McLUHAN

Voice is the foundation for role-playing among men in the sense that the use of voice and its understanding . . . forces man to enter into others.

—WALTER J. ONG, S.J.

Every phenomenon of nature was a word—the sign, symbol, and pledge of a new, inexpressible, but all the more intimate union, communication and community of divine energy and ideas. Everything that man heard in the beginning, saw with his eyes, contemplated, and his hands touched was a living word. With this word in his mouth and in his heart, the origin of language was as natural, as near, and as easy as child's play.

—JOHANN GEORG HAMANN

All things were made by the Word. In the beginning there was neither mind nor matter. In the beginning was the Word. St. John was properly the first Christian Theologian because he was overwhelmed by the spokenness of all meaningful happening.

—EUGEN ROSENSTOCK-HUESSY

Names are not intended to express the nature of things. . . . Their real task is not to describe things but to arouse human emotions; not to convey mere ideas or thoughts but to prompt men to certain actions.

—ERNST CASSIRER

We make deductions, as poets, as orators and as philosophers. The former are more often closer to reason than those in the logical form. When the heart speaks, our understanding is nothing but quibbling.

—JOHANN GEORG HAMANN

Language as the Lifeblood of Existence

ALTHOUGH SKETCHY, WHAT we do know about the earliest beginnings of language as rhetoric and communication confirms the essentially social nature of preliterate man and his dependence upon communication, if only in the form of gestures, rough ejaculatory noises, and the like. Perhaps more so than even today, the realization of the psychosomatic unity of man was accepted to the extent that every gesture, movement, and bodily odor was a vehicle for expressing danger, need, desire, satisfaction, or pleasure. From a later period, the antiphonal wooing of the lovers in the *Song of Solomon* and their fascination for the smell of love is an excellent illustration of this. "Because of the savor of thy good ointments thy name is an ointment poured forth, therefore do the virgins love thee," or ". . . how much better is thy love than wine! and the smell of thine ointments than all spices!"

A marriage counselor recently offered this relevant piece of wisdom: "The wiser we become, the more we pay attention to what people say without words—say with their eyes, muscles, body odors, skin temperatures, their habitual ways of moving, the tones of their voices." Despite the impersonal and complex nature of our society, we today hang on words and gestures in all their configurations and tones in much the same way as lovers from the beginning of time relied on a movement, a smile, an odor.

Since man's earliest beginnings—though the form of expression may have differed—he has relied upon communication in order to survive and shape the reality about him. In Defoe's *Robinson Crusoe*, Friday is taught to speak and is introduced to civilization not out of any sense of missionary zeal, but in order that his teacher might be relieved of the intolerable burden of loneliness. Until Friday's arrival, Crusoe would race daily to the Valley of the Echoes where upon a mountaintop he would yell repeatedly in order to hear another voice—albeit but the echo of his own. Though the way of the spirit changes with time and necessity, it has forever been a fact that truth, meaning, and existence are garbed in the power of some form of communication. Rabbi Heschel notes this when he says: "We shall never be able to understand that the spirit is revealed in the form of words unless we discover the vital truth that speech has power, that words are commitments."[1]

Job knew this when he asked, "Is there any wrong on my tongue? Cannot my taste discern calamity?" and later when he said, "But it is the spirit in a man, the breath of the Almighty that makes him understand."

In order to grasp what is meant by speech, we might note that in French and German, for example, there is a word for language (*langage* and *Sprache*) as well as for the spoken word (*parole* and *Rede*). The most common meaning of language refers to the more than four thousand tongues that are spoken on this planet. Similarly, speech refers to the oral form of a particular language. Generically, however, man is human to the extent that he is capable of *speech*— of speaking in a particular tongue, which is his means of establishing his social identity. Thus, language consists of more than simply the tongue one speaks—English, French, or German. Language is our historical and social identity card, and speech, the spoken word, is the means whereby we vote as members of the human race. The fact that all men have a language and all are capable of speech also means that when we speak as Americans, as Russians, as Germans, as Frenchmen, we do so at the same time as members of the human race, with all the obligations, responsibilities, rights, and privileges that entails. Human speech is therefore the means whereby humanity can transcend national allegiances and be either linked together or torn asunder. When the dominant speech and value patterns of a particular tongue ring out with sounds that threaten our essential humanity, we are often forced, as World War II proved, to fight on behalf of human speech—to be willing, if need be, to die, on behalf of the freedom of speech which is our sacred tie with God and His creation.

The speech-dependent view of reality presented here parallels closely that of the Biblical view of reality, which was also governed by *davar*, the word.[2] Our interest is not, however, with assertions about the Bible as normative for all times and aspects of the human condition, but rather with the seriousness with which, during various historical periods, men regarded certain events as crucial or sacred because significant speech had taken place. This view enables us to regard such events as having the same sacred quality as was recognized among Biblical men without denigrating the testimonies of our own linguistic experience.

Unfortunately, throughout history men have insisted, as was popular at the turn of the century, that "Language is the expression of

human thought by means of words." This is a one-sided and emascu-
lated view of language because it relegates speech and language to
the ancillary role of the mind's handmaid without once asking the
simple question, "What is the source of the mind's knowledge?"
This travesty on speech, committed in the name of the many gods
of scientists, scholars, and educators, whether it be empiricism,
knowledge, fact, or objectivity, is still the accepted view of language by many professional educators, including teachers of speech
and language. In an oft-cited classic among professional elementary
and secondary school educators, *Taxonomy of Educational Objectives*, it is significant that the authors' hierarchical classification begins with knowledge rather than with either the sources of knowledge or the selective principle employed in determining what it is
that shall be taught as knowledge.[3] Related to this misunderstanding
is the unwarranted assumption that the written word is somehow
more trustworthy and, in some sense, truer than the spoken. This is
maintained despite the fact that only 5 per cent of the world's
languages have a written counterpart. Few moderns realize that the
art of writing was at first nothing more than a means of keeping
trading records among Sumerians and Egyptians about five thousand
years ago. This is significant in view of the fact that man existed as a
social creature for at least five hundred thousand years before he
discovered the art of recording knowledge by means of visual symbols inscribed upon or impressed in papyrus or clay. In any society,
whether preliterate, literate, or that of our own electronic age, it is
some mode of the spoken word that determines *what* it is that shall
be remembered, taught, or programmed. Someone has to tell, in-
struct, order, or command before we know what it is that shall be
offered up in any given age upon the high altar of knowledge.
Consciously or unconsciously our intellects have always been servants of speech and not vice versa. We think, we speak, because we
have first been spoken to, addressed.

"No man is an island unto himself," said John Donne. Where this
is known to have happened—as in the cases of children isolated and
deprived of speech and social contact, or those reared among wild
animals—such individuals never fully achieved their potential humanity. This is true not merely of isolated cases, such as Wild Peter
of Hanover, or the wolf-girls of India, and Kamala and Amola in
1920, but bears directly upon a disease among children known as

marasmus, a Greek term meaning "wasting away," which generally afflicts them in their first year of life, and which, until forty years ago, accounted for more than half the deaths in that age group. Isolation in the form of lack of motherly love and affection was found responsible for this atrophy. Even with the best of care, the ability to speak was retarded or slow in developing. As Margaret Ribble's studies indicate, it is impossible to overestimate the importance to the total development of the infant of caressing, singing, speaking, rocking, and fondling.[4] Note the bearing upon the foregoing of a recent statement by a psychologist about the connection between language and consciousness:

"Reality" becomes a meaningful part of consciousness only through the interpretation of reality-contents by language. The importance of auditory experiences for the interpretation of reality is proven through observation of deaf children. . . . A world without sound is a dead world: when sound is eliminated from our experience, it becomes clear how inadequate and ambiguous is the visual experience if not accompanied by auditory interpretation. . . . Vision alone without acoustic perceptions does not provide understanding. Deaf persons are prone to paranoid interpretations of outside events.[5]

In the adult world it is by means of speech and those stylistic forms that originate in speech that a civilization comes into being, history becomes a fact, and men become conscious of time. Through speech the past may be affirmed and continued into the present, or it may be terminated by virtue of the power inherent in new speech patterns. Speech, as Rosenstock-Huessy has developed it in his *grammatical* approach, "is the power to frame an act as being the communal experience of two different people, and yet one act of either one of them." He illustrates this with reference to the story in Hinduism about the son who is commanded by the father: "Break this twig!" and who must respond: "Father, the twig is broken." These two separate sentences, consisting of imperative and response, constitute two phases of a temporal event—one before, one after the act. One purpose of grammar, which for Rosenstock-Huessy is the lifeblood of speech, is that it "identifies the tenses through which the same event passes in human experience." In this instance imperative and response determine the meaningfulness and content of time; they determine whether something has occurred which should or should not be remembered by a tribe or society.[6]

To believe in a future that can be more than a mere casual projection of past events into the tomorrow is to believe in the transforming power of speech. To believe that our lives can have significance beyond death and the grave is to know that our words and names are able to survive us and live in other persons and institutions. Through speech we are conscious that life has significance that antedates birth and overcomes death. Through song, one of the oldest forms of speech—through, for example, the chanting of "We Shall Overcome"—men are bound together in their attempts to wipe out oppression, discrimination, and poverty—all forms of man's inhumanity toward his fellowman.[7] Through song and powerful rhetoric we usher in new ages and human conditions, and create new value systems. Through speech we have the possibility of realizing that for which we have hoped. To overcome one time sense and to create a new time sense, a new eon, is inherent in the privilege and power of speaking.

There are those who will resist accepting such an assertion on the grounds that for them "time is time"—*e.g.*, an absolute with which no mortal can tamper. It is a truism that most men associate time with chronos—with a sense of absolute chronological time—*e.g.*, with what happened in the twelfth, thirteenth, or seventeenth century. Indeed, the structuring of many college and university courses in the humanities reflects this reverence for a chronological time sense without much mention of the fact that several other time senses have determined what it is that shall constitute the substance and content in retrospect of these centuries. Since the concern of many, if not most, critical and objective historians is with evidence —*e.g.*, with *written* recorded history—the speech-conditioned time sense of those who have determined the content of human recorded history is accorded, from the perspective of the twentieth century, the subordinate and, implicitly, less trustworthy role of mythical time. Few critical historians seem to appreciate the fact that just as speech precedes thinking, so too, speech-conditioned time and speech-conditioned space determine what it is that shall become part of Western man's autobiography.

What we refer to as history would be an empty shell were it not for the wide variety of time-oriented ideologies and mythologies which have guided men's private and corporate existences from the very beginnings of human tribal life until now. The writings of

Mircea Eliade and others have shown how deeply ingrained in Western man's heritage is this respect for sacred times and sacred spaces. What Eliade and some of those involved in history-of-religions studies seem to have overlooked, however, is the extent to which this tribal mentality is still part of our modern mentality despite the fact that traditional sacred/profane distinctions are being universally questioned, and despite Eliade's regret that modern Western man takes seriously terms like faith and history.[8] Although we no longer appear to respect traditional fixed forms of sacred speech, which were felt to bring about a sense of the holiness of certain kinds of time and space, it does not follow that modern tribal man no longer regards certain speech patterns and tones as sacred or sacramental. Those concerned with hermeneutics (problems of interpretation) are acutely aware that men in every age attach special significance to certain stylistic speech patterns despite the fact that many hermeneuticists still appear more at home with the written than with the spoken word.

The Re-emergence of Tribalism in an Electronic Era

IF WE DISCARD terms like modern man or the modern mind and focus rather upon our existence as tribal man, it may be easier for us to recover our respect for the spoken word and those written styles that have arisen in response to those who, like J. G. Hamann, have gnawed continually upon the bone of speech. All too frequently we assume that to live in the twentieth century requires that we discard all our links with the past—even those ties that identify us as *humans* in the generic sense. We fail to realize at the juncture of the conclusion of a mechanical technological age and the beginning of a computer or electronically oriented age that we still have recognizable tribal ties and customs that are uniquely ours and not merely holdovers from the past. Whereas the mechanical technology through which we are passing "exerted a fragmentary force, psychically and socially," just the reverse will be true in an electric age of circuitry. This is Marshall McLuhan's thesis; "Today we appear to be poised between two ages—one of detribalization and one of retribalization."[9] Tribal existence is a particularly important theme for us today for many reasons. Whenever the term is used it usually implies that human succession and the transmission of cultural mores and values are serious considerations. Tribal life historically has meant just the opposite of barbaric existence. A sense not only of the relevance but of the nobility of tribal life for today was described by Eugen Rosenstock-Huessy, one of those whose preoccupation with speech occasioned originally the writing of this book. In an essay entitled *Tribalism* he said:

> We are entering now a thousand year period in which the rudiments of tribalism will serve us as a refresher course, for the family is destroyed today and speech is destroyed today; and speech and the family, being the creations of the tribes, we will find again at their fountainhead, where they were most intensified, because it is there they were first created.[10]

To live in a tribe means that there is a respect for law and order, for peaceful means of discarding the old in the light of new situations and problems. To live as a member of a tribe means above all that our social and religious life is guided by speech patterns which determine what it is that we shall one day remember as history—*i.e.*, as important, if not sacred. Each tribe has its own code of conduct and way of life which language betrays. The term language as used in this context denotes that which is most alive in a group's existence. And by its very nature language automatically signifies that which concerns a people. Language, in this context, is the shaper of reality—it carves out and creates the milieu for a people's existence. Thus, language is a mighty power, a force, a tool. Within tribal life, language is never a neutral or lifeless substance. Furthermore, in tribal life the *spoken* word rather than the *written* or other forms is the dominant force. One might be tempted to use the phrase *a people's rhetoric* to denote this force, were it not for the fact that the history of the *trivium* and general usage have often caused the term *rhetoric* to fall into disrepute as something artificial and stilted. Language within the context of tribal life means speech, from which evolves all other cultural and linguistic configurations of the tribe. In a tribal setting, speech is more than a single linguistic concern— such as the sacred or religious. This is Eugen Rosenstock-Huessy's point when he says that:

> To speak . . . means more than to be a scientist or a poet or a demogague or a narrator. It means to insist on the essential unity of all

these four types of language. They all are needed, they all interpret each other. It is nonsense to believe that the scientist or the historian or the politician or the poet alone can know the truth. The truth is in the man who can speak all four languages with sincerity by using one and the same materials for all, and who does not disrupt the unity of speech by running away into a merely scientific, a merely poetical, a merely petrified or a merely revolutionary language.[11]

That which is singled out as the sacred as against the profane is itself conditioned and shaped by the tribe's total linguistic experience. Speech embraces all the manifold utterances possible to each member—son, husband, father, friend, worker, and so on. The interrelatedness of those roles is not only the best clue as to the tribe's style, but it automatically suggests that no single role makes any sense when viewed apart from its relationship with all the other roles. Tribalism is a dynamic concept which enables us to make sense out of the larger social fabric both in terms of the present as well as in terms of our links with the past and our views and hopes about the future. The tribal background also enables us to give speech the recognition it deserves as *the* force *par excellence* in determining a people's destiny.

One reason for infrequent references to tribal existence today is that the basis for the fragmented classified approach to life, which marks a highly technologically oriented society such as ours, appears at cross-purposes practically as well as theoretically with the salient characteristics of tribal life. One interpretation might be that this indicates the phasing out of tribal life as Western man gradually matures. Another interpretation, which I find more congenial, is that this hiatus only illustrates some of the important shortcomings, with respect to a totally unified life, that mark existence in a mechanical technological society. For some, the advent of a computer age will only heighten this disparity and complete the phasing out of tribalism. Concern over the impersonal aspects and effects of auto-instructional teaching devices upon students is just one example. As noted earlier, there are others today who view the passing of a mechanical technological society and the advent of an electronically oriented one as marking a definite return to many aspects of tribal life. In his address at Vision 65 Marshall McLuhan said that in an electronic age we will find ourselves "playing the tape backward." He was referring to the tape that recorded human development from "tribal man to individual man."[12] In an electronic age we will find ourselves playing the tape in reverse; we will see ourselves moving from a mechanical technological society geared to the individual to one that stresses tribal characteristics. In an electronic era of computerized knowledge and pattern recognition we are moving away from the classification of knowledge and data that resulted from the technology of the written word. He suggested that this time men will enter the tribal environment aware even of the possibility of liquidating the unconscious.

> . . . we could quickly reach a state in which we had no unconscious. This would be like dreaming awake. Such may well be the prophetic meaning of *Finnegans Wake* by James Joyce: his idea . . . that tribal man lived a dream and modern man is "back again Finnegan" into the cycle of the tribal involvement, but this time awake.[13]

In *Understanding Media: The Extensions of Man*, Professor Mc-Luhan discusses the salient features and new vocabulary of what, for lack of a better term, I choose to call tribal-electronic man. Similar characterizations were reflected in the other addresses delivered at Vision 65, a conference held in 1965 at Southern Illinois University and sponsored by The International Center for the Communication Arts and Sciences. For example, according to Professor McLuhan, awareness and dialogue are "cool" terms appropriate to an electronic environment where the stress is upon pattern recognition rather than on understanding classified data and fragments of information as is common in a technological era. He states that our children ". . . grow up in an electronically configured world . . . a world not of wheels but of circuits, not of fragments but of integral patterns." Whereas our students live "mythically and in depth" they are confronted in the classroom with "classified information . . . visually conceived in terms of a blueprint."[14] Under such conditions the student in the classroom, having no sense of involvement comparable to that in everyday group life, experiences a sense of estrangement and irrelevance about the educational process and frequently drops out. One remedy McLuhan suggests is that education be "programmed for discovery rather than instruction." He warns us that "we would be foolish not to ease our transition from the fragmented visual world of existing educational establishment by every possible means."[15]

The contrast presented between education geared to pattern recognition rather than data classification is captured in his remarks such as those about the meaning of the slang word "cool" as used by today's young people. For most adults a cool attitude refers to "one of detached objectivity and disinterestedness." However, among today's youths just the opposite is true. Cool ". . . indicates a kind of commitment and participation in situations that involve all of one's faculties." Hence, automation is cool "whereas the older mechanical kinds of specialist or fragmented 'jobs' are 'square.' " A square is one who cannot totally involve his powers and faculties in a given situation. Jokes, for example, are rarely cool, since they incline "us to laugh *at* something instead of getting us empathetically involved *in* something."[16]

In an age accustomed to separating reality into subjects and objects—one which prides itself in its ability to view things in isolation and detachment—the implications of the electronic revolution are bound to come as a bit of a shock to many. For example, it has been customary for students to regard with considerable skepticism, if not amusement, the suggestion that in the mythopoeic tribal mentality of the ancient Near East one viewed objects, like trees and even salt, as persons—as *Thous*. Or when presenting Martin Buber's I-Thou approach to the life of dialogue, it is exceedingly difficult for modern technological man to grasp what Buber means by the realm of the there-in-between I and Thou. Now, suddenly, on the threshold of an electronic age, we hear communications specialists refer to man's dialogue with computing and programming machines. In an electronic age many of the key themes and motifs common to earlier tribal existence are being reintroduced—particularly many of those generally associated with the ancient Near East, with Semitic culture, and with Homeric antiquity.

After reading the twenty-five papers delivered at Vision 65, one sensed that the cool terms among those interested in communication in the arts and sciences are equally cool among those interested in the religious significance of human speech, in speech thinking and the life of dialogue. Both groups, for example, assume that style is a creative force in shaping one's environment and culture; both groups are concerned with relational living, with the effect of external address—*i.e.*, the medium as the message—upon our oral and aural powers; both have delved into questions pertaining to the origin of language; and both are quite at home with the dynamic relativism inherent in the views of men like Homer, Heracleitus, Bergson, or Whitehead. Each side has recognized the need to do away with fragmented and classified approaches to learning, which mark a mechanical technological society and are creations of what McLuhan earlier referred to as the "technology of the written word." Implicit in this is a common renewed respect for the spoken word, which "involves all of the senses dramatically" as well as a drastic de-emphasis upon our visual powers, which play such a prominent role in the present technological period.

Lastly, each has looked upon the effects of the fragmented approach to reality—*i.e.*, the subject-object distinction, as inadequate and obsolete. For example, men like Emil Brunner, Martin Buber, Rollo May, and Ludwig Binswanger are unanimous in their agreement with A. A. Bowman, who long ago said that "The tacit assumption that experience is all of the subject-object type has played havoc with much European philosophy."[17]

More recently Rollo May defined existentialism as "the endeavor to understand men by cutting below the cleavage between subject and object which has bedeviled Western thought and science since shortly after the Renaissance."[18] Ludwig Binswanger described the "cancer of all psychology" as "the cancer of the doctrine of subject-object cleavage of the world."[19] In the Biblical field, Emil Brunner stated that "The Biblical understanding of truth cannot be grasped through the Object-Subject antithesis: on the contrary it is falsified through it."[20] Particularly relevant for our purposes is Buber's contrast: "The duality of I and Thou finds its fulfillment in the religious relationship; the duality of subject and object sustains philosophy while it is carried on. . . . I and Thou exist in and by means of lived concreteness; subject and object, products of abstraction, last only as long as that power is at work."[21]

Even with these remarks about the relevance of tribal mores to an electronic era, it is obviously not suggested that, for example, all of ancient man's ways are to be reintroduced without their being subjected to updatings and modifications appropriate to the times. The papers devoted to "the electronic revolution" delivered at Vision 65 are especially worth reading by all those whose interests are primarily religious and theological, and especially by those within this group concerned about the role of the word and human speech not only in a post-Christian age but also in a computer age. Somehow, the ferment and revolutions occurring in religious circles will have some bearing upon, and naturally, be affected by, the computer revolution in an electronic age. In the same breath it should be said that those more at home in a computer atmosphere and also lacking in philosophical and religious sophistication or concern may find the interest in the word and speech of those personalities discussed in this book a complement to their scientific interests in communication. Perhaps both revolutions, the theological as well as the electronic, will be regarded by an increasing number of individuals as manifestations of the word for those on the threshold of a new cultural millennium.

Regardless of whether men live in a preliterate, literate, technological, or electronic age, few would deny that the dynamics of human speech and human communication will determine where we humans go and how we proceed, whatever our cultural mentality. The spoken word today, as in every age, is the direction finder, the spark, the key to human progress and development. The Athenian orator, Isocrates, (436–338 B.C.) knew well the power of the art of discourse as that which shapes reality and determines the content of history. Isocrates said that:

> We ought, therefore, to think of the art of discourse just as we think of the other arts, and not to form opposite judgments about similar things, or show ourselves intolerant toward that power which, of all the faculties which belong to the nature of man, is the source of most of our blessings. . . . generally speaking, there is no institution devised by man which the power of speech has not helped us to establish. . . . in all our actions as well as in all our thoughts speech is our guide, and is most employed by those who have the most wisdom.[22]

Speech in the context of any age provides the valuation which will determine how our technological or electronic know-how can best be applied—whether to destroy mankind, or to create an enduring and meaningful social order.

The balance of this chapter will be devoted to a presentation of a number of themes characteristic of tribal societies, particulary those in the ancient Near East, in Biblical and pre-Biblical times as well as during the Homeric and Platonic periods. An examination of these themes, especially those that bear upon the importance of speech, of our oral and aural powers, of names, history, and time will serve as an introduction and background to the contributions of J. G. Hamann, Eugen Rosenstock-Huessy, Franz Rosenzweig, Martin Buber, and Ferdinand Ebner. It is hoped that the introductory remarks about tribal existence in an electronic age will add to the importance that many already, particularly in Europe, have attributed to the works of these men. The American religious climate today warrants a serious examination of these writings not only because of our inescapable participation in all forms of social and scientific revolutions (the electronic being but one) but also because of current interest in the writings of Dietrich Bonhoeffer, Bishop Robinson, Paul Tillich, Harvey Cox, William Hamilton, and Thomas J. J. Altizer. For those concerned about the shape of spirituality in the Johannine Age, for those interested in religionless Christianity, radical theology, and hermeneutics, the writings of our dialogicians and speech-thinkers may be especially relevant.

The Oral and Aural Climate of the Ancient Near East and Israel

ANCIENT MAN STOOD in awe of language. Language for him was spirit, being, reality—a powerful force in his life. Throughout Assyria, Babylonia, Egypt, the early West, and the ancient Orient, language—the word, and not only the Divine Word—was creative energy, a dynamic force. Words had the power to produce events rather than, as for most moderns, merely to describe them or articulate private thoughts. The same was especially true for ancient Israel. Hamann's disciple, Herder, dealt at length on this theme in his essay *The Spirit of Hebrew Poetry, an Introduction for Lovers of the Same and of the Most Ancient History of the Human Spirit.* Compare, for example, verses from the prophets Isaiah and Jeremiah with those from the great bidding prayer to Marduk-Ellil:

> For as the rain and the snow come down from heaven,
> and return not thither but water the earth,
> making it bring forth and sprout,
> giving seed to the sower and bread to the eater,
> so shall my word be that goes forth from my mouth;

it shall not return to me empty,
but it shall accomplish that which I purpose,
and prosper in the thing for which I sent it.

—ISAIAH 55:10

Is not my word like fire, says the Lord,
and like a hammer which breaks the rock in pieces?

—JEREMIAH 23:29

  3 His word, which proceeds like a storm . . .
12—13 The word which destroys the heavens above
14—15 The word which shakes the earth beneath
20—21 His word is a rushing torrent against which there is no
      resistance
24—25 His word destroys the mother with child like a reed
32—33 The word of Marduk is a flood that breaches the dam
34—35 His word breaks off great mesu-trees
36—37 His word is a storm bringing everything to destruction
60—61 His word, when it goes about gently, destroys the land.[23]

Though the imagery may vary—in Assyria and Babylonia the
word is like a strong wind; in Egypt, a corporeal emanation—the
word is looked upon as the sustaining force behind natural, spiritual,
and cosmic processes. It had an independent power capable of de-
structive consequences not only when uttered by the deity or ruler
but when used as a weapon between families. For example, take
the case of the power of curses and blessings. A curse was so objectively real for primitive man that when father and son engaged their
enemy in combat, the father often threw his son to the ground to
avoid his son's being struck by his opponent's curse. Ancient man,
like the later prophets of Israel, "treated the curses . . . just like the
blast of a bomb." One ducks, hides, shields oneself, in order not to
be struck by them.

A solitary Benedictine monk, occupying the hermitage of the late
founder of the Society of Little Brothers, Père Charles de Foucald,
in the desolate Hogar Plateau in Algeria, once described the sense of
communion he felt with God and the universe, mediated by the
sounds of the desert winds, which he likened to the breath and
Spirit of God. It is a good example for us moderns of the sensitivity
men have had for the way in which the Spirit reveals itself in the
animate quality of the universe. Early man was unable to look upon

his words as symbols, as designations or representations of a higher reality. The word, speech, language, for them was identical with reality, and men partook in the unity of the universe to the extent that they were capable of speech and aware of its dramatic, concrete powers. Against this setting, man does not control speech; rather speech literally seizes a man.

Throughout the ancient Near East the universe was personal and alive. What we moderns would refer to as the things and objects around us had a personal existence for early man equal to his own. Andrew Lang's disapproving characterization of this situation is most apt. He referred to "that inextricable confusion in which men, beast, plants, stones, stars, are all on one level of personality and animated existence." For a Mesopotamian, ordinary kitchen salt is never merely a mineral and inanimate substance, but rather a source of help, another person, whose aid could be invoked should one fall under the spell of witchcraft and sorcery. Thus the petition:

> O Salt, created in a clean place,
> For food of gods did Enlil destine thee.
> Without thee no meal is set out in Ekur,
> Without thee no god, king, lord, and prince
>   do not smell incense.
> I am so-and-so, the son of so-and-so,
> Held captive by enchantment,
> Held in fever by bewitchment.
> O Salt, break my enchantment! Loose my spell!
> Take from the bewitchment!—And as my Creator
> I shall extol thee.[24]

The foundations of Western civilization, in both the ancient Near East and the Hellenic world, have their origins in a mentality that looked upon reality as essentially personal and dominated by ancient man's reliance upon his oral and aural powers. The phenomena of reality confronted men in terms of speech and address—as *I* and *Thou*. Hence, the characterization of the ancient oral mentality as mythopoeic—where myth as a form of poetry is the means whereby early man's memorable encounters with the phenomena of reality were shaped and preserved. Ancient man was absolutely incapable of the kind of impersonal reflection and distance from reality that characterize the more modern logical, scientific, and mechanical mentality. The ability to understand reality by distinguishing between the perceiver and the thing perceived—by dividing reality into subject and object, or appearance and reality—in a word, to look upon reality as an It, was totally unknown to ancient man. Understanding for the mythopoeic mentality was an activity of involvement and identification which in most cases especially involved men's aural powers. With respect to the Jew of antiquity, Martin Buber said: "We may state it thus, that the Jew of antiquity was more acoustically oriented (*Ohrenmensch*) than visually (*Augenmensch*), and more temporally oriented (*Zeitmensch*) than spatially (*Raummensch*). Of all his senses he relied most heavily upon his hearing when forming his picture of the universe."[25]

In the ancient Near East the force of the king or suzerain's word, his command, was regarded as the power that conditioned and shaped social existence. In every one of those communities founded upon the suzerainty-type covenant, the suzerain's word was like the womb from which a nation's life poured forth. It controlled and permeated, but still transcended, all the individual languages, whether of soldier, statesman, or priest. Ultimately it gave unity and meaning to their individual roles, and none could speak meaningfully apart from its influence and without the king's command and blessing.[26]

Among the Israelites Yahweh is distinguished from the nearby nature gods not only as the transcendent One who immanently speaks creation into existence, but as the One who singles out a particular creature to be fashioned after His own image and likeness and permits His creatures to partake in the Word. Their partnership or covenant was established upon their respective abilities to converse and co-operate with one another in the task of creation. The relationship between Creator and creature among the Israelites follows the suzerainty-type covenant to the extent that without God's Word—without the sustaining power of *davar*—men would wither and die, and human history would become meaningless. Hence the prophet is a *nabi*, literally a "mouthpiece" of God, who warns, persuades, cajoles, and ultimately provides direction for Israel's destiny. However, unlike Egypt, for example, the quality of the divine-human covenant is such that men are able to respond to or, as with Job, to resist God's word and contend with Him.

Davar is derived from a form meaning simply "speak," although some scholars contend that it is originated from a stem meaning "to be behind and drive forward." *Davar* also means "deed" and "event," the deed or event being the natural consequence of the word that is spoken. Goethe, in the poodle scene in *Faust*, says "In the beginning was the deed," rather than the word, which suggests better than "word" for the modern mind the powerful ramifications of a word spoken out of the divine-human partnership. *Davar* has significance as word and event only if we look at it not as a single word or single unit of speech but rather in the context of a situation. Thus Buber writes: "Not things, but situations are primary. Out of different situations of different kinds that early man experiences emerge similar, so-to-speak similar-remaining, things and beings, events and states that want to be conceived as such, named as such."[27]

At the beginning of Israel's history *davar* serves as a kind of seal or testimony of an encounter between God and His creatures or between two or more living creatures. Thus, *davar* cannot be translated simply as "word" unless we realize that whenever spoken, *davar* signifies a happening, a situation that is spoken into existence. The exact process whereby the divine *davar* and human speech are blended remains for all practical purposes a mystery. Human speech is permeated with that which, in one sense, is nonhuman, and yet there is no definite way of distinguishing between human speech which partakes of the creative word and that which is not permeated with this sacramental quality. *Davar* is, Biblically speaking, a constant instrument of revelation, wherein, as Buber writes, ". . . the human substance is melted by the divine fire which visits it, and there now breaks forth from it a word, a statement, which is human in its meaning and form, human conception and human speech, and yet witnesses to Him who stimulated it and His will. We are revealed to ourselves—and cannot express it otherwise than as something revealed."[28] Against the oriental and Israelitic backgrounds, which stress the pervasive character of the divine word, it is more correct to say that man is seized by the word than to say that man possesses the word. Speech, in this setting, is like the *ruah Yahweh*, the Spirit of God, which possesses man and pervades every fiber of his creatureliness. "*Davar* is Yahweh as he is recognizable to mortal man."[29]

Davar is also the key to Biblical man's recognition of concrete spiritual time and space. We know that his awareness of time and

space differed decidedly from our own, but what we seldom understand is the degree to which holy events (time) and places (spaces)
were created where a holy action or conversation had occurred
between God and His people. A particular time or place is significant because significant acts occurred there and then between God
and His people, and these deeds needed to be retold in order for
their lives to have individual and collective meaning and direction.
Speech not only makes a particular time or place worth remembering; speech also creates memorable times and memorable places. The
early Israelite depended upon his speech in order that the tomorrow
become incorporated into the divine-human spatiotemporal consciousness, as signified by the importance of memory. Without significant words uttered, conscious of the divine-human partnership,
there would be little worth remembering of the day and place except, perhaps, that it might have been an occasion so ignominious
that man could not forget his waywardness, his vanity, and his
pride, which were responsible for creating what took place. Here
the curse of memory enters in, and man remembers the words uttered apart from the divine-human partnership. He feels the misery
and curse of his solitariness; he bears the cross of isolation and
despair. For such an individual, tomorrow's words must redeem
today's sins. Though able to sin, the Israelite could hope that the
tomorrow might be God's, that his speech might not be as today's.

For the early Israelite, time was concrete, filled with content.
Time and space as abstractions were unknown to Biblical man. He
would not have known, for example, the meaning of Macbeth's
statement, "Come what come may, Time and the hour runs through
the roughest day." Pedersen states that "the colourless idea of
'hour', measuring time in a purely quantitative way, is far from the
old Israelite conception."[30] There were three divisions in a day—
morning, noon, and evening (Jer. 6:4), and the year was known by
its seasons and seed and harvest periods. The Feast of Unleavened
Bread was significant not for its being a natural annually recurrent
agricultural event, but rather because at that time the Exodus, a holy
event in the lives of Jews, took place. Similarly, the Feast of Weeks
occurring during spring harvest is important because it was associated with the giving and receiving of the Torah on Sinai. Hence the
Jews have become identified not with a cyclical view of time but
with a sense of the irreversibility of time rooted in significant events

that took place at a specific time in a specific place and constitute the spiritual history of Jews. Memory, "Remember O Israel!" is an admonition not to forget the significant words spoken, the covenants made, the declarations proclaimed, which have become associated with Israel's name. Memory, name, events, times and timing, Holy Places, and covenants are all related to sacramental speech. Thus, God's Word, His *davar*, was not exclusively His; it belonged to those with whom He had made a covenant. Their speech, their actions, partook of His *davar*, His Word. To the outsider, the early Israelite might well be regarded as a member of a chorus of holy voices whose statements are seemingly discordant and contradictory. However, for the insider, these voices contain a divine melody that only those can appreciate who have the curse and the blessing of memory, and the awful privilege of having their words determine their destiny by speaking and singing new times and new places into existence.

Throughout the oral climate of the ancient Near East, whether in Egypt or in Israel, neither men nor animals are fully recognized as creatures until a *name* is bestowed upon them. The powers possessed by an individual were regarded as gifts bestowed upon one who is essentially unworthy of them. To be given an order by a representative of the authoritative word was a sign of favor, since it meant that one's name was recognized: hence, one's existence was meaningful. To be excluded from assigned tasks and responsibilities was ignominious, since it meant in effect that one's name, and therefore one's person, had no significance. For an Egyptian, Accadian, Sumerian, or Israelite, the very notion of not having a name sent chills up one's spine. As Professor Wilson has noted, "The utterance of a name is in itself an act of creation." Among Egyptian literature, the interior dialogue carried on by the would-be suicide illustrates this admirably. On the one hand, he recognized that he was nothing, and yet he realized that he dared not tamper with his life for fear of endangering that which had been bestowed upon him and gave him value—namely, his name. In contemplating giving himself over to a life of pleasure, he worries about the effect of this act upon his good name:

> Behold, my *name* will reek through thee
>   More than the stench of fishermen,
>   More than the stagnant swamps where they have fished.

Behold, my *name* will reek through thee
More than the stench of bird droppings,
On summer days when the sky is hot.[31]

Although it was certainly true that the universal concreteness of primitive symbolism suggested that *pars pro toto*, a part can stand for the whole—a lock of hair, a shadow, could represent the whole individual—names were of a higher order. Among Egyptians, as is true in any age, to destroy or to malign one's name was equivalent to destroying the person. For the Egyptian kings of the Middle Kingdom, one destroyed one's enemy simply by inscribing pottery bowls with the names of one's enemy and then smashing them during an appropriate ritual. In our own time, without the inscribing and smashing of bowls, there have been many who have known the effect upon one's person of having one's name maligned. Ernst Cassirer summed up the significance of names when he said, "Names are not intended to express the nature of things. . . . Their real task is not to describe things but to arouse human emotions; not to convey mere ideas or thoughts but to prompt men to certain actions."[32]

A glance at the Genesis narrative of man's creation quotes God as saying, "Let us make man in our image (*tselem*), after our likeness (*demuth*). . . . So God created man in his own image, in the image of God he created him." (Genesis 1:26–27) Despite the injunctions to man against making images and likenesses of God, God creates man in His own image and likeness. According to Professor Heschel, "Human life is holy, holier even than the Scrolls of the Torah. Its holiness is not man's achievement, it is a gift of God rather than attained through merit. Man must, therefore, be treated with the honor due to a likeness representing the King of Kings."[33] Or as Thorleif Boman put it, "With the aid of *imago dei* God gives man his stamp and thereby puts his seal upon his creation."[34] In the Bible, in Genesis, for example, man is not complete until a name is bestowed upon him. Each *imago dei* bears a unique name, the importance of which is attested to by the frequent genealogical passages throughout the Bible. In Genesis it is Adam, a concrete individual as well as humanity, who is the first *imago dei* mentioned.

According to Franz Rosenzweig, Adam becomes self-conscious and fully aware of his actions when God first calls him by his name. The condition and limitation of Adam's status is determined by his responding to an external address. A man becomes "enthused" (*en-*

theo), fully divine, and human, when he admits the priority of Thou over I and the impossibility of separating the I from relationship signified by his bearing a name. Our authentic spiritual grammar might rather begin, as Rosenstock-Huessy contends, with the recognition that Thou rather than I is Adam's first real grammatical posture. Martin Buber touches upon the same theme (without reference to names, however) in *I and Thou*, in his discussion of the Inborn Thou in the child and the child's early efforts to establish relation as signified by the outstretched hand. Thus, the importance of the mythical saying of the Jews, "In the mother's body man knows the universe, in birth he forgets it."[35] To be conscious of one's name in Genesis is to be at once aware of the relational character of all existence.

To the responsibility of bearing a name is added the privilege of naming—a sign of man's true partnership with God in the shaping of creation. "And out of the ground the Lord formed every beast of the field, and every fowl of the air; and brought them unto Adam to see what he would call them. And whatsoever Adam called every living creature, that was the name thereof." (Genesis 2:19) From the standpoint of the Genesis narrative, the difference between man and animal is not that the former possesses reason, as Aristotle said, but rather that the animals were named by man through his power of speech. Inherent in the bestowing of names and our powers of speech was the establishment of certain permanence and order in the world; memory and places become significant; the past and the future are united and partly determine one another. Creation then means life, order, and permanence in a sacramental universe where man's ability to speak plays a decisive role.

The pride and vanity of man are displayed in the Tower of Babel narrative in the eleventh chapter of Genesis. Originally, as the writer notes, "the whole earth was of one language and of one speech," until God observes man making brick to construct a tower "whose top may reach unto heaven." The writer then adds, "and let us make us a name, lest we be scattered abroad upon the face of the earth." The tower and the name were symbols of a desire for knowledge and power in addition to what had already been bestowed upon them. God beholds this and notes that, having already one language, they still do this: "now nothing will be restrained from them." His reaction is to confound the language of all the

earth and then "to scatter them . . . upon the face of all the earth."
The one way to curb man's vanity at that time was to curb his
speech. This was effectively accomplished by creating a confusion
of tongues. It should be carefully noted that nowhere does the
writer (or writers) actually say that God gave man speech. The
Genesis story begins simply with Adam's naming powers, and it is
solely on the basis of this and man's being created *imago dei* that the
divine authorship is assumed. Nor is there explicit reference to the
divine origin of language. The later assumption of the divine origin
of language is more implicit in the narrative than explicitly stated.

Although the controversy over the origin and meaning of the
Divine Name, Yahweh Elohim, will never be settled, some of the
interpretations afford one further insight into the close connection
between oral speech and names. Buber's and Rosenzweig's investigations of this subject make possible a feeling that the divine is somehow related to all that is implied in anthropomorphic terms like
personal, encounter, exclamation, and invocation. For example, the
origin and meaning of the Divine Name in Exodus 3:14, where
Yahweh reveals Himself, illustrates the dynamic flexibility with respect to the nature and character of divine revelation. Although the
more familiar rendering of the text is "I am what I am" or "I shall
become what I shall become," a number of reputable scholars have
translated the text as "I am wont to be that which I am wont to be"
(A. B. Davidson, W. R. Smith), and Buber renders it, "I am He
who will be there at the appointed time"—*e.g.*, "When *I* determine
that you need Me." Professor Driver, for example, suggests that the
text "declares that while He is, as opposed to non-existent heathen
deities, He exists not simply in an abstract sense (e.g. LXX, *ego eimi
ho on!—ho on, to on*), but actually, it is His nature ever to express
Himself anew, ever to manifest Himself under a fresh aspect to the
world. . . ."

Ancient man literally sang his unity: it was through song that
men were reunited by re-experiencing a common event and thereby
given the power to face the unknown. In the time of the great
Patriarchs during the first half of the second millennium B.C., we
have little in the way of accurate dates and written sources. Whatever we know of this period, of the great historical events upon
which great traditions have been established, is through song and
legend. The renarrating of great events or the singing of great hap-

penings, such as the Song of Deborah, brought to a great emerging people unity, courage, and life, which sustained them over three thousand years ago, and recently in the face of Nazi oppression. When put to a life-or-death test, these songs and legends, which play such havoc with historical chronology, nevertheless touch the wellsprings of those forces that create and determine history and yet transcend merely chronological history in favor of a force and tradition that is selective and seemingly arbitrary, but nevertheless of one mind with respect to sources, dates, events, people.

Buber cautions us wisely against withdrawing in the face of the historian's retort that "there is nothing here but legend." For Buber it is not history that is significant but rather the particular voices that created the event that needed to be retold and resung in order to keep a people alive. Buber puts it quite simply when he writes:

> Historical song and legend are to a large extent—and often too in the Ancient East—the natural forms of the popular oral preservation of "historical" events, that is to say events of vital importance for the tribe. They all represent a vital kind of history memorizing as it happens, so long as the force of tribal life is greater than that of state control; only when the latter becomes stronger is the former obscured by the variegated history written to government order.[36]

Voices proclaim, preserve, glorify, but never merely describe, events. For these ancient peoples it was through song and verse—through the hearing of heroic tales narrated by the tribe's story-teller—that generations of peoples were bound together and instilled with a common spirit and purpose. In this connection Buber noted that the best description of Hebrew style is that it is essentially an acoustical art. "Tone is the simplest form of expression, rhythm the foundation upon which her art is established, and lyrics, the most adequate means of embodying her style."[37] In early Jewish culture, the faculty of hearing, a sense for tone and rhythm, were developed long before the Jews had any kind of significant pictorial art.

Early Christianity as a Speech Event

THE RESPECT SHOWN throughout the ancient Near East not only for the Word but for words, for speech, for men's oral and aural powers, as well as for names, time, history, and the relational quality of all life was certainly not minimized among the early Christians. If anything, interest in these themes was heightened by virtue of the effect of the Christian affirmation that Jesus was the Word, that God had assumed human form and had instituted by His incarnation, death, and resurrection a new era in human history. Although it can be argued that the statement "In the beginning was the Word" applies to everything just discussed, certainly the early Christian communities invested it with new rhetorical meaning and vigor.

Professor Amos Wilder's *The Language of the Gospel* is an excellent study of the importance of language for the early Christians. The power of the Word as human spoken word is not just one element in the "good news"; it *is* the Gospel, and speech is its instrument. Christianity was essentially a speech revolution founded upon a new *genus homo:*

. . . The Gospel represented a new outburst and plenitude of human utterance and communication in all aspects of language. Language is so primordial a gesture of living things that any radical renewal of it . . . points to an epoch-making moment in the human story. The early Christian consciousness of this break in culture comes to expression in its eschatological imagery as well as in its novel speech forms. The grasp upon ultimate reality coincident with this revolution in speech constituted no less than a new *genus homo,* and one capable therefore of unprecedented moral energies and cultural creativity.[38]

In this study the implicit and until recently unnoticed rhetorical elements in the preaching and spreading of the "good news" receive just as much, if not more, attention as the explicitly theological and doctrinal themes that have preoccupied the faithful down through the centuries. *How* the gospel was preached, *how* men were persuaded, is intimately bound up with the fact *that* Jesus died and rose in behalf of mankind. The advent of a new oral form of discourse is presented as our most valuable clue when assessing the secret behind the fact of Christianity and its development. Against this setting one's attention is drawn immediately to the oral impact that created the documents and literature. The oral tradition the Gospel writers appropriated is thus not simply a prolegomena to the Gospels, but is in fact the actual medium wherein the gospel took effect. To approach New Testament literature with this in mind suggests that we are vitally concerned with stylistic elements, with that which was extremely personal and, of necessity, subjective.

In an address in 1858 before the School of Philosophy and Letters, while Rector of the Catholic University of Ireland, John Henry Newman set the tone for approaching literature of this kind. Although literature "implies writing, not speaking," he said that the voice, rather than handwriting, is its primary vehicle of expression. "Speech, and therefore literature which is its permanent record, is essentially a personal work." As such, literature expresses thoughts rather than things, is subjective rather than objective. Newman identified science with things, literature with thoughts, science with the universal, and literature with that which is essentially personal, and noted that "Literature is the personal use or exercise of language." In this sense, the style, idiom, and phraseology a person employs attend on one's own "inward world of thought as its very shadows. . . . Style is a thinking out into language." *Logos* quite appropriately has the double meaning of "reason" and "speech," which though distinct may never be separated. The poet and the orator who take the power of speech seriously have, despite the varieties of tongues, periods, and national backgrounds, "a catholic and ecumenical character, . . . what they express is common to the whole race of man, and they alone are able to express it."[39] Speech for the poet is thus the mirror of man's total energies.

Newman, theologian and Roman Catholic, had the seeming audacity and yet humility to recognize that full testimony of the spirit is personal and catholic in the Greek sense of being forever open and searching, penetrating all that is personal, social, and thoroughly human. He saw in literature the testimony of the spirit in man. The genius of Newman has been characterized in many ways by countless men. From one perspective his genius lay in his high regard for the sacramental quality of style as one form of man's conversations with destiny. Though lengthy, his concluding remarks in this address are an appropriate means whereby speech and literature, the personal and human, the timely and social, become a proper arena of study and spiritual inquiry.

If then the power of speech is a gift as great as any that can be named,—if the origin of language is by many philosophers even considered to be nothing short of divine,—if by means of words the secrets of the heart are brought to light, pain of soul is relieved, hidden grief is carried off, sympathy conveyed, counsel imparted, experience recorded, and wisdom perpetuated,—if by great authors the many are drawn into unity, national character is fixed, a people speaks, the past and the future, the East and the West are brought into communication with each other,—if such men are, in a word, the spokesmen and prophets of the human family,—it will not answer to make light of literature or to neglect its study; rather we may be sure that, in proportion as we master it in whatever language, and imbibe its spirit, we shall ourselves become in our own measure the ministers of like benefits to others, be they many or few, be they in the obscure or the more distinguished walks of life,—who are united to us by social ties, and are within the sphere of our personal influence.[40]

Against such a setting the words of a former moderator of the Church of Scotland and great social reformer, George McLeod, are appropriate: "In the light of the Incarnation, nothing is secular." The significance of the Incarnation—the Word becoming flesh and dwelling among men—is intimately related to what the early Church fathers referred to as "the economy of salvation," with that speech that both affects and effects every sphere of our personal influence.

Admittedly, the style and idiom of New Testament times—even the conceptual apparatus, as Bultmann and others have shown—are in many respects not the same as ours today. The three-decker view of the universe, for example, is totally foreign to our contemporary ways of thinking. And yet in New Testament times as in every period in man's development, language in a rhetorical and dramatic garb has been decisive for human progress and development. "It is significant," says Professor Wilder, ". . . how large a place the dramatic mode has in the faith of the Bible and in its forms of expression, even though we find no theater-art as we know it in the Bible or among the early believers."[41] In poetry, in drama, in rhetoric of all kinds, the destiny of a people is made plain. In syntax, vocabulary, articulation, and discourse the range and depth of mankind's resources are revealed. Suzanne K. Langer's reference to "the language line" as the line which separates men from beasts was also recognized by Aristotle, who described man as a "speech-possessing creature." From the beginning of human history, every people in each stage of their development has captured the uniqueness of their culture in terms of new speech forms—of a new vocabulary. This was especially true in the early Church, where the incarnate Word for both John and Paul was one that shone in darkness and was attested to in the words and acts of the apostles. The birth of the Christian Church was indeed a *speech event*.

When the day of Pentecost had come, they were all together in one place. And suddenly a sound came . . . from heaven like the rush of a mighty wind, and it filled all the house where they were sitting. And there appeared to them tongues as of fire, distributed and resting on each one of them. And they were all filled with the Holy Spirit and began to speak in other tongues, as the Spirit gave them utterance. (Acts 2:1–4)

Traditional representations of this event in early and medieval art usually show the dove, symbolizing the Spirit, hovering over the apostles, with the outpouring of the Spirit descending upon opened mouths and waiting ears. It was in this event that a new depth was achieved in recognizing the unity of all men under the fatherhood of God. Thus Psalm 40:6 reads: "Sacrifice and offering thou dost not desire; but thou hast given me an open ear."

It was Jesus who as a layman and, from the standpoint of the times, a *secularist,* but also the Word, introduced new speech patterns in his time. The early Church spoke of his coming into a time of darkness and silence. Thus writes Ignatius of Antioch: "Jesus Christ, his son, who is his word proceeding from silence"; and "He is the mouth which cannot lie, by which the Father has spoken truly." Note the parallel to a recent statement by Professor Fuchs, "Could one perhaps say that the Easter faith proclaims to all the world that previously was believed only quietly in silence?"[42]

Current interest in hermeneutics, not only among Biblical scholars but among philosophers, theologians, and literary critics, reflects a growing tendency to give stylistic considerations top priority. The description by a leading scholar in Biblical hermeneutics of the Good News (the Gospel) as a speech event attests to this.

Primitive Christianity is itself a speech-phenomenon. It is for that very reason that it established a monument in the new style-form which we call a *gospel*. The Johannine apocalypse and, indeed, in the first instance the apostolic epistle—*literature*, these are creations of a new utterance which changes everything that it touches.[43]

At the heart of the proclamation of the good news was "exhortation," and as Professor Fuchs notes, it meant that "a person is called upon to listen and is told he has to listen with regard to himself."[44] The experience of faith in the Biblical period involved men in a linguistic revelation in which the temporal element of *timing* was central. "Faith has a particular relation to language that is all its own. This experience is the most characteristic experience of faith."[45] Not only does Jesus come at the *kairos*, at the "proper season" or "right time," but a glance at the syntax of the Gospels indicates a new and unparalleled propensity for verbal as against substantive forms of expression. Traditional Hellenistic preoccupations with concepts such as knowledge, truth, belief, and the like are recast in a verbal, hortatory, active, personalist setting—*e.g.*, "Know ye! Believe! Say! Come! Follow! Pray! I am the Truth," etc. The power of the event and its imperative consequences are revealed most acutely in its temporal-linguistic cast, where the hortatorical setting infects and creates unique literary forms such as the gospel, epistle, parable, and canticle. The linguistic context admits that time is crucial and produces a new sense of urgency and direction to those who have been converted—*i.e.*, those who literally have turned from one time and speech pattern to another. Implicit in all of this is a new sense of the essentially relational and social character of all life, which increased men's dependence upon oral discourse. A new people had been created and communication was the lifeblood of their existence. Hence Fuchs' affirmation that "the New Testament is itself a textbook in hermeneutics," since historically it is rooted in preaching and proclamation. As such, our guides and norms are inclined to emphasize our powers of hearing rather than seeing: ". . . we must find out to what extent our mental activity, our seeing, is bound to a hearing. That is the hermeneutical problem!" To speak of hermeneutics—of the message and meaning of the New Testament proclamation—is therefore an oral and aural problem. "The New Testament speaks the language of hearing."[46]

While all of men's senses are touched by the Spirit, those of hearing and speech are of far more significance than one's visual powers. In the tenth chapter of Romans, for example, all these themes are accentuated. In 10:13 we read, "every one who calls upon the name of the Lord will be saved." In 10:14–18 the story is completed:

> But how are men to call upon him in whom they have not believed? And how are they to believe in him of whom they have never heard? And how are they to hear without a preacher? . . . So faith comes from what is heard, and what is heard comes by the preaching of Christ.
> But I ask, have they not heard? Indeed they have; for
> "Their voice has come out to all the earth,
> and their words to the ends of the world."

It is particularly significant that Jesus' style as well as that of the apostles was free and spontaneous, conditioned by the necessities of the situation—*extempore*, "immediate, reckless of posterity; not coded for catechists or repeaters."[47] It was the *viva voce* quality of Jesus' entire life and ministry that ushered in that tremendous speech revolution known as Christianity.

When followers like Paul did write, it was with the voice of a speaker personally directed to a particular group, distressed that circumstances would not permit a personal encounter. Thus in Galatians Paul's statement, "I could wish to be present with you now, and change my tone, for I am perplexed about you." (Gal. 4:20) What is commonly referred to as Pauline theology is, it must be remembered, an extraction and abstraction from numerous oral-epistolary encounters the content and style of which, like those of Jesus, were determined by the needs of a specific community at a specific time.

Whether Jesus, Paul, Augustine, or even Luther, the content of their theology is understandable only in terms of the biographical temporal context of various encounters the style of which is modeled upon oral engagement, whether it be petition, admonition, supplication, or wise counsel. This is admirably summed up in Professor Wilder's statement:

> . . . it is significant that the emotional dynamics of the Gospel were always controlled by the meaningfulness of speech. To this, visionary and psychic phenomena were subordinated. And the language in question was not only the spoken word but personal address; it was not only

in the indicative mode but in the imperative; it was not only in the third person but in the second and the first; it was not only a matter of declaration but of dialogue.[48]

Further, and this cannot be repeated too often—as with the oldest of the patriarchal traditions among the Israelites, so too among the early Christians—considerable time elapsed before a specifically religious or holy language was adopted. "Though early Israel knew nothing of any 'holy language,' yet its utterance took on new features as over against the speech-forms of Canaan."[49] Before fixed forms of celebration with their attendant linguistic formularies had been developed, the power of the good news was proclaimed, simply shouted amid ecstatic joyous enthusiasm. The fact that Jesus was the Christ was revealed by enthusiastic souls—literally *en theo*, those in and through whom God worked and spoke. Ordinary human qualities were suddenly consecrated, made sacred vehicles of the New Creation. The profane, in this setting, was simply that which the Word must yet touch and transform. The profane, in the sense of an absolute which is opposed to the sacred, no more existed for the early Christians than it did for the early Israelites.

The use of the word intercession in the King James and other versions is an example of an artificial sacred-profane distinction in the Bible with respect to the potentially sacramental quality of all human discourse. The term intercession appears twice in the New Testament—in I Timothy 4:5 and 2:1. In the Revised Standard Version the relevant passage is translated "For Everything created by God is good . . . it is consecrated by the word of God and prayer." The Greek for both "prayer" and "intercession" in the New Testament, (as in the Septuagint in II Mac. 4:8), is *enteuchsis*, which can mean, according to Abbott-Smith: "1. a lighting upon, meeting with. 2. conversation. 3. a petition." The close association of intercession and prayer with ordinary discourse is undeniable. Plato once used the same term to describe the boldness with which pirates board a ship. Implicit in the term is not only an intimate association with normal oral discourse; the elements of encounter, address, engagement, struggle, are equally present.

These few remarks serve to heighten our awareness of the oral dependence of men in antiquity and in the early Church. Our purpose in doing this was not to suggest that each of the various forms

—*e.g.*, story, parable, poem—should serve as a paradigm for modern man. It is one of the achievements of Bultmann and those concerned with hermeneutics that they have urged us to employ the oral forms of our own day rather than those of antiquity. Such an appropriation presupposes, however, that oral discourse—the spoken word—is the lifeblood of change among humans in every age. It should be further apparent in the light of our introductory remarks that we today are being given and asked to assume greater responsibility for the control and direction of our culture than primitive man could possibly have envisioned. If the Johannine vision and other millenarian expressions are at all relevant about the increasing role humans may play in the conduct of society, then it is particularly imperative that we weigh carefully the lessons and evidence of earlier men in the area of language.

It has been suggested that the poetry and rhetoric of the New Testament have a quality of naïveté about them comparable to the references to modern man's total sensuous life in the poetry, for example, of Rilke, Yeats, Donne, Blake, or Wallace Stevens. One explanation would be that this is as it should be as long as the language event caused by Jesus' birth, death, and resurrection is regarded not as a finished prototype but rather as a new linguistic beginning.

One among the many virtues of the contributions of men like Amos Wilder, Eugen Rosenstock-Huessy and Franz Rosenzweig, to mention but a few, is that they suggest that any authentic revolutionary movement must affect men's imaginations and speech patterns differently in successive generations. Professor Wilder captures this quality when he says:

> The poetry of the New Testament . . . can best be seen as the voice not of an established culture and sensibility, but of an iconoclastic moment and crisis in culture. Primitive Christian poetry is spoken . . . at the beginning of a world, indeed, at the world. Its substance and forms are eloquent, then, of this hour, an hour, indeed, which ever renews itself for faith.[50]

It is to the credit of interpreters like Bultmann, Fuchs, Ebeling, Wilder, and all those interested in hermeneutics that they begin with this assumption in mind. One wonders, however, whether the hermeneutical task must forever be bound, however demythologized one's categories be, by the New Testament pattern. One alternate emphasis would be to focus upon the dynamics of contemporary ordinary language, keeping in mind the various historical legacies without, however, being bound by them. One reason for doing this, with Christianity especially in mind, stems from a slightly different appreciation of the character and scope of Christianity in our time. All those interested in this problem should note that the concerns of hermeneutists for everyday language have been perennial concerns of all those who stress the Johannine element in Western thought. Fuchs hinted at this when, as was noted earlier, he cited the Johannine apocalypse as an example of "creations of a new utterance which changes everything that it touches." Traditionally, a Johannine thinker combines a number of elements in his thinking which make him ideally prepared for taking seriously the potentially sacramental character of everyday discourse in successive eras and aeons. This stems from the Johannine stress upon the importance of the Incarnation viewed as a speech event that totally changed the character of all that came into being in subsequent millennia and aeons. Among the marks of Johannine Incarnational thinking are the following, many of which are taken from Rosenstock-Huessy's truly Johannine work entitled *The Christian Future or The Modern Mind Outrun*, as well as from his *Out of Revolution*.

In *Out of Revolution*, Rosenstock-Huessy proposes a sequel at the end of time to Michelangelo's portrayal in the Sistine Chapel of God creating man. "In the beginning" when God said "Let us make man in our image" man is shown reclining naked and helpless while God is depicted as strong and mighty, containing all his angels or helpers in the folds of his robe. In the proposed sequel man is depicted with all of God's angels having descended to him to give him greater powers in accord with his increased powers and responsibilities.[51] Thus, Rosenstock-Huessy's statement: "In this light, the Church Fathers interpreted human history as a process of making Man like God. They called it 'anthropurgy': as metallurgy refines metal from its ore, anthropurgy wins the true stuff of Man out of his coarse physical substance."[52]

The anthropurgical process takes place in the three great epochs or millennia of human history, the first represented by the Christian Church symbolizing the triumph of one God "over the many false gods." In the second, of which we are still a part, man's energies were devoted to the unification of the many peoples and lands all over the earth. But while the earth is one, its members still have not been united. In *Out of Revolution*, Rosenstock-Huessy coined a motto which he offers as a means of the realization of the focus of the third millennium, which is concerned with the creation and preservation of a truly human society: *"Respondeo etsi mutabor"* (I respond *although* I will be changed).[53] Inspired human speech will be the vehicle and power for the accomplishment of this task, one that cannot be achieved except the Holy Spirit rule the hearts and lips of men for whom the Christian Church must become incognito. Several passages from *The Christian Future* define the task of the third millennium as well as the conditions for its realization.

> The double concern of this epoch will be the revivification of all dead branches of the single human race, and the reinspiration of all mechanized portions of the single human life.
>
> Though I believe that the Church is a divine creation and that the Athanasian Creed is true, I also believe that in the future, Church and Creed can be given a new lease on life only by services that are . . . incognito. The inspirations of the Holy Spirit will not remain inside the walls of the visible or preaching Church. A third form, the listening Church, will have to unburden the older modes of worship by assembling the faithful to live out their hopes through working and suffering together in unlabelled, undenominational groups, thereby to wait and listen for the inbreak of a new consolation which shall redeem modern life from its curse of disintegration and mechanization.
>
> The tree of everlasting life can grow only through successive generations of men reaching their hands to each other in one spirit across the ages. And each *generation has to act differently precisely in order to represent the same thing*. Only so can each become a full partner in the process of Making Man; only so can life be as authentic in the last age as in the first.[54]

These brief excerpts illustrate most of the Incarnational elements in Johannine thinking which, as is appropriate for those who live by the inspiration of the Holy Spirit, find a company of kindred spirits throughout Western thought. Mention of some representative Johannine thinkers will indicate that their ranks, beginning particularly in the nineteenth century, have been filled by those whom the Church regards mostly as secularists and religious heretics—but whose chief preoccupation nevertheless is mostly with man, humanity, and society—*e.g.*, Fichte, Hegel, Schelling, Feuerbach, Compte.

Naturally, not all Johannine thinkers have been Christians in the classical sense of the term. Many of these Johannine thinkers have contributed much to our present difficulties when attempting to define religion and the sacred. Many of them, especially those twentieth-century death-of-God theologians, if forced to employ the term religion—in a positive and constructive way—would identify religion with that which for many is the secular and profane. It is suggested that the concerns of these men, notably those of the nineteenth century and after, might be the kinds of concerns to which New Testament hermeneutic scholars will ultimately have to speak. It is quite possible that some New Testament hermeneutists may never be able to leave the New Testament paradigm when attempting this task. This inability may well handicap their ultimate goals.

Ancient Greece Revered Speech

To CONTINUE OUR presentation of those themes from antiquity that bear directly upon the importance of speech, of our oral and aural powers, upon names, time, and timing, let us next examine certain aspects of the legacies of Greece and Rome. This is especially important in view of the tendency among some Biblical scholars to accept Tertullian's conviction that Athens has absolutely nothing in common with Jerusalem. It is suggested, contrary to Tertullian, that the distinctions often made between Athens and Jerusalem also exist within each legacy. For example, the differences between the Homeric and Platonic mentalities, as well as those between Heracleitus and Parmenides, represent opposing attitudes on a number of key issues and especially on matters germane to our interests in language. These mentalities ought not simply to be lumped together as constituting a unified Greek outlook. Without too much difficulty, a similar case could be made with respect to the differences between the Hebraic and Hellenistic Jewish mentalities within that tradition Tertullian labeled Jerusalem.

During the last decade considerable attention has been devoted to

the oral character of early Greek culture.⁵⁵ Because so much attention has been devoted to the legacies of Plato and Aristotle, we are
just barely beginning to recognize in the humanities the implications
of Cassirer's insights in his *Essay on Man* and more particularly in
Volume I of his *Theory of Symbolic Forms*, where he stated that
speech is the key to our understanding of the universe. "If we fail to
find this approach—the approach through the medium of language
rather than through the physical phenomena—we miss the gateway
to philosophy."⁵⁶

The classical scholar and devoted friend of Cassirer, Ernst Hoffmann, raised the problem in all its seriousness in 1925 when he
wrote, "To natural philosophy and cultural philosophy belongs a
third—the philosophy of language. As far as we can look back . . .
from Pythagoras and Heracleitus on, the object of Greek philosophy is not only the *world*, but also human *speech* about the world.
. . . Can human speech be the vessel for truth?"⁵⁷

In order to pursue the language theme the reader is requested to
focus upon certain aspects of Greek culture prior to Plato's times,
to an inheritance as rich and significant in insights into the power of
the word as that supplied by the legacies of the ancient Near East,
ancient Israel, and the early Christian communities. The reader is
also requested to appreciate the fact that prior to Aristotle, Greek
terms like *logos, dialogismos,* and *dialogos* were closely associated
with conversation, discourse, and dialogue, and lacked the association with logical and purely rational and abstract considerations
later accorded them. Pauly-Wissowa, for example, states that the
interests of the Greeks in grammar, rhetoric, and philosophies of
language stem from an interpretation of *logos* that was closely associated with "dialogue, conversation, discussion"—*i.e.*, with the vocal
qualities of language. "The origin and meaning of *Logos* teaching
can be discovered if one traces it back to its original meaning as
speech (Rede), out of which linguistic philology and grammar
arose."⁵⁸ The statement "In the beginning was the Word" was just
as appropriate to Heracleitus, for example, as it was to the author of
the Johannine Prologue.

Beginning with Homer and the Homeric tradition, which per-
sisted throughout Plato's lifetime, Greek culture was sustained by
the oral power of poetry and rhetoric. The spoken word was the
chief instrument of Greek culture, whether in the senate, in the give
and take between citizens and magistrates, or in litigation between

lawyers. There were no handbills, circulars, newspapers, or journals and magazines; all information depended upon the spoken word. In the field of entertainment the human voice, whether on the stage, in informal conversation, or in the listening to the tales of the glory of Greece, provided the communities' diversion. Where written literature existed it was designed to be read aloud even when reading to oneself. It should also be remembered that in earliest times the art of oral narration allowed for considerable flexibility in much the same way that the teacher in the classroom repeats certain points again and again, using illustrations and digressions which make sense only within the context of the classroom. The seemingly disjointed character of many recorded tales makes sense only when viewed originally in its oral context, where the ears and eyes of the group actually shaped the quality and structure of the tale. In his discussion of Homeric oral tradition, Albert Lord writes:

> Each theme . . . each formula—has around it an aura of meaning which has been put there by all the contexts in which it has occurred in the past. It is the meaning that has been given it by the tradition in its creativeness. To any given poet at any given time, this meaning involves all the occasions on which he has used the theme, especially those contexts in which he uses it most frequently; it involves also all the occasions on which he has heard it used by others, particularly by those singers whom he first heard in his youth, or by great singers later by whom he was impressed. To the audience the meaning of the theme involves its own experience of it as well. The communication of this supra-meaning is possible because of the community of experience of poet and audience.[59]

The teller, as well as his audience, was under the spell of oral discourse, and this affected the audience's sense of time, which often was presented as the reverse of ours—*i.e.*, frequently the latest and most recent events were recited first because they were freshest to the ear, and then one proceeded to those events that actually preceded the ones already told. Chronological time was reversed so that what is normally the last in a series of events becomes the first for the storyteller in an oral culture. Education in the Homeric tradition began at an early age in the home, where the ear was trained to listen by the singing of lullabies, by employing a teacher or slave whose accent was pure, and by listening to the nurse's tales of the heroes, of Aesop's fables, and naturally, of witches. Marrou sums up the oral dependence of ancient Greece when he writes, "In modern times the spoken word has given way to the all-powerful written word, and this remains true even today, despite the great strides made by the radio and the gramophone. But in ancient Greece, and especially in its political life, the spoken word reigned supreme."[60]

To have existed in an oral culture required a tremendous auditory sensitivity, which is lacking in our own visually oriented technological society. Among the merits of the studies of Parry, Lord, and Whitman is their evidence and conclusion that it is wrong to suggest that oral sensitivity is exclusively a primitive mentality. Thus, Cedric Whitman's statement:

Homer's mind is the archaic mind, prephilosophic, primarily synthetic rather than analytical, whose content is myths, symbols and paradigms. It is not a primitive mind, however, for the archaic, preconceptual way of thinking has a maturity of its own, fully as valid as later modes, and, to judge from Homer, perhaps more valid. In any case, such mentality is a more fruitful source for poetry than the mind trained to logical and philosophical analysis, for its meanings cluster iridescently around unclear images, with the complexity, and explosive power of high-valence atoms. It is the function of poetry to compress meaning, where prose expatiates upon it, and the *Iliad* seems like a brief poem in the light of its meaning.[61]

For modern man, the technique of memorization is largely a private activity consisting of first reading, using the visual senses, and then shutting our eyes and translating them into sounds, which we repeat over and over to ourselves until we have mastered the text. A tremendous amount of individual energy is involved in what is essentially a solitary, quite asocial activity. In oral society, such as the Homeric, oral memorization did not require the expenditure and drain of personal energy involved in today's private act of translating from the visual into the auditory. Not having the material before him to be read and seen, preliterate man relied exclusively upon the power of the sounds heard in a mouth-to-ear environment. Like children, the audience simply had to submit to the hypnotic spell of the storyteller. In our time the nearest analogy is perhaps that of the ability of young people to pick up the melodies and words of jazz and pop hits. In their jargon, "no strain" is required—it "comes naturally." Contrast this with the difficulties many of the same children have in concentrating, learning their ABC's, and avoiding becoming dropouts. They may not be able to spell and read, but they will dance the latest rhythm almost unconsciously when approaching the teacher's desk to account for their unpreparedness. Whether in the Homeric period, among Yugoslavians listening to the story-teller accompanied by his *gusle,* or in an electronic age, "the medium," as Marshall McLuhan points out, "is the message." In each milieu it is appropriate to speak of instantaneous communication.

The psychological principles involved in this process are such that the entire nervous system is geared so that not only is the uncon-scious intimately tied up with the conscious, but the response of all the reflexes involved produces a feeling of relaxation and pleasure at the deepest levels of awareness and stimulation. In a unique way, pleasure and recreation were combined with the appropriation of the tribal encyclopedia—of those stories and legends regarded as worth remembering by each generation. The poet's utterance is likened to a "flowing" or "gushing river," or perhaps to "arrows," where Hesiod speaks of "feathered phrases." This *Mousike* is thor-oughly enjoyed, as evidenced by names for the Muses such as "the Enjoyable," "the Passionate," and by references to the utterances as "sweet-dewed" and "honeyed" and to the dances and chants as "desireful."[62] Eros here is hardly noble reason; it refers to the in-tegrated powers of the most thoroughly human and creative aspects of personality brought to life, aroused by the spoken word. The reciter as well as the audience unconsciously had committed them-selves, placed themselves under the spell of speech. In the process something of the identity of each participant was surrendered in the submission to speech, just as each departed enriched and nourished by this re-creation.

Dependence upon speech was similarly matched by the depend-ence and proximity of the gods with whom the people continually conversed. Characteristic of the *Iliad,* for example, was the constant penetration of the human by the divine as a result of human prompt-ing, and the common apotheosis or elevation of humans like Achilles to the rank of gods. Aeschylus' words appropriately describe the divine-human partnership; "God is well, whenever man himself takes action, joins with him." Thus, Whitman's statement:

Homer's divinities depend on human prompting for their deeds; their knowledge is independent and transcendent, but their action as a rule is immanent in human action, or character. Hence all divine participation has something of the effect of *apotheosis,* and this is true no less of Homer's system of the continuing images than it is of action itself.[63]

In the fields of history, drama, or philosophy, the oral foundation is at once apparent. History began with the stories and genealogies of famous families, told around the campfire, which were passed on to the listening ears of the younger generation or sojourner from a foreign land or province. History was oral and had to be told; its lifeblood depended upon its need to be retold, memorized, and in turn transmitted to others. For centuries Greek history was identified with the oral Homeric legacy, with epic poetry, with the events of the Trojan War, with the valor of the men of Athens and the acts of the gods.

Whether one considers epic or hymnic, elegiac or lyric poetry, in each instance the content was oral, although the shape could be address, persuasion, deception, and the actors both divine and human. Similarly, what we moderns refer to as drama had its beginnings in the addition of dialogue to the chants of the chorus. Greek drama, among the tragedians, had the character of trial where "speech matched against speech" was the basic device.[64] The conflict of sounds issuing forth from the masks of the actors constituted, as it did among the Sophists in the lawcourts and for Heracleitus, a warring—a battle of words. There was particular importance attached to the *agony* and war of words in each of these mediums. The actor as a *persona* who wore many masks (*persona* meaning literally "one-through-whom-sound-passes") was engaged in an antiphonal agonistic exchange involving discordant sound (*antiphonos*) and strife (*agones*). In Homer, it is interesting to note how the personality of Odysseus is revealed. For the Homeric mentality, identity was defined through recollection of the various roles or masks worn by Odysseus. Thus, Whitman's statement:

> Meanwhile, the self *per se* lies hidden. Odysseus can rebuild his world only out of those prepared by their own knowledge-ability to penetrate the disguise, and he begins at the lowest rung with Eumaeus, the swineherd. And now the self-revelations begin again, not indeed with Eumaeus, but with Telemachus. The modes of revelation tell more than the identity of the stranger; they rehearse his roles as father, hero, king, husband, and son. Telemachus, though he could have had no recollection of his father, had often imagined him.[65]

The social and relational basis for defining personality, rooted as it is in human genealogy and biography, stands in sharp contrast to

Plato's recognition of selfhood *per se*, completely shorn of human, transitory existence. That which in Plato's time was only tentatively separated from reality later became an accomplished fact in Descartes' world of isolated mind. In each instance, whether for Plato or for Descartes, human experiential language became a barrier to true recognition and authentic identity. Cicero, in the *Orator*, noted this when he reflected on the low esteem into which rhetoric had fallen as a result of Socrates' and Plato's attack upon it and the Homeric tradition in Plato's *Republic*. "From the scorn of Socrates for rhetoric arose the unnatural separation of rhetoric from philosophy. . . . That divorce as it were of the tongue from the heart . . . that one class of persons should teach us to think, another to speak, rightly."[66]

One effect of that separation of tongue from heart, said Cicero, is that "philosophy has suffered." For Cyrenaic philosophy it meant "incompleteness because men were dissuaded from participation in public life." Among the Stoics, their "dry abstractness of address" is "quite ineffective" and their philosophy "makes wisdom practically unattainable." "Rhetoric, on the other hand, has suffered by being reduced to maxims of pleading. In a word, training in rhetoric, to be adequate, must include philosophy, and philosophy remains ineffective without rhetoric."[67]

The Clash between Parmenides and Heracleitus

WITH THE POSSIBLE exception of Heracleitus, the Greek Enlightenment contributed little toward our interest in oral discourse. What it did illustrate, however, was the perennial propensity of the human mind, amid an atmosphere that questioned traditional modes of discourse, to devise a single abstract and artificial language and method to explain the unity implicit in reality. What was happening was important from the standpoint of language because men boldly proclaimed their trust, if not their faith, in a single mode of discourse. Parmenides contributed significantly to a seemingly indefatigable tradition which believed so firmly in the autonomy of thought that men were forced to deny the hierarchical and multiform character of ordinary sensuous speech. From the standpoint of interest in

everyday speech, Parmenides is a classic example of the devil's ad-
vocate, for as Burnett put it so well, "he showed once and for all
that if you take the one seriously you are bound to deny everything
else."[68]

With Parmenides, wisdom is reduced to thought in such a way
that myth and legend and all the vocal and visual imagery associated
with them became meaningless. "But do thou restrain thy thought
from this way of inquiry, nor let habit by its much experience force
thee to cast upon this way a wandering eye or sounding ear or
tongue; but judge by argument (*logos*) the much disputed proof
uttered by me."[69] It is noteworthy that, according to Burnett, this
is the earliest use of *logos* in a logical or dialectical sense.[70]

Despite the testimony of the senses, Parmenides was able to deny
the reality of concrete change and all forms of becoming. With
Parmenides' selection of thought as the only reality, idealism was
established. What took place in the sixth and fifth centuries B.C. in
Greece in the name of the intelligibility of the universe is then but a
series of footnotes to Parmenides. In this context Karl Reinhardt's
evaluation of Parmenides is most appropriate, since he described him
as "a thinker who knows no other desire than knowledge, feels no
other manacle than logic, and is left indifferent by God and by
feeling."[71]

The pluralistic presentation of Biblical reality—*i.e.*, God, man,
the Creation—was, in contrast to Parmenides' monistic outlook,
much closer to the testimonies of the senses and to a commonsense
approach. It is well to remind ourselves that an appreciation for the
spoken word in all its configurations—*e.g.*, song, narration, divine
and human speech—and the importance of names, were the themes
that held together the pluralism inherent in most tribal life. By
contrast, with Parmenides the way is established wherein detachment, speculation, and the visual discernment of truth by reason as
the mind's eye is fully established, with the corollary that the testimonies of the spoken word which impinge upon the mind from
without, in an antecedent sense, as well as from within the soul of
man, in an equally antecedent sense, become meaningless, yea obsolete. The real meaning of idealism as established by Parmenides
within the context of this study is that it became an unfortunate
canon of the Western modern mind that thought precedes speech,
rather than vice versa as common sense tells us.

Parmenides' assertion that the "roadway" (*hodos*) is a way of salvation not to be found on earth was the forerunner to the use of the term *methodos* or method (methodology), with which the heirs of Parmenides preoccupied themselves. For all practical purposes, Parmenides' use of *hodos* is the same as the later formal concern for methodology, since dialectics was the chief instrument one employed. Parmenides' rendering of *logos* as dialectics is a suitable point of departure to appreciate the radical differences between Parmenides and Heracleitus.

Heracleitus was one of the earliest Greek thinkers not only to stress a pluralistic rather than monistic unifying principle, but to incorporate an appreciation for change, flux, strife, paradox, and contradiction as inherent in the very nature of the universe. Ernst Cassirer interpreted Heracleitus as standing on an anthropological threshold wherein man rather than the cosmos is central: ". . . for him the particular word is related to *speech* as a whole. . . ." Elsewhere he says, "Only in the mobile and multiform word, which seems to be constantly bursting its limits, does the fullness of the world-forming logos find its counterpart."[72]

Martin Buber in *What is Common to All* noted that "Heracleitus always remained in accord with the thoroughly sensuous living speech of his time. For this reason the logos, even in its highest sublimation, does not cease to be for him the sensuous, meaningful word, the human talk which contains the meaning of the true."[73]

For Heracleitus *logos* and *cosmos* (world) were the medium within which men lived. The logos is not the private property of an individual; rather it is by virtue of the logos which is "common to all" that men are united. Men stand within it, are possessed by the logos, and yet possess the logos in much the same way men are related to the air that they breathe. As Heracleitus put it, "So we must follow the common, yet though my *Logos* is common, the many live as if they had a wisdom of their own."

The theme of *strife* is integrally related to that of the logos, and interests us, not only for its importance to Heracleitus, but for its bearing upon the importance of themes such as encounter, conflict, war, and revolution in the thought of Buber, Rosenzweig, and especially Rosenstock-Huessy. In *Fragment* (43–47) Heracleitus states that the cosmos must be understood in terms of the law of strife and opposition, which manifest themselves in the "upward and downward" path. Reality consists of a constant tension of forces. This tension—*strife*—accounts for "the attunement of opposite tensions, like that of bow and the lyre." "As the arrow leaves the string the hands are pulling opposite ways to each other, and to different parts of the bow." Hence, war or strife "is the father of all and the king of all."

In Plato's *Cratylus* (402), Socrates suggested at one point that Homer and Hesiod would agree about all things being in motion, or as Heracleitus is supposed to have believed: "Everything changes, war is the father of all things, and a man cannot step into the same stream twice." Heracleitus criticized Homer for praying that "strife might perish from among the gods and men," because Homer "did not see that he was praying for the destruction of the universe." Harmony exists in the ostensible chaos of the exchange between man and man. We have in Heracleitus' thought a view of reality quite unlike that found in Parmenides. Process and change, strife and conflict are basic to reality conceived absolutely and are not merely part of the unreal world of semblance and becoming as against the essential reality of the world of unified being.

Plato's Attack on the Homeric Legacy

WHAT HAPPENED IN Athens in the sixth and fifth centuries B.C. is of particular significance to our interest in language because, as Karl Popper has noted, that was the period when "The strain of civilization was beginning to be felt."[74] It was a period of liberation, transition, and revolution, to the extent that old established tribal legacies, largely oral in character, were facing dissolution and obsolescence through new interest in critical inquiry in every field of endeavor. Whether in the field of human relations or natural science it is true, as the biologist T. Q. Young has shown, that ". . . great changes in ways of *ordinary* human speaking and acting are bound up with the adoption of new instruments."[75] The tension in the Greek world was due partly to the encounter of the largely oral and preliterate tribal culture of Greece from Homer to Socrates with what Marshall McLuhan has described as a culture attuned to "arrested visual analysis, namely our phonetic alphabet," which, he adds, "was as new to the Greeks as the movie camera to our century."[76]

The tension became quite acute in Athens in Plato's time, because Plato incorporated in his thinking the main presuppositions of a number of traditions, including the Parmenidean and Pythagorean, which dated from men's earliest efforts to understand the sustaining element behind the world of appearances. It was inevitable that Plato's unique synthesis, with its recognition of the significance of our critical and analytic powers woven as they were into his philosophy of forms, should find the Homeric legacy intolerable. From the perspective of Greek cultural history it can be argued that Plato simply brought into sharp focus a number of elements which had been in existence for centuries. Plato provided the impetus that enabled his heirs to pretend complete freedom from all authority except reason. E. R. Dodds noted this when he said, "Plato is almost the last Greek intellectual who seems to have real social roots; his successors, with very few exceptions make the impression of existing beside society rather than in it."[77] Against this cultural background and from the standpoint of our interest in the spoken word it is appropriate to examine the significance of, first, Plato's attack upon poetry as embodied in the Homeric legacy; and secondly, Plato's differences with the Sophists as represented by Socrates' attack upon them. An examination of the character of Plato's and Socrates' use of dialogue is an important aspect of our consideration of the importance of everyday concrete speech in antiquity.

In the tenth and last book of Plato's *Republic*, Socrates identifies the role of the poet with that of the painter and suggests that the work of each is but a distant and imprecise facsimile of reality in its essentiality. The poet, as an imitator of appearance, is "a long way off from the truth, and can do all things because he lightly touches on a small part of them, and that part an image." (598) Homer and the tragedians are mere imitators, as is evident in the fact that no "State was ever better governed by his help," nor would he ever have been allowed by his fellowmen to starve had his poetry been anything more than a third-hand imitation. The effect of poetry is "a crippling of the mind whose only antidote consists in a knowledge of things as they really *are*." (605) At stake here is an issue that is more than philosophical in the narrow, more technical use of the term; it represents a questioning of the entire tradition upon which Greek culture had been established. As such, the issue was at once cultural, political, and especially educational.

For Plato reality is rational, scientific and logical, or it is nothing. The poetic medium, so far from disclosing the true relations of things as the true definition of the moral virtues, forms a kind of refracting screen which disguises and distorts reality and at the same time distorts us and plays tricks with us by appealing to the shallowest of our sensibilities.[78]

The appeal to reason is nothing more in the final analysis than an appeal to the absolute criterion provided by the eternal forms which exist absolutely and independently of human language. Poetry and rhetoric, being grounded in the ordinary language of commonsense, everyday experience, and hence a third-hand kind of *mimesis*, cannot possibly be trustworthy when judged by such criteria. Against the framework of this kind of realism the poor poet could not help but come out not even second, but third best. Against this background, that which is real is objective and exists independently of language, except for mathematics and logic, which are permitted what Hamann later referred to as having a "magic castle" all their own.

The Platonic revolution, which made philosophy rather than poetry the supreme music, could not have been achieved had not Plato in effect made a totally arbitrary and completely unverifiable distinction between human and nonhuman language. Somehow, the beautiful *per se* and the just *per se* are more real than "that beautiful woman" and "this just action," and somehow, those nonhuman disciplines such as logic and mathematics are the keys to the doors of that wonderful world of *per se*.[79]

The new language Plato introduced in the fifth century B.C. created literally a new world with its own laws, its own values, its own attitudes toward the senses, its own concept of time and space. While Plato would probably have resented reference to his efforts as a new language experience, it is only fair to our poets to suggest that what Plato achieved was nothing more than a human decision to use human language in a different human manner. To have been caught in the fifth century between such formidable linguistic enterprises must indeed have produced tensions which our own time is only gradually resolving—and then, in the sciences and in the arts, ultimately on Homeric rather than Platonic terms. Very few, if any, reputable scientists, whether physical or social, employ the terms truth, beauty, or goodness as Plato did. In a word, the linguistic revolution today includes a rejection of the linguistic world of *per se.*

Somehow, things never turned out as Plato had anticipated. The free and open society founded upon the music of philosophy never achieved its desired goals. Perhaps T. H. Huxley's remark fits the situation: "A man's worst difficulties begin when he is able to do as he likes." As Dodds and others have shown, the Age of Reason was for all practical purposes the beginning of a period of intellectual decline which lasted until the Turks captured Byzantium. The legacy of the third century was indeed a pitiful one: ". . . in all the sixteen centuries of existence still awaiting it the Hellenic world would produce no poet as good as Theocritus, no scientist as good as Eratosthenes, no mathematician as good as Archimedes, and . . . the one great name in philosophy would represent a point of view believed to be extinct—transcendental Platonism."[80]

The names Nock, Nilsson, Jaeger, Festugiere, and Dodds are but a few of those whose interests have been devoted to an understanding of the real causes for the failure of Greek rationalism. Dodds, for example, suggests that "the fear of freedom—the unconscious flight from the heavy burden of individual choice which an open society lays upon its members" was a principal factor in this decline. The burden produced by the "fear of freedom" was so great that men no longer utilized philosophy as an instrument of free inquiry, but rather transformed it into quasi-religious dogma which in the end resisted change and produced, as Nock put it, a willingness "to accept statements because they were in books, or even because they were said to be in books."[81]

While the scholar will shudder at this telescoping of causes and effects, our purpose is simply to amplify the fact of strain, tension, and eventual decay, which set in in Plato's time and took effect shortly thereafter. The reader is asked to keep in mind the earlier suggestion that the conflict in Plato's time between the music of poetry and that of philosophy was an important factor in this transformation.

If a general comment may be permitted, it is suggested that language offers a clue toward one possible approach to the problem of the analysis of the decline of Greek culture. Certainly, all of us today are interested in normative guides to aid in the creation and survival of a truly human society. We might begin with the assumption that a healthy society, to use Popper's all too convenient distinction, in order to remain healthy must be at once open and at the same time closed. This suggests that men cannot live off the proceeds of a single linguistic legacy, whether it be that of poetry or that of philosophy, to mention but two possibilities. In presenting the problem in this fashion, it is suggested that the problem of the survival and health of societies is fundamentally a language and communication problem—to wit, the problem of knowing to what extent and when man must obey those kinds of language that bear upon his past and future and those that must be spoken in order to cope with the needs of his present place and space.

Dodds referred to the heirs of Plato as those who used tradition, rather than being used by it. The problem can never be an either/or, but is rather a both/and, and language is the only instrument that enables us to live in more than one space or world or time sequence without schizophrenia resulting. If Aristotle was correct in describing man as a *zoon echon logon*, which Heidegger in *Being and Time* translates as a "speech-," rather than "reason-possessing animal," both were shortsighted in assuming that man is uni- rather than plural or multi-vocal. Cast in this way, the issue no longer revolves around viewing man as essentially rational or irrational.

From a linguistic standpoint, the roles we play, the masks we wear as persons, assume that both passion and reason are necessary and healthy qualities to personal and collective existence. For all their insights, both Aristotle and Heidegger seemingly missed the insight that our lives consist of a rhythmic interchange between one language role and another, between living alternately in one mythical time or space sphere and another. To be fully human from this standpoint would require that one live in both, even though this would vary among individuals and be disproportionate depending upon the circumstances. We have to wear many masks and play many roles, not as an evasion, but as a prerequisite for being full persons.

Plato's Differences with the Sophists

Plato was not content to challenge merely the entire oral legacy of Greece, beginning with Homer. With equal vigor and on related grounds, and again through Socrates, he attacked the Sophists. The problem was different with the Sophists because, unlike the Homeric preliterate tradition, they were committed to a prose style, although in the courtroom they were masters of the art of oral persuasion. It must be remembered that their view of poetry or prose was exempt from Plato's attack; he regarded them, in fact, as his allies, at least during his educational battle with Homeric tradition. They had followers (which Plato accused Homer of not having) and they were popular champions of poetry, but they were not identified with Homer, except that they, like Homer, were educational leaders in their time.

The Sophists in the fifth century B.C. were mostly lecturers who traveled about discoursing on the virtues of political excellence. Their goals were largely practical, their concerns were with the immediate. The effect of their views caused them to be charged with philosophical relativism—Protagoras being the best-known example. In the *Theatetus* (152aiff) and in the *Cratylus*, Plato mentions Protagoras' axiom that man is the measure of all things. In the *Cratylus*, Socrates asks whether Hermogenes agrees with Protagoras, or would he say that things have a permanent essence of their own?

Their views were clearly opposed to the Platonic belief in the existence of a world of permanent essences, or the world of *per se*, as it was referred to earlier. Given such views, it is understandable that the Sophists should find themselves at home in the courtroom and in the political arena generally, where the issues are never clearcut and the give-and-take of debate and decision is the only final, absolute judge. They believed in the power of language, but they also recognized its frailty within any given situation. Their reliance upon the *agony* of debate and the importance of agonistic elements in Greek and Roman rhetoric suggests, as Ernst Hoffmann and others have shown, a *Sprachphilosophie* which differed radically from Plato's views, not only on the nature of language—*per se*—but with respect to the nature of reality—*per se*. In the ancient division between theory and practice, their concerns were devoid of epistemological considerations, not because they were charlatans and tricksters, but because they were interested primarily in the practical affairs of political life. The differences between Plato and the Sophists were not peculiar to their time; they had come up earlier in the opposing views of Heracleitus and Parmenides and have become apparent in our own time in the field of ethics, theology, jurisprudence, and all our present concerns for language. In his valuable study, *The Art of Persuasion in Greece*, George Kennedy writes:

> The disagreement between Plato and the sophists over rhetoric was not simply an historical contingency, but reflects a fundamental cleavage between two unconciliable ways of viewing the world. There have always been those, especially among philosophers and religious thinkers, who have emphasized goals and absolute standards and have talked much about truth, while there have been as many others to whom these concepts seem shadowy or imaginary and who find the only certain reality in the process of life and the present moment. In general, rhetoricians and orators, with certain distinguished exceptions, have held the latter view, which is the logical, if unconscious, basis of their common view of art as a response to the rhetorical challenge unconstrained by external principles. The difference is not only that between Plato and Gorgias, but between Demosthenes and Isocrates, Virgil and Ovid, Dante and Petrarch, and perhaps Milton and Shakespeare.[82]

Plato's attack on Gorgias illustrates some of his fundamental differences with the Sophists. In *Gorgias,* written about 487 B.C., Plato is perhaps his bitterest on the subject of rhetoric. Gorgias states that he is a rhetorician and that rhetoric is the art of discourse, that art which is pre-eminently concerned with the verbal element and with the best of human things. The chief end of rhetoric is summed up in Gorgias' statement (450) that "rhetoric is the art of persuasion in courts of law and other assemblies . . . and about the just and unjust." In the course of the discussion, Socrates places rhetoric and cooking in the same class and refers to rhetoric not as an art but a knack, a sham, a kind of flattery, "the habit of a bold and ready wit, which knows how to manage mankind." Later on Socrates says (465) that sophistry is to legislation as tiring to gymnastic; rhetoric to justice as cooking is to medicine. The philosopher is ultimately the better guide for political life because he alone has experienced the *fruitio dei* and has a knowledge of absolute justice *per se.* The practicing politician must forever take a backseat to the true political scientist, the philosopher. Whether or not Plato was correct in distinguishing between the true philosopher and the Sophist—"a paid huntsman of rich and distinguished youths"—is not our concern here. Of greater interest is the preoccupation of the Sophists with the theme of strife in their fundamentally speech-centered universe.

After Heracleitus, *logos* usage developed in two directions. For the Pythagoreans logos became associated with the impersonal concepts of number, category, and quantity. The Sophists, on the other hand, stressed the vocal persuasive and mediating qualities of the logos inherent in human speech. For Cassirer, the Sophists realized the anthropological insights germane in Heracleitus' suggestion that speech is the new gateway to philosophy. In Sophistic thought, man and his speech have indeed become the center of the universe. In place of the universality of the logos, the Sophists developed a new science—namely, that of rhetoric, which attempted to treat linguistic problems in a systematic fashion. Rhetoric, not grammar or etymology, became their chief concern. In their definition of wisdom (*sophia*), rhetoric maintains a central position. The most important result of their newfound science was that "all disputes about the *truth* or *correctness* (*orthotes*) of terms and names became futile and superfluous." No longer was there any correlation between names and their eternal essences or forms. The task of language is "to arouse human emotions; not to convey mere ideas or thoughts but to prompt men to certain actions." The Sophists recognized only the agonistic or struggling element in language as the key to their understanding of truth and reality. The guilt or innocence of the defendant was decided on the basis of the striving or contending by the litigants in the courtroom. The litigants were primarily concerned with the effect of the word upon the listener: hence, rhetoric became a form of "enchanting the mind by arguments." (*Phaedrus*, 261a) As Cassirer has noted, the Sophists "were very much at home in that middle region of words that is situated between man and things."[83] The agonistic aspects of the rhetorical tradition emphasized the function of the logos as "that which is capable of bringing the listener under the power of the speaker."[84] In the blending of the agonistic elements with the rhetorical, the give-and-take character of conversation attained classic form. Jaeger referred to them as the "heirs of the educational tradition of the poets; . . . the successors of Homer and Hesiod, Solon and Theognis, Simonides and Pindar." They were preoccupied with the whole man in the modern sense of the term, out of which there developed an interest in cultural humanism of the kind that saw all the traditional absolutes as relative to their humanistic emphasis. Jaeger also notes that ". . . the conscious ideal of humanism could not have been produced by the Greek educational tradition except at a moment when the old standards which had once meant so much to education began to be questioned."[85] Protagoras' assertion that "Man is the measure of all things" must be seen in the light of his times as a bold attempt at preparing men, in the sense of "caring for the soul," for a future in which the existing standards and absolutes would become questionable.

The Socratic Method of "Midwifery"

ERNST HOFFMANN saw in the eristic and agonistic elements of the Sophistic tradition a greater concern for the personal, for confrontation, and for the reaching out to the other over against one than was present in Socratic maieutics, which Hoffmann contends was chiefly concerned with objective truth. "While it is true that the versatility of the individual was the 'standard' for the agonistic logos, the socratic logos stressed an objective standard, namely 'the truth'; the agonistic never fought 'in behalf of' (e.g. an objective standard), but rather 'against' persons."[86] The maieutic method and also the dialogical literary form used by Plato were from this standpoint but a foil, an art, a *techne*, a device, which had as its aim not the realization of truth within and between man, through give-and-take, but rather the separation of absolute objective truth from subjective relative fiction. Were Plato's ideal realizable, men would through this method eventually see, literally behold, the true forms. From Plato's and Socrates' standpoints the absolute relativism of Protagoras' humanistic concerns smacked of pure subjectivism. It is indeed unfortunate that we do not have Protagoras' *Antilogies*, since the title suggests a treatise defending the nobility of all those elements and ideas one associates with his name.

One ought to distinguish between Plato's literary style in his dialogues and the conversational model used by Socrates. Platonic dialogue is a literary technique similar to the dramatic form in the theater, where several voices betray the mind of the author. It is a fixed and very closed style from beginning to end. The dialectic of clear thinking rather than the probability and uncertainty of the clash of words is supreme in most areas of Platonic investigation.

In the case of Socrates, the style is more open in that each response takes its cue from the word of the listener, so that there is more of a clash or contending of words—much in the same way that the words of the Sophists clashed in the courtroom. Never forget that Plato's teacher Socrates never published, never wrote anything down; that, unlike his disciple Plato, he chose to remain in the arena governed by the uncertainty of speech. Genuine dialogue, open give-and-take, were normative for the role of midwife which Socrates strove to maintain. Hence his style was maieutic, like that of a midwife (a *maieutikos*). However, unlike the Sophists, whose outlook assumed that the truth had to be discovered amid the agony, the clash of words, Socrates assumed that truth nevertheless existed absolutely and independently of human language. Hence, his role of midwife was to use the question-and-answer method as a means of enabling his adversary to distinguish—literally to see—the difference between truth and falsehood. Language here is not the vehicle within which truth is revealed, as was the case with the Sophists and all politically and practically oriented Athenians; rather, language was a device by means of which incorrect opinions could be replaced by a true vision of the eternal ideas. Plato and Socrates, each in his own way, were interested in the dialectical pilgrimage of the soul from the darkness of its sensory world of illusion to the bright light of intelligible forms. This assumption colored their view of language as it did their view of education and political life. Amid current interest in the term dialogue it is suggested that from the standpoint, for example, of Martin Buber's thought, Plato and Socrates were dialecticians rather than dialogicians. Buber's attitude toward Socrates is brought out most succinctly in his exchange with Robert M. Hutchins. Hutchins' concern for the great truths in the history of ideas caused Buber to associate Hutchins' position with that of Socrates. While admitting great "trust and veneration" for Socrates, Buber questioned the Socratic method as an educational device. "Socrates overvalued the significance of abstract individual experiences. . . . Socrates conducts his dialogue by posing questions and proving the answers that he received untenable; these are not real questions, they are moves in a sublime dialectical game that has a goal, the goal of revealing a not-knowing."[87] In contrast to Socrates' emphasis, Buber insisted that educators should begin with the living experience of concrete individuals. Buber was not denying the validity of conceptual truths; rather, he was insisting that *truth* lies somewhere between the realm of ideas and a pupil's life-situation. Conceptual truths are irrelevant apart from those situations in which the ideal, according to Buber, "has to authenticate itself."

It is noteworthy that in his concluding remarks in the *Phaedrus* (279) Plato mentions that venerable student of rhetoric, Isocrates, and expresses the desire that "he will not be satisfied with rhetoric . . . that there is in him a divine inspiration which will lead him to things higher still. For he has an element of philosophy in his virtue." How unfortunate that Plato could not see a connection between the madness of love, which he respected, and the art of discourse, which he mocked and despised. For noble Isocrates had, as noted earlier, bequeathed to mankind an eloquent testimony on the power of the art of oral discourse, in the fifth century. Speech, as understood by Isocrates, was the womb out of which the thoughts of a civilization poured forth; speech was more than a mere means for the expression of private thoughts. A people pondered and thought because they had been confronted by new forms of address. Rhetoric was a noble word in Isocrates' vocabulary and lacked the limited role later assigned to it as a mere vehicle for private thoughts. Remember that Cicero spoke his speeches before writing them down and that Schleiermacher in his *Dialektik* noted that he had to teach students in the classroom in order to develop his private thoughts. Implicit in Isocrates' outlook and that of the Sophists is recognition of an absolute relativity that must influence our every endeavor—particularly our view of language. Had Isocrates known of Schleiermacher, he might have entitled some of his addresses *Lectures on Language to its Cultured Despisers,* for under the influence of Plato and his followers oral discourse was rapidly falling into disrespect. Behind Plato's attack, in each instance, is his insistence that timeless abstract absolute standards exist absolutely.

Against this, the language of the poet and rhetorician are imperfect vehicles whose content can only lead the soul astray. The soul and its cultivation have become the chief end of instruction. In the process of education for Plato or for Aristotle, distance, complete independence, emancipation, wisdom, and correct knowledge of the eternal verities have produced a creature whose entire focus is upward, away from the bodily and material, the worldly and political, the temporal, the changing and corruptible. In a word, Plato demanded the surrender of one language experience in favor of a new language experiment guaranteed to give ultimate and absolute answers where human language had hitherto failed.

The Sacramental Character of Speech

BEFORE PROCEEDING TO an examination of the significance of speech in more recent times, it is appropriate to summarize from the preceding remarks a number of points that are particularly relevant for contemporary interests in oral discourse. Reference to these themes will, one hopes, provide a background against which the following chapters might have particular relevance.

The first insight into the role of the word in antiquity made it clear that men in the ancient *world* were aware, despite their own insignificance, of the role of the word in the shaping of the universe wherein they lived. As tribal men they feared and revered the power of the word just as they revered names, oaths, blessings, curses, and the like. These elements can be referred to as having a magical quality for ancient man, if by this is implied a reverence for them and an inability and fear either to account for their power or to achieve conscious mastery over their source. Given ancient man's mythopoeic environment, speech was a powerful force in the shaping of reality.

The situation was somewhat different for the early Israelite, due to his acceptance of the high status he at once achieved as one created in the image of God. As a man with a *name*, he was conscious of his part and status in the life of Israel, in its fate and destiny as this manifested itself in the constant conversations held between Yahweh and His people. The Israelites had a much greater sense of personal and collective history than most of their contemporaries and predecessors. Like ancient man, the Israelite was still dependent upon the word, but it was Yahweh's Word, and on occasion he took the liberty of answering back, protesting, and arguing. In common with earlier men, his oral and aural powers were the sensitive organs whereby reality was shaped and given meaning. Although like Homeric man he lived in a dominantly oral preliterate society, it has been repeatedly suggested that the future of a civilization is intimately tied to its use of speech. We have investigated these periods because it was there that the formative speech patterns were established which not only provided the framework for the shaping of modern Western attitudes and outlooks but, in the case of Judaism, Christianity, and the Platonic influence, provided normative speech patterns which many in these traditions still look upon as relevant for our present situation. Just as Western religious theologians speak of the authoritative character of the Word and mean by that Biblical Judaism and Biblical Christianity, so too, as Whitehead pointed out, it is exclusively to Plato and Aristotle that modern man looks when seeking out his intellectual and cultural roots. Each of these traditions had a particular regard for speech, whether it was positive indebtedness or critical reserve. The Homeric storyteller, Heracleitus, the Sophists, and the Roman rhetoricians are useful examples of men and traditions in the Graeco-Roman world who regarded speech as a power or force within which men live, move, and have their being, in a way not too different from the power and cohesive character of the Word in early Jewish and Christian communities. They have in common a kind of tribal respect for the unifying character of oral discourse, although this varies from tradition to tradition in substance as well as in stylistic representation. In each instance, however, it was necessary, despite definitions of the term, that a community participate in the spell or magic of speech in order for their lives to have direction. Furthermore, it was noted that some kind of give-and-take, or in the case of Heracleitus and the Sophists, a clash, struggle, or war of words was an essential quality of meaningful discourse. In the case of Jews and Christians particularly, but also for the Sophists and Homeric oral tradition, a respect for time in the sense of *timing*, i.e., doing things at the right or proper time, was characteristic of speech-centered existence.

As these characteristics are brought out it should be remembered that we were not concerned with the degree to which people were conscious of their dependence upon speech, or with whether, in the obvious case of Heracleitus or the Sophists, they had a philosophy of language (*Sprachphilosophie*), as Hoffmann suggests. If they did, it lacked the precision and concern for definition which mark interests in language dating, for example, from Max Müller's investigations at the turn of this century. The fact that they quite simply accepted the power of ordinary language as a force in their lives would, quite understandably, make it a difficult subject matter for examination by devotees of linguistic analysis. Inherent in their acceptance of the power and mystery of everyday discourse was a largely unconscious acceptance of the diverse forms of speech and the numerous roles that ordinary language contains and combines. While there were numerous events to be remembered and retold, whether in the Homeric period or in the case of Jesus' or Paul's missionary activity, there was considerable flexibility with respect to the appropriate style to be used when telling, calling, exhorting, etc. The phenomenon of a fixed language, of an orthodox vocabulary, was by and large a product of necessity, not arising out of the fact that one was in an oral or literate society; rather, as was the case in the development of Christian doctrine, a fixed style arose out of the need of the faithful for defining the correct position, way, or truth.

In what I regard as their most vital periods, whether dealing with religious or secular matters, variety of expression and recourse to speech patterns appropriate to the occasion were the rule rather than the exception. In this connection it was noted that in the Homeric period, in the time of the ancient Israelites, and in the early Christian communities, it was exceedingly difficult to single out a particular way of speaking which was viewed as a sacred as against profane mode of discourse. How speech was used rather than what words were said was ultimately significant. It is suggested that everyday speech and timing were the matrix or medium for correct or sacred speech during most vital periods in these traditions.

Our use of the term sacred or sacramental speech as employed here is not determined by whether a tradition or situation was one necessarily involving a relationship with a particular god or gods, but rather in a much broader sense—*i.e.*, by the way speech was

used to give meaning and direction to people's lives. This certainly
would include, for example, the sacred exchanges between Yahweh
and Abraham, as well as those between Abraham and Isaac. As used
here, to suggest that all speech is potentially sacramental applies to
all forms of discourse under every possible temporal condition.
Against this background the canons of necessity, appropriateness,
and timeliness are better guides for determining sacred or sacramental speech than are those which would measure a man's words
against fixed sacred forms or holy writ. The fact that Zeus is or is
not mentioned in the telling of a Homeric tale is incidental to the
fact that the tale had to be told in order for the community to be
sustained. The terms sacred or sacramental may include whatever is
meant by either sacred or profane language from a historical, literary, or theological standpoint. Words uttered too early or too late
rather than those conditioned by the time and ears of the audience
might well be profane words because they have missed their intended mark. To live under the spell of a poet's, statesman's, or any
man's word suggests, but only upon reflection, that something
sacred or, in Tillich's words, of ultimate concern, has happened.
Sacred happenings or meetings are sacred insofar as the partners in
the event, the cor-respondents (literally those who respond from
the heart), actually do so and give themselves (part of their indenti-
ties) up to the words which out of necessity have been spoken.

Sacramental speech is speech uttered at the right time. The inadequacies of all definitions are particularly true here. Immediately, the
horrors of relativism, the difficulties of knowing whether such and
such a word and time are correct or not, come to mind. Such
ambiguity is consistent with serious discourse today in every area,
whether in jurisprudence, ethics, or in the case of such issues as civil
disobedience, the use of nuclear weapons, or even when placing
responsibility for a partnership, project, or marriage that has failed.
In many cases we cannot define the correct position because we
aren't even sure if there *is* a single correct answer which can be
settled upon and then subjected to definition. If the reader can bear
the admission of the inadequacies and frailty of definitions when
dealing with ultimate questions—as many intellectuals seem to be
doing when discussing, for example, transmoral values—then the
natural limitations as well as the unnatural sacred potential of speech
can begin to be appreciated.

The reader may have discovered by now that the term sacred or sacramental speech can apply potentially to almost any kind of discourse under almost any conditions; and secondly, that the term religion or religious, as normally used, is of as little use as is the term profane or secular. Our use of the term sacred or sacramental speech suggests, however, that certain irreligious, neutral, or profane utterances and exchanges may under certain conditions have religious significance in the traditional sense in which religion and sacred are used. This requires, however, a broadening of our understanding of the realms of experience that now in a nontraditional sense may be regarded as religious. The anthropologist and student of language Edward Sapir, in an early essay entitled *The Meaning of Religion* (1929), illustrated this when he discussed our modern conception of religion, which almost by definition creates fixed sacred and profane realms by equating religion with a "selfconscious church," with "carefully guarded rituals, with sacred texts, and with followers of a charismatic leader." Contrast this, he suggests, with religion among primitive peoples. "If we leave the more sophisticated peoples and study the social habits of primitive and barbaric folk, we shall find that it is very difficult to discover religious institutions that are as highly formalized as those that go under the name of the Roman Catholic Church or of Judaism." His next words are particularly appropriate to our interest: "Yet religion in some sense is everywhere present. It seems to be as universal as speech itself and the use of material tools."[88]

Today, the term religion has become an increasingly meaningless term, primarily because it can apply to almost every situation area, ideology, and discipline. If this is so, then our difficulties with sacred or sacramental speech are just as real. However, it is precisely because of this situation and these ambiguities that we have focused upon speech as the potentially sacred driving and unifying medium for modern fragmented man. To say this is not to deny the fact that we are modern men living in a modern world, rather than ancient men living in an earlier milieu. However, one of the chief concerns today of concerned clergy and laity, as well as of those in almost every nonreligious discipline and profession, is with the effects of fragmentation upon modern man. While the situation cannot be corrected overnight, many feel the need for providing a sense of unity, meaning, and direction, given the existing situation. One at-

tempt of clergy in response to this situation is to break down socially conditioned distinctions between sacred and profane and to
encourage a realization that everyday concerns and actions are potentially sacramental concerns. If this be so, then the traditionalist is
encouraged to stay with us and explore the potentially sacred character of ordinary speech as reflected in the writings of those who in
subsequent periods spoke in an unorthodox fashion and out of a
deep sense of the meaning of orthodoxy. It has been said of Edward
Sapir's influence upon the social sciences that "his writing is programmatic and pioneering rather than definitive." In a similar sense
this effort is offered as programmatic and pioneering, or to use an
appropriate term from within this tradition, it might serve as a
prolegomena for subsequent investigations.

A last observation relevant to subsequent chapters, and certainly
to some of the problems of definition just raised, again bears upon
our interest in speech. The interests of Cassirer and Hoffmann indicate a conscious interest in outlining a philosophy of language in a
manner not totally unlike the efforts of Martin Heidegger. Certainly, as will be seen, J. G. Hamann and Eugen Rosenstock-Huessy
have made similar efforts. In each instance, normative judgments are
made with respect to meaningful language. While this cannot, and
from our standpoint should not, be avoided, there are differences
with respect to the manner and scope of the undertaking. Ernst
Hoffmann's investigations discerned in the pre-Socratics—*e.g.*, Heracleitus—and again in the Sophists, a preoccupation with language
in a way overlooked, for example, by the natural philosophers.
What Hoffmann in turn seems to have overlooked is an awareness
of the fact that language was the instrument of the natural philosophers as well, despite their ostensible disregard, if not disdain, for
ordinary discourse. This seems relevant from our standpoint because
in each instance little attention was devoted to whether the language
was primarily oral or not, ordinary or speculative, the language of
the common man or that of the intellectuals. More importantly,
little attention was given to the place of these various forms of
speech within the total social framework. What distinguishes, for
example, the interests in language of a Hamann or a Rosenstock-
Huessy is the absence of a philosophy of language in the narrow
sense and a recognition of the place of every possible kind of speech
in the life of a people. Traditional philosophers of language seem to

have failed precisely at the point where the beauty of language becomes most apparent—namely, in the fact of its diversity. Along with this, they seem to have failed to recognize the hierarchical and tonal character of speech—*i.e.*, that there are tonal hierarchies as well as various levels of discourse befitting the countless situations that confront us. Not only is there a time and place for various levels of discourse, but more importantly, an awareness of the hierarchical and tonal character of speech is essential to the creation of new times and memorable places. Hence, it is assumed that no single pattern of language is adequate for every level of concern, whether to express or to analyze it. For example, certain forms of expression having nothing to do with time are true irrespective of time—*e.g.*, two and two are four. Other forms of speech create new times— *e.g.*, "I take thee, John, to be my wedded husband"; "The battle is won, the ridge has been taken"; or, more obviously, "The governor has granted you a reprieve." Some forms of expression, to paraphrase Abraham Heschel, are devoted to men's conquest of space, others to his sanctification of time. No one language pattern is appropriate to both. Needless to say, it would be an oversimplification to suppose that we had but two linguistic options—one dealing with space and one dealing with time. A moment's reflection indicates that there are many forms of space, *e.g.*, abstract, physical, and concrete or geographical place; and in the case of time, at least the language tense prior to an event, while it is happening, and after an event. And then too, there are many kinds of time—*e.g.*, mythical, chronological, biographical, revolutionary, evolutionary, eschatological, messianic, and so forth. Each of these spheres has its own indigenous vocabulary. While many Jews and numerous Christians are hence indebted to Professor Heschel for *The Sabbath*, wherein he illustrates the Jew's understanding of the meaning of time, space, and eternity from the standpoint of the language of the Sabbath, there are still countless others who come to these same insights from other perspectives. Somehow, all of those who do so betray an indebtedness to language; and then certainly not as a mere technical means of expression.

One of the difficulties arising out of the strain of civilization in the sixth-century clash between the music of poetry and that of philosophy stemmed from a lack of awareness of the various themes and problems which each music is capable of treating. It is suggested that a healthy civilization is polyphonic, which is different from Karl Popper's diagnosis of it as a cacophony. Of all the men considered in this work, Rosenstock-Huessy's insights into speech are perhaps most relevant, since he is one of the few to have undertaken an analysis of the autobiography of Western man from the standpoint of language.

In presenting the sacramental character of speech in the next chapters, it is at once apparent that each of those considered is credited with stressing a particular quality or aspect of speech. The assumption that no single individual can exhaust the implications of taking speech seriously is at once apparent. It is to the credit of each of these men that while developing in varying degrees an approach based on speech—in one instance a methodology—yea, even a system or *Programm*—each has done so completely under the spell of language. However, they are not on top of the problem, as much as the problem, in Hamann's words, is language, the bone upon which they gnawed continually. In view of the kind of problems which we face today, it is significant that there are those thinkers whose approach is an open rather than a closed one. By open is meant a tendency to ponder—mindful of the limitations of human thought and systems—when dealing with ultimate questions in such a way as to exclude nothing, to consider the fragmentary character of human speculation, and to be ever mindful of Tennyson's words:

> Our little systems have their day
> They have their day and cease to be
> They are but broken images of thee
> And Thou, O Lord, art more than they.

Hopefully, there is a middle ground between, on the one hand, the pessimism about speculation of a Tennyson and a Nietzsche who in his *Twilight of the Idols* said, "I hate systems; the will to a system betrays a look of honesty" and, on the other, those whose use of language is bound by a reverence for language. Assuming that all speculation takes place within the limitations of language, is it not important to consider especially those speculations whose foundations are built upon a reverence and awe for language rather than upon a kind of intellectual *hutzbah* which assumes at a crucial juncture, and then falsely, that thought precedes speech, rather than vice versa? The open form of philosophizing that characterizes the following speech thinkers and dialogicians takes for granted that all are, as the title of H. H. Farmer's book on Martin Buber suggested, *Servant[s] of the Word*, and in no way intellectually or humanly superior to the complex super-individual, or *meta-noetic* nature of the problems facing us. In the early nineteenth century, some of these men probably would have been referred to as faith-philosophers, in the oversimplified sense in which F. H. Jacobi said that faith precedes reason. The difference here is that this is a twentieth-century setting and no longer a faith-reason nor even a speech-reason problem; rather, it is at once a religious, social, and technological problem no longer susceptible to the kind of neat, parochial faith-reason categories which worked in previous ages. J. G. Hamann recognized this when in a letter to the faith-philosopher F. H. Jacobi he said, "What you refer to as *Being*, I prefer to call the *Word*." While secularists can appreciate that each age poses different questions and solutions, the traditionalist, and in this sense the religiously parochial thinker, too often assumes, and then unfortunately, that the questions facing us in the twentieth century are identical with those which faced members of the early Christian Church.

NOTES

CHAPTER I

1 Abraham J. Heschel, *Man's Quest for God* (New York: Charles Scribner's, 1954), p. 25.
2 One of the best presentations of the significance of *davar* for the Hebrews is James Muilenburg's *The Way of Israel* (New York: Harper Torchbooks, 1965).
3 Benjamin S. Bloom (Editor), *Taxonomy of Educational Objectives* (New York: David McKay Co., 1964).
4 Margaret Ribble, *The Rights of Infants* (New York: Columbia University Press, 1953), p. 5 ff.
5 Clemens E. Benda, "Language, Consciousness and Problems of Existential Analysis *(Daseinsanalyse)*," *American Journal of Psychotherapy*, 14, 2 (April 1960), p. 262.
6 Eugen Rosenstock-Huessy, from a privately printed monograph on grammar.
7 *Negro Slave Songs in the United States* (Ithaca: Cornell University Press, 1953).
8 G. Mircea Eliade, *The Sacred and the Profane* (New York: Harcourt, Brace, 1959) and Eliade's *Cosmos and History* (New York: Harper Torchbooks, 1959).
9 Marshall McLuhan, *Understanding Media* (New York: McGraw-Hill, 1965), p. 343.
10 Eugen Rosenstock-Huessy, "Tribalism," *Exodus*, No. 2 (Fall 1959), p. 14.
11 *Ibid.*
12 Marshall McLuhan, "Address at Vision 65," *The American Scholar*, (Spring 1966), p. 198.
13 *Op. cit.*, p. 200.
14 McLuhan, *Understanding Media*, p. vii.
15 *Ibid.*, p. ix.
16 *Ibid.*, p. vi.
17 A. A. Bowman, *Studies in the Philosophy of Religion* (London: Macmillan, 1938), Vol. II, p. 239.

18 Rollo May, *Existence* (New York: Basic Books, 1958), p. 11.
19 *Ibid.*
20 Emil Brunner, *The Divine-Human Encounter* (Philadelphia: Westminster, 1943), p. 21.
21 Martin Buber, *Eclipse of God* (London: Victor Gollancz, 1953), p. 45. *Cf.* also: John Baillie, *Our Knowledge of God* (London: Oxford University Press, 1952), pp. 217–18; James Brown, *Subject and Object in Modern Theology* (London: SCM Press, 1955).
22 Iscocrates, *Antidosis*, 253–58.
23 Thorleif Boman, *Hebrew Thought Compared with Greek* (Philadelphia: The Westminster Press, 1960), pp. 58–73.
24 Henri Frankfort, *Before Philosophy* (Middlesex: Penguin Books, 1951), pp. 142–43.
25 Martin Buber, *Die jüdische Bewegung* (Berlin: Jüdischer Verlag, 1916), Vol. I, p. 245.
26 George E. Mendenhall, "Law and Covenant in Israel and the Ancient Near East," *The Biblical Archeologist*, XVII, 2 (September 1954), pp. 49–76.
27 Martin Buber, "The Word That is Spoken," from *The Knowledge of Man* (London: George Allen and Unwin, 1965), p. 116.
28 Martin Buber, *Eclipse of God*, p. 173.
29 Thorleif Boman, *op. cit.*, p. 67.
30 Johannes Pedersen, *Israel* I–II (London: Oxford University Press, 1946), p. 489. *Cf.* also: H. Wheeler Robinson, *Inspiration and Revelation in the Old Testament* (Oxford: Oxford University Press, 1953), p. 107.
31 Henri Frankfort, *op. cit.*, p. 113.
32 Ernst Cassirer, *An Essay On Man* (New Haven: Yale University Press, 1944), p. 114.
33 Abraham J. Heschel, *op. cit.*, p. 124.
34 Thorleif Boman, *op. cit.*, p. 112.
35 Martin Buber, *I and Thou* (New York: Charles Scribner's, 1958), p. 27.
36 Martin Buber, *The Prophetic Faith* (New York: The Macmillan Company, 1949), p. 5. *Cf.* also: H. Wheeler Robinson's remarks in *Inspiration and Revelation in the Old Testament*, p. 123 ff.
37 Buber, *Die jüdische Bewegung*, p. 245.
38 Amos Wilder, *The Language of the Gospel* (New York: Harper & Row, 1964), p. 136.
39 Raymond Macdonald Alden (Editor), *Readings in English Prose of the Nineteenth Century* (New York: Houghton Mifflin, 1917), p. 439.
40 *Ibid.*, pp. 444–45.
41 Wilder, *op. cit.*, p. 13.
42 Robinson and Cobb (Editors), *The New Hermeneutic* (New York: Harper & Row, 1964), p. 120.
43 Wilder, *op. cit.*, p. 18.
44 Robinson and Cobb, *op. cit.*, p. 122.

45 *Ibid.*
46 *Ibid.*, p. 144.
47 Wilder, *op. cit.*, p. 21.
48 *Ibid.*, pp. 19–20.
49 *Ibid.*, p. 15. Note also Wilder's comment: "Christian utterance and writing did have charismatic power and prestige, but not in the sense of esoteric holy texts. The *common* language of men was itself the medium of revelation." (*Ibid.*, pp. 26–27.)
50 Wilder, *op. cit.*, p. 124.
51 Eugen Rosenstock-Huessy, *Out of Revolution* (New York: William Morrow, 1938), p. 727. The reader should note the existence of a paperback edition of this work: (New York: Four Wells, 1964).
52 Eugen Rosenstock-Huessy, *The Christian Future Or The Modern Mind Outrun* (New York: Harper Torchbooks, 1966), p. 108.
53 Rosenstock-Huessy, *Out of Revolution*, p. 741.
54 Rosenstock-Huessy, *The Christian Future*, pp. 116, 127, 130.
55 The contributions of Parry Whitman, Albert Lord, Eric Havelock and George Kennedy have enriched immeasurably our knowledge in this area. If taken seriously, along with the works of E. R. Dodds, Werner Jaeger, Philip Wheelwright, Ernst Hoffmann, and others, these studies, mostly historical and literary in character, represent a fundamental change in attitude toward the legacies of Greece and Rome.
56 Ernst Cassirer, *The Philosophy of Symbolic Forms*, Volume I, *Language* (New Haven: Yale University Press, 1953), p. 145.
57 Ernst Hoffmann, "Die Sprache und die archaische Logik," *Heidelberger Abhandlungen zur Philosophie und ihre Geschichte*, No. 3 (Tübingen: Mohr, 1925), p. vii.
58 Pauly-Wissowa, *Real encyclopaedie der Classischen Altertums-Wissenschaft*, Vol. 13 (1905), p. 1035 ff.
59 Albert Lord, *The Singer of Tales* (Cambridge: Harvard University Press), p. 148.
60 H. I. Marrou, *A History of Education in Antiquity* (New York: Mentor, 1964), p. 84.
61 Cedric H. Whitman, *Homer and the Homeric Tradition* (Cambridge: Harvard University Press, 1963), p. 13.
62 Eric Havelock, *Preface To Plato* (Cambridge: Belknap Press, 1963), pp. 153–55.
63 Cedric H. Whitman, *op. cit.*, pp. 149–50; 238 ff.
64 George Kennedy, *The Art of Persuasion in Greece* (Princeton: Princeton University Press, 1963), p. 6.
65 Whitman, *op. cit.*, p. 301.
66 Charles Sears Baldwin, *Ancient Rhetoric and Poetic* (New York: Macmillan, 1924), p. 54.
67 *Ibid.*
68 John Burnett, *Early Greek Philosophy* (4th ed., London: A&C Black, 1952), p. 179.

69 Frankfort, *op. cit.*, p. 261.
70 Burnett, *op. cit.*, p. 173.
71 Karl Reinhardt, *Parmenides und die Geschichte der griechischen Philosophie* (Bonn, 1916), p. 256.
72 Cassirer, *The Philosophy of Symbolic Forms*, pp. 120–21.
73 Buber, *The Knowledge of Man*, p. 98. The centrality of language to the differences between Parmenides and Heracleitus has been treated by Rosenstock-Huessy in "Herakleitos an Parmenides," in *Festschrift für Victor von Weizsäcker* (Göttingen, 1956), as well as in his book *Züruck in das Wagnis der Sprache* (Berlin: Käthe Vogt, 1957).
74 *Cf.* Marshall McLuhan, *The Gutenberg Galaxy* (Toronto: University of Toronto Press, 1962), p. 8.
75 *Ibid.*
76 *Ibid.*, p. 6.
77 E. R. Dodds, *The Greeks and the Irrational* (Boston: Beacon Press, 1957), p. 192.
78 Havelock, *op. cit.*, p. 25.
79 *Ibid.*, pp. 225–82.
80 Dodds, *op. cit.*, pp. 236, 244.
81 *Ibid.*, p. 252.
82 George Kennedy, *The Art of Persuasion in Greece*, p. 15.
83 Cassirer, *Philosophy of Symbolic Forms*, p. 122.
84 Hoffmann, *op. cit.*, p. 29.
85 Werner Jaeger, *Paideia*, Vol. I (New York: Oxford University Press, 1943), pp. 296, 315.
86 Hoffmann, *op. cit.*, p. 32.
87 Sydney and Beatrice Rome (editors), *Philosophical Interrogations* (New York: Holt, Rinehart and Winston, 1964), p. 67.
88 David G. Mandelbaum, *Selected Writings of Edward Sapir* (Berkeley: University of California Press, 1963), p. 346.

Johann Georg Hamann (1730-1788): Speech Is Sacred

Speak that I may see thee! This wish was fulfilled in the creation, which is a speaking to the creature through the creature.

—J. G. HAMANN

He who does not enter into the world of language, which is the Deipara of our reason, is not adept for the baptism of a church and state reformation.

—J. G. HAMANN

I speak neither of physics nor of theology: with me language is the mother of reason and revelation, its Λ and Ω.

—J. G. HAMANN

What in your language is being, I should prefer to call the Word. It is the Word which unites Moses and John, Christianity and Judaism, the living and the dead—whose society was scattered and spoiled by the tower of Babel, but who are of one mind through the dovelike innocence of the Spirit which has no tyrannical fetters—it is the Word which turns fellow-sinners into brothers of one mind.

—J. G. HAMANN TO F. H. JACOBI

The oldest language was music and with it the perceptible rhythm of the pulse beat and of the breath in the nose,—the physical prototype of all *measurement of time* and its numeral proportion. The oldest writing was *painting* and *drawing*, concerning itself even so early with the *economy* of *space*, and its boundaries and determination through figures. Therefore the concepts of *time* and *space* through the abundantly persevering influence of both the noblest senses (sight and hearing) have made themselves so "universal" and "necessary" in the entire sphere of the understanding, as light and air are universal and necessary for eye, ear, and voice, so that space and time would appear to be not innate but "maternal" ideas, the "mother" of all intuitional knowledge.

—J. G. HAMANN

Silent Interregnums

THE RECORD OF Western man's achievements between the first and eighteenth centuries is a notable one, particularly in the fields of mathematics, science, exploration, and political thought. Through a wide and rich variety of styles he attempted to employ language both to conquer space and to sanctify time. However, when responding to his challenges, he frequently confused his styles thereby losing some of the richness and uniqueness of the phenomena, as well as opportunities for exploration and application. This was particularly true in the areas of literature, poetry, and theology. It is to the credit of the scholarship of Walter J. Ong, S.J., and Basil Willey that they have shown, for example, the effect upon "theological and poetic beliefs" when "exposed to the 'touch of cold philosophy.' "[1] In the seventeenth century, according to Professor Willey, "a great effort was being made by representative thinkers, to see things 'as in themselves they really are,' and the ideas of Truth and Fiction which were then evolved seem to have exerted a decisive influence upon the poetic and religious beliefs of succeeding times."[2] Father Ong sums up one aspect of this theme when he says that:

In many ways, the greatest shift in the way of conceiving knowledge between the ancient and modern world takes place in the movement from a pole where knowledge is conceived of in terms of discourse and hearing and persons to one where it is conceived of in terms of observation and sight and objects. This shift dominates all others in Western intellectual history, and as compared to it, the supposed shift from a deductive to an inductive method pales into insignificance.[3]

During this period, especially in the seventeenth and eighteenth centuries, because of a preoccupation with methodologies based upon observation, measurement, and quantifiable language, men frequently devoted little if any attention to those themes and media rooted in oral discourse. Where they were considered, it was usually against the physical scientific paradigm of the period. Against such standards the richness of those themes involving a sensitivity for the spoken word in all its configurations was either demeaned or found unworthy of scholarly investigation. Quite unmindful of

Aristotle's admonition that every realm of reality must be examined in terms of its own inner logic and uniqueness, men blithely assumed that religious and poetic themes of any consequence could be dealt with in the same way that men treated problems in the natural and physical sciences. These were the times when any scholar of substance had to apply a rigorous method and above all produce a system. In the seventeenth and eighteenth centuries it was a sign of the merit of one's work if the word "system" appeared in the title. It gave one's endeavors an aura of scientific and intellectual respectability. Thus we have *The New Intellectual System of the Universe, A System of Rhetoric, A New System . . . for a General Peace*, and even *A New System of the Gout and Rheumaticism*. The Scottish minister friend of Sir Isaac Newton, The Rev. Mr. John Craig, was so taken by the spirit of the times that in 1699 he wrote a book entitled *Mathematical Principles of Christian Theology*, which he offered as a companion piece to Newton's *Mathematical Principles of Natural Philosophy*.[4]

Such periods were what I choose to label *silent interregnums* from the standpoint of our interest in the spoken word. They were times of "freedom from the customary authority" of the spoken word. These were periods during which men relied most heavily upon the silent language of mathematics and logic. The throne originally occupied by living speech was vacant because there were few during these silent interregnums who believed in its powers and might. Fortunately, the autobiography of Western man is a record of revolutionary conversations and events. The Italian philosopher Luigi Pareyson recognized this when he described the differences in political or philosophical theory in terms of "a dialogue rather than a dispersal, a communion rather than a monologue, an itinerary rather than a history of errors . . . a co-presence of voices freely talking, questioning and answering one another."[5] Unlike dialectics, historical dialogue rests upon the assumption that, consciously or unconsciously, the historical alter egos or partners in dialogue will affect one another and subsequent generations. A statement by the aging Goethe about Faust appropriately captures these sentiments and provides an introduction to the response made by J. G. Hamann and the *Sturm und Drang* movement toward the latter part of the eighteenth century. Goethe referred to "the history of the world and man, in which the solution of every problem gives rise to a new problem which needs to be solved."[6] Let us turn now to those in the eighteenth century, particularly Hamann, who regarded speech as sacred or sacramental. Any introduction to the intellectual climate to which Hamann addresses his energies ought to include a brief discussion about the *Sturm und Drang* movement, about prevailing and subsequent theories of the origin of language, and finally, a word about the involvement of Hamann's disciple, Herder, in these matters.

On the Origin of Language

TO SAY THAT speech is sacred—that it is our link with God and His creation—does not require necessarily that we prove scientifically, as many have attempted, the divine origin of language. Some fifty years ago The Linguistic Society of Paris passed a rule which excluded from consideration papers devoted to the theory and origin of human language. They did this because no admissible empirical evidence existed to support the various theories which were proposed. While certainly a sound declaration for such an august group, this does not rule out the possibility of studying both the mythical accounts and the actual structure of language where a body of literature exists, as is the case for classical antiquity, the ancient Near East, or even our own personal experience. Evidence for the sacred character of language is not only attested to in these literatures, but more significantly, interest in this phenomenon is commonplace among contemporary scholars whose attention is devoted to problems involving communication, propaganda, identity, and social unity. Rather than prove historically the truth implicit in Genesis 11: "And the whole earth was of one language and one speech," we need only examine the human situation as it exists today for confirmation of the main fact in the Genesis account—namely, that speech is sacred for all men; that it can divide or reconcile men, destroy or build them up, bring life or death, enable them to be slaves or free. It is of no concern to us, for example, as it was to Reuchlin, that Hebrew alone was God's language. We can agree, however, with Reuchlin's assertion in 1508 that "The mediator between God and man is . . . language."[7] An amusing variation on this theme was the assertion by a Swedish scholar, Andres Kemke, in the seventeenth century, that "in the Garden of Eden the Lord spoke Swedish, Adam spoke Danish, and the serpent spoke French."[8] While no evidence exists to support a theory that all men "in the beginning" spoke a single language, that an *Ursprache* ever existed, few will deny the fact that men have always needed some form of communication and the power of speech in order to survive. If sacred may be defined as the power which enables men not only to exist but to establish and perpetuate communities and societies, then speech certainly is one of men's most sacred and precious powers.

The history, particularly in the nineteenth century, of efforts to speculate upon the genesis of language is not only fascinating but, according to the classifications of one recent commentator, highly entertaining. The seven most notable theories characterized by one scholar are the Bow-wow, Pooh-pooh, Yo-he-ho, Ta-ta, Ding-dong, Sing-song, and finally the Goo-goo theories. Of these efforts, it is noted that "Standing alone, each of these theories reveals flaws which are implicit in the baby-talk names by which they are contemptuously known. Each has been thoroughly criticized, rebutted, tarred-and-feathered, and ridden out of the pale of modern linguistic research."[9] It has been suggested, for example, that language developed as a result of men imitating natural sounds; hence, the onomatopoeic or echo quality of certain words. One of the earliest was the Bow-wow theory, which has been associated over the years with man's prerogative in the Bible of naming "every beast of the field and every fowl of the air." Another theory explains the development of language as having evolved from "reflex vocal utterances" associated with physical exertion. Sir Richard Paget offered a different theory when he suggested that speech developed as a kind of vocal accompaniment to various bodily gestures; gradually "gestures become audible."[10] Still another theory affirmed the existence of a kind of harmony between sense and sound, so that "tree" was the natural sound for that which one saw nearby. Darwin and Jespersen provided the basis for a different theory; one to which Hamann, Herder, and other *Sturm und Drang* representatives would have been sympathetic. They associated the first utterances of speech with song, with the wooing associated with courtship; hence the name, the Sing-song theory of language. Kittredge, and also Darwin, had stressed the purposive character of speech, and the latter suggested that as an animal might imitate the sound of a beast of prey in order to warn his own of impending danger, so too humans developed speech in order to announce a particular set of circumstances.[11]

Among these theories, the Pooh-pooh, for example, is close to the view advocated by Martin Buber and Franz Rosenzweig when they undertook to translate the Hebrew Scriptures into German. The notion that speech originated as a result of "spontaneous exclamations and interjections of the human animal; cries of fear, surprise, anger, pain, disgust, despair, or joy" is close to Buber's view of the origin of the Divine Name as an elemental cry, as a Presence which, as Buber notes, requires gestures for its completion and is "more suitable for evocation than for invocation."[12] Although grammatically a name is a noun, the Divine Name for Buber, Rosenzweig, and also Rosenstock-Huessy ought to be regarded more in its oral-aural setting as an ejaculatory utterance, an exclamation, a convulsive response arising from the depths of a man's being.[13] The way one emits spontaneously a sound when taken by surprise, or even better, when the wind is taken out of one's sails by a sudden blow—this captures, perhaps, the spontaneity associated with this quality of speech.

Closely related to the Pooh-pooh theory, and especially to that of Rosenstock-Huessy, is the well-documented thesis of A. S. Diamond, an English lawyer and anthropologist. He maintains that the earliest forms of human speech were "nothing more than exclamations, grunts, or gasps uttered in the course of violent or strenuous action" which developed into imperatives like "Break!, Kill!, Eat!, Come!," as soon as more stable social patterns developed.[14] Whatever their actual origin (and here we can do no more than speculate), in more advanced cultures, such as those prevalent in the ancient Near East, discernible speech patterns and stylistic preferences developed which confirm many of the insights of theorists like Diamond. While the personalities discussed in subsequent chapters have engaged at times in this kind of speculation, it is hoped that an interest in these insights into the sacred character of speech will not rest upon their having engaged in what for many is but a controversial academic mare's nest.

The Sturm und Drang Movement

DURING THE LATTER part of the eighteenth century, there existed a group consisting mostly of young German intellectuals who regarded oral discourse, poetry, and religious rhetoric as seriously as did their Enlightenment alter egos quantified language modeled upon mathematical analogues. Critics and historians have identified them with the *Sturm und Drang* ("Storm and Stress") movement, which began to take shape in 1770; the personalities involved began to go their separate ways around 1778. Regarded by some as politically affecting German culture in a way comparable to Luther, they represented an effective bourgeois challenge to the European stereotype of the culture of the polite society. They were forerunners not only of nineteenth-century romanticism and realism, but also of much twentieth-century interest in existentialism, language, and other religious, philosophical, and literary themes. Although German in makeup, they reflected a renewed enthusiasm throughout Europe, in France as well as Britain, for the values and rights of the growing middle class and for those outbursts which attacked and questioned traditional norms, whether in religion, politics, the stage, or, especially, poetry and prose.

Beneath the surface, a new response to Shakespeare and folksong, to wild nature and grandiose feelings, to melancholy and mystery, was shaking the serenity of classical poise. If in Locke, Hume, Voltaire, Diderot and the Encyclopedie, Richardson, Lillo, and Fielding, the intellectual challenge to traditional thought and values became explicit, in Young, Gray, the Wartons, Sterne, in Percy we see a groping after a new type of feeling. Rousseau summed up in its most provocative form the problematic of the new man, at loggerheads with his times, capable of new rapture and tortured by new, obscure desires.[15]

The personalities whose writings are particularly relevant for our interests and who were either precursors of the *Sturm und Drang* or were directly or indirectly related to it include Justus Moser, Herder, Goethe, Lavater, F. H. Jacobi, Lenz, and, especially, J. G. Hamann. Characteristic of their common bond was a tremendous drive in those areas of life most affected by instinctive feeling, intuition, revelation, and the sensuous concrete testimonies of everyday life. For life to be meaningful and authentic it had to be invested

with one's total energies and united powers. According to the norms
of a serene and polite society, most of the *Sturm und Drang* personalities were looked upon as confused, emotionally unstable, irrational, slaves of their passions, and given to spontaneous and often
violent outbursts and displays of arrogance which not only kindled
criticism from among their opposites but produced divisions and
conflicts within the group itself. To a man they had a congenital
disdain for abstract systems and rigorous methodologies modeled
upon the physical sciences. What had such abstract and impersonal
systems to do with a man's passions and energies? In their age they
represented in many ways the modern counterpart to the ancient
poets and rhetoricians and constituted a significant effort to regain
for oral discourse the respect and reverence accorded it in Homer's
time as well as throughout early Israel and the ancient Near East.
However, unlike the low estate into which oral discourse and
poetry had fallen during the Greek Enlightenment, the *Sturm und
Drang* was to their age what Plato was to his. But as far as language was concerned, the shoe was now on the other foot. Unfortunately, like their ancient and immediate critics, like Plato and
many of their predecessors, they too eventually succumbed to the
tendency to revere one form of discourse at the expense of all
others. However, despite this and other criticisms, their interests,
particularly those in the fields of religion, language, and poetry, are
worthy of serious consideration in view of their similarity and, in
many cases, their acknowledged influence upon the contributions of
men like Rosenstock-Huessy, Rosenzweig, Ebner, and to a lesser
extent, Buber.

For most of the *Sturm und Drang*, it would have been inappropri-
ate to distinguish religion or religious concern from poetry, sensuous language, or those movements and concerns that evoked a total
commitment from men regardless of traditional sacred-profane distinctions. This is rather surprising in view of the fact that most of
them had strong connections with German Protestantism. Klop-
stock was an orthodox Lutheran; Herder, the chief pastor in his
state; Lavater, also a clergyman; Lenz, a theological student; Jung-
Stilling, a known pietist; Goethe had been raised a Protestant; and
Hamann, despite his unorthodoxy, was a precursor to the kind of
Christian existentialism one finds in Kierkegaard. Despite this, there
developed among them an almost pathological abhorrence of any

form of religion that reflected the rationalism of a Lessing, excessive intellectualism, clericalism, rigorous theological orthodoxy, or a fundamentalist piety, which in Goethe's words, in *Poetry and Truth*, had little relevance for "social morality." Their antipathy toward the religious views of the Enlightenment is captured in Merck's statement:

Now we have got the freedom of believing in public nothing but what can be rationally demonstrated. They have deprived religion of all its sensuous elements, that is, of all its relish. They have carved it up into its parts and reduced it to a skeleton without colour and light . . . and now it's put in a jar nobody wants to taste it.[16]

Johann Gottfried von Herder (1744-1803)

HERDER, FOR EXAMPLE, could never reconcile completely his clerical function with his own inner convictions. Nicolai once joked about Herder's "very secular theological articles" and the latter admitted his difficulties when he told his fiancée that "My sermons are as little clerical as my person, they are human sentiments of a full heart."[17] Herder's orthodoxy was constantly "in question" and his writings suspected as those of an "atheist, a free thinker, a Socinian, and enthusiast."[18] For Herder as for the Sophists, truth can never be known *per se;* it manifests itself here and there, constantly changing from individual to individual and people to people, given their respective unique social situations. Herder's account of the Creation narrative in his essay *The Oldest Work of the Human Race* illustrates the questionable quality of his religious orthodoxy judged by Enlightenment standards.

Two influences are at work; the first betrays an earlier realization that the intuitive and emotionally loaded poetical style of the Bible is *sui generis* in contrast to that of actual scientists and rationalists. His essay rejects two assumptions current during his lifetime; the first, the suggestion by Voltaire that the Bible is a ridiculous mass of contradictions; and the second, as represented by the German Biblical theologian Michaelis, that it was possible allegorically to square Genesis with the results of modern science. He also rejected the allegorical method of reconciliation put forward by Buffon in France, which maintained that the days of Creation correspond to larger subsequent ages or epochs in Biblical man's development.

Rejecting apologetical approaches, he chose to rely upon a historical approach based not only upon his interest in poetry, but more especially upon his studies of the languages of primitive peoples. From a historical standpoint, Herder insisted that Genesis reflected the style of a primitive pastoral people, and as such, is totally devoid of the language of physics and metaphysics. The principle of historical relativism made any attempt to judge the truth of the Genesis account by modern canons foolhardy. Herder respected, however, the outlook of the Newtonian cosmology, but argued that the Mosaic or Biblical was preferable because it reflected better than the Newtonian the power of Creation as it affected men's senses at every level of their being. Biblical style reflected the creative power and vitality of God's encounter with His people in a way which the abstract style of Newton or Leibnitz was incapable of. Thus, Herder writes of Leibnitz:

> For our philosopher, God is a metaphysical Something, an exalted Somebody, and this feeling is so sublime that he can say and think nothing about him: the Deist-religion scorns the simple who have to make a Something, an image, a symbol of the God to whom they pray, in whom they trust, who has created them and who preserves them every moment through his might.[19]

Genesis remains the "oldest document of the human race" as well as one of the noblest because it portrays in a unique way God as being organically involved with every element of His creation. The completely untheological character of Herder's approach to Scripture, as well as to every facet of human concern, is captured in Volume I of his *Letters Concerning the Study of Theology* (1779):

> One must read the Bible in a human way: for it is a book written through human agency for human beings; human is the language, human were the external means whereby it was written and preserved; human, finally, is the sense with which it must be grasped and every aid that elucidates it as well as the entire purpose and use to which it should be applied. You can, therefore, safely believe that the more humanly (in the best sense of the word) you read the Word of God, the closer you will come to the purpose of its Artificer, who created man

in His image and acts humanly for us in all works and benefices in which He shows Himself to us as God.[20]

Herder's interest in all our human powers and his antipathy toward artificial systems and constructs marked every aspect of *Sturm und Drang* expression. He deplored any identification of the religious or sacred with any particular human faculty or power, such as one finds later in Schleiermacher or Rudolf Otto's presentation of the numinous. In a work, whose title he borrowed appropriately from Pascal, entitled *To Preachers: Provincial Letters*, Herder speaks about the "history of religion" as "the great vehicle of education" intended not "as a primer of sugary moral examples but for the whole development of human powers through the revelation of God." The task of the preacher is to strengthen "the whole man." Essentially, religion for Herder was fact, history, lived "on the witness of the senses and not merely of the higher mental powers; upon faith, which embraces all powers."[21] Religion is directed to the "common people, the largest, more sensual portion of mankind" rather than to an intellectual elite, and has as its purpose the transformation of their being and language. The faith-philosopher Jacobi objected to this stress upon God's immanental activity and accused Herder, Goethe, and others of Spinozistic tendencies. Having planned a work not only on Spinoza but on Shaftesbury and Leibnitz as early as 1775, Herder freely admitted being guilty as charged. In 1784, Herder wrote that "God works through all things . . . as sensuous expressions for sensual creatures." Later that year, he wrote in a tone similar to that of his teacher Hamann, "But what is a God, if he is not in you and you do not feel and taste his Being in an infinitely inward fashion, and if he does not enjoy himself in you as an organ among his thousand million organs?"[22] To the end of his life, Herder's religious outlook arose from his love of life, from the vital energies in the universe which he interpreted as the speech of the divine to the human through the human; and lastly, from his regard for poetry and sensual language as the means for understanding the Divine Place in history. Against the background of eighteenth-century deism how ridiculous if not blasphemous it must have seemed when men like Herder and Hamann asserted that concrete sensuous human experience and existence could at the same time be a revelation of God's existence.

Herder on the Origin of Language

IT WAS UNFORTUNATE, not only from the standpoint of the close relationship which existed between them but also from the perspective of their mutual respect for the sacred character of language, that Hamann and Herder should have become divided as a result of Herder's prize essay *A Treatise on the Origin of Language*, which appeared in the spring of 1771. Hamann maintained that Herder had succumbed to the rationalist tendencies of his age by rejecting the higher hypothesis—namely, that speech had a divine origin—without really offering any positive solution. The background to the debate sheds light upon the issues involved. Herder later admitted to Nicolai in 1772 that he had written the essay "fleetingly, in haste," and had misgivings about his effort, which if fact, did not constitute a rejection at all of Hamann's attitude toward the sacramental power of the Word. The subject had been widely discussed as a result of Michaelis' prize essay in 1769, *On the Influence of Language on Opinions*, and other contributions by Maupertius, Rousseau, Mendelssohn, Sulzer, Premontral, and last but not least, by the Biblical fundamentalist Süssmilch, whose position was clearly stated in the title, *Essay to Prove That the First Language Had its Origin, Not From Man, but Solely from the Creator* (1766). Herder interpreted his invitation to submit an essay as reflecting a desire on the part of the committee that a view be expressed which avoided on the one hand the mechanistic interpretation of Rousseau and Condillac about the origin of language, and on the other, the extreme reactionary view of Süssmilch that language as we know it was God's special direct and fully developed creation. Süssmilch had recently died and the Academy was anxious that Condillac's view be offset by a more moderate position, lest they lend further support to Condillac's views on the origins of human inequality. In his letter to Nicolai of Felsung (1772), Herder recognized that the Academy desired that the question be saved from both extremes. Actually, Herder's task was a formidable one; how to avoid the shortcomings inherent in the views of theologians, idealists, and materialists? Was there an alternative to Süssmilch's view that language was a finished, ready-made product given by God to his creatures? Was language more than a creation of the mind as idealists insisted? And finally, was language as the materialists maintained, nothing more than a product or invention arising out of sense experience? Though displeasing to Hamann, Herder's answer has been recognized as "the first rude foundation of the science of comparative philology and of the deeper science of the ultimate nature and origin of language."[23]

Of the three positions, that of the theologians could be most easily discredited and dismissed, leaving the field to the idealists and materialists. On the basis of Herder's spirituality, it could be assumed that he was not prepared to accept the solutions offered by either group, whether they be the views of idealists and rationalists like Mendelssohn and Maupertius or those of empiricists and sensualists like those associated with the German historian Gatterer, with the *Encyclopedie*, or those associated with the Scottish followers of Adam Smith. It is unfortunate that Hamann was unable to distinguish between his own position and that of the orthodox theologians who in every other respect had little affection and respect for that bumptious unpredictable soul in Münster. That Herder had not given in completely to reason, as Hamann maintained, is evident from Herder's comment that Süssmilch was incapable of explaining the origin of language as "a development of reason and a product of the spiritual forces of man."[24]

What, in fact, was it that Herder offered as a solution to the thorny question of the origin of language in his prize essay? As might be assumed, he began by reiterating his rejection of the doctrinaire views of men like Süssmilch. This he did by appealing to data about the speech habits of primitive peoples and also by suggesting that such a thesis not only anthropomorphizes God but detracts from man's power as the most precious of God's creatures to create and act on his own. In dealing with the claim of men like Condillac, who asserted that language began as ejaculatory expression in which were blended onomatopoeic elements, Herder referred to these qualities as only the sap and not the roots of speech. Herder refused to look upon man simply as an animal crowned with reason, and he rejected the implied suggestion that human language had the same narrow orbit of activity that exists among beasts. In contrast to animals, man's physiological makeup is *sui generis* and the range of his powers also unlimited. "Language is a natural organ of the understanding, a sense of the human soul, just as the instinct of the bee builds its cell." What instinct is in the animal realm, language and reason are in the human; "there is no reason without language, no language without reason"; both are expressions of man's essential humanity and distinguish him from all other creatures in the Creation.[25]

Implicit in this position was a rejection both of the Cartesian view of man as a rational, autonomous, solitary creature and also Rousseau's views about natural man, which Herder described as a "phantom notion." For Herder, reason and experience were inextricably blended together in all forms of human consciousness and language. "We are one thinking *sensorium commune*"; we discover our identity by means of language. "The sense for language has become our sense of mediating and combining; we are creatures of language."[26]

By Herder's time nouns were thought to be the original and basic forms of language. This was due to a number of factors, one of which certainly stemmed from the Genesis preoccupation with names, another from the rationalist preference for nouns as against verbs. Herder attacked the view that maintained the primacy of nouns and insisted that verbs expressed best the interaction between man and his environment. Language is an expression of man's creatureliness as a social animal. His approach was based more on a comparative study of the history of language from earliest times, on its development rather than upon its genesis, and his preoccupation with language as a unified center for both reason and experience reflected the disdain common among *Sturm und Drang* thinkers for any dualistic, fragmentary view of man. What Herder did achieve was to put to rest any metaphysical explanations of the genesis of language, as well as any view that regarded it simply as a "mechanical reflection of the environment." The relationship between men and their environment is one of mutual interpenetration; a dynamic interaction viewed as continually in flux and incapable of division. Language, as the testimony of this process, can never be identified exclusively with either the individual or his environment. Man and his universe are conceived essentially in relational and linguistic terms.

Hamann was less than happy with this statement. Having little of Herder's concern for comparative philology and linguistics, for the views of idealists and materialists, Hamann felt that if the topic was the origin of language, then speak to the subject, rather than around it. Above all, show language to be of *divine* origin, though in a way that avoids the pitfalls of Süssmilch's position. In essence, all of Hamann's total life's energies were absorbed in this task.

Johann Georg Hamann (1730-1788)

ONE OF THE loudest apologies in behalf of the sacramental character of speech during the eighteenth century was that which poured
forth from the pen of Johann Georg Hamann. Though to many a
confused romantic completely unattuned to the main intellectual
currents of his age, his insights into language mark a significant
beginning in the attempts of men in modern times to give to the
spoken word and everyday sensuous speech the prominent creative
place it deserved in the shaping of human destinies. His writings
were as much a protest against the silent interregnum produced by
the eighteenth century as they were prescriptive; *e.g.*, he suggested
criteria for determining authentic from unauthentic speech. The
link between authentic speech and true religion was such that the
proper and timely word was a mark of sacred involvement. While
he offered no systematic philosophy of language, the words he uttered were listened to with respect in his own time not only by
admirers like Herder, Jacobi, Lindner, Behrens and Goethe, but
even by men like Kant, who were either unsyspathetic to his criticisms or confessed an inability to fathom the meaning behind his
sensuous metaphors and frequently crude verbal ejaculations. During his lifetime he was a thorn in the flesh to theologians as well as
philosophers. Besides, what sort of pietist would dare to place the
head of a satyr on the title of a book and delight in being called
Pan?

In fairness to both our interest in speech and also to Hamann's
contribution to our subject, the reader is asked to listen to him
against the background of his age. In many respects his thought is
incomplete when viewed from the concerns of our own period. For
example, for Hamann, poetry alone was the most perfect form of
language. He failed, for instance, to recognize the potentially sacred
character of political discourse or even of alternatives to traditional
forms of religious rhetoric. The lack of sensibility for the latter was
due not only to his general disdain for orthodox theologians but
perhaps also to his awareness at an early age that his tongue was too
thick for preaching, which incidentally was a significant factor in
his decision to give up preparation for the ministry and to devote his
life to scholarship, the mastery of languages, and above all, to use

the written word as the main vehicle for expression his insights into the spoken word. Though he lacked the rhetorical powers one associates with a Cicero, a Churchill, a John F. Kennedy, or a Martin Luther King, those today who recognize in the spoken word a unique vehicle for effecting personal human and collective social change would do well to read Hamann in order to enhance their own confidence in the potentially sacred character of speech.

Despite various handicaps, not the least being his general unpopularity among his fellow intellectuals, Hamann's life is a record of his own involvement with the mystery and sacramental power of language. Speech and the word were practically synonymous for him; they were the bone upon which he gnawed all his life. "I speak neither of physics nor of theology; with me language is the mother of reason and revelation, its A and Ω."[27] It is Hamann's life, the bodily man, flesh and blood, that is the key to understanding his thoughts. In the twelfth book of his autobiography Goethe said of Hamann: "The main principle to which all Hamann's statements may be referred is the following: 'All that a man undertakes to perform, whether by deed or word . . . must proceed from all his powers united; everything isolated is worthless.' " Hegel suggested a similar insight when he stated that "Hamann's writings do not so much have style as that they are style through and through."[28] Kierkegaard once remarked about Hamann, "with all his life and soul, to the last drop of blood, he is concentrated in a single word."[29] The Kierkegaard scholar Walter Lowrie once remarked that he felt Hamann had exerted the greatest positive influence upon the shaping of Kierkegaard's thinking.

Among the men of the nineteenth century who were profoundly influenced by him was Kierkegaard. In this author, who lived a hundred years before his day, Kierkegaard recognized his *alter ego*, and he discovered him just at the time when he most needed the help H. could give. It was in his student days when he had registered in his *Journal* the conviction that Christianity could not endure the searching light of philosophy. He hailed him at once as "Emperor!", and he remarked that everything he wrote bore his own image and superscription. In my *Kierkegaard* I registered the opinion—which has perhaps more truth than evidence on its side—that no other author influenced him so profoundly.[30]

The issue between Hamann and the philosophers of his age involved many of the same factors which marked those earlier debates in classical antiquity between Homeric defenders of the music of poetry and the Platonic espousers of the music of philosophy. Then, and in Hamann's time, tradition, experience, and the problem of language were central to the differences among the protagonists. The similarity is especially apt in view of both Hamann's and Homer's high regard for poetry and oral discourse. Consider, for instance, Hamann's statement that "We make deductions, as poets, as orators and as philosophers. The former are more often closer to reason than those in the logical form. When the heart speaks, our understanding is nothing but quibbling."[31] *Aesthetics in a Nutshell* is a development of this theme. "Poetry is the mother-tongue of the human race," and "the whole treasure of human knowledge and happiness consists of nothing but images," essentially poetic in character.[32] The entire Creation narrative constitutes an unfolding of the divine plan through poetic speech. Thus he states: "Speak that I may see thee! This wish was fulfilled in the creation, which is a speaking to the creature through the creature." Creation, nature, is "but a confusion of verses and *disiecti membra poetae* left for our use."[33] Plato's feud with the Homeric legacy and Hamann's sympathies with Plato's opponents are summed up in Hamann's reversal of the Platonic hierarchy which gave to the philosopher, rather than the poet, the keys to the kingdom of truth. "To make sense out of the confusion of words is the task ultimately of the poet. To collect them is for the scholar; to expound them, for the philosopher; to initiate them or even more audaciously to bring them into order is the poet's modest part."[34] At an earlier point in his essay he observed that the poetic art was called botanic and suggests, following a line from Bacon, that it is our key to understanding the mystery in nature, since for Bacon, ". . . poetry is a plant, which has germinated . . . from the luxuriant earth and from a sure seed, it has increased beyond other learning and spread through them."[35]

Speech, for Hamann, is above all "translation—from the language of angels into a language of men"—i.e., "thoughts into words, things into names, images into signs, which can be poetical or kyriological, historical or symbolical or hieroglyphical, philosophical or characteristic."[36] Every exercise of our speaking powers is for Hamann a tribute to the divine; every response to our fellowman, a sign of the Divine Presence.

This analogy of man to the Creator gives to all creatures their content and their character, from which depend loyalty and faith in the whole of nature. The livelier this idea, the image of the invisible God in our heart, the more capable we are of seeing and tasting, looking at and grasping with our hands, the loving kindness of God in the creatures. Every impression of nature in man is not only a memento but also a pledge of the basic truth—who the Lord is. Every reaction of man towards the creature is a letter and a seal of our share in the divine nature, and that we are of his race.

O for a muse like a refiner's fire, and like fuller's soap! She will dare to purify the natural use of the senses from unnatural use of abstractions, which mutilate our ideas of things as badly as they suppress and blaspheme the name of the Creator. I speak with you, O Greeks, because you think yourselves wiser than the chamberlains with the gnostic key; just try to read the Iliad after excising, by abstraction, the vowels alpha and omega, and then tell me what you think of the poet's understanding and harmonies.[37]

For Hamann the dichotomy between Athens and Jerusalem was an impossible one, since both the "Word became flesh" and the medium of the muses of antiquity had much in common. The richer, more universal claim of the Gospel was for Hamann but an extension of the ancient poetic legacy to all mankind. Within each tradition, however, Hamann found something lacking, and where he did, a speculative philosopher—whether Greek, Christian, or Jew—usually bore the brunt of his invective and criticism. In a letter to Jacobi (April 9, 1786) he extended the range of his criticism to include both Lessing and Mendelssohn. "You must expect that every systematic thinker looks upon his system as a Roman Catholic does on his church, and the same principle that was Lessing's and Mendelssohn's seems to be Kant's *proton pseudos*—although he . . . speaks more modestly and without hypocrisy of revelation." Hamann's *Golgotha and Scheblimini* (1784) is a violent reaction to Mendelssohn's *Jerusalem;* in particular, to Mendelssohn's and, indirectly, to his friend Lessing's presentation of the truths of Judaism as a form of rational religion. For Hamann this was incompatible with the temporal, historical, and linguistic style of Biblical faith. Moreover, it seemed like a complete accommodation to the demands of eighteenth-century philosophers for a rational religion consisting of universal intelligible truths. Thus Hamann's remark; "I know of no eternal truths save those which are unceasingly temporal."[38]

In retrospect, it was indeed unfortunate that Hamann came to know and hence to criticize traditional Judaism on the basis of Lessing's and Mendelssohn's presentations. Had he experienced a different introduction to Judaism, Hamann might well have shown the same veneration for Hebraic poetry and style as he did for Homeric. For example, Hamann distinguishes between Judaism and Christianity neither on the basis of differences involving "immediate" or "mediate revelation," nor eternal truths and dogmas, nor ceremonial and moral laws, but simply "temporal historical truths which occurred at one time, and shall never return—*facts*, which . . . became true at one point of time and in one place, and therefore can be conceived as true only from this point of time and space. . . ."[39] In this connection both O'Flaherty and Fritz Blanke have noted that "It is indeed striking that as profound a believer in the transcendence of ultimate reality as Hamann could nevertheless adopt a philosophy of historical relativism. Blanke has commented on his acceptance of a relativistic and yet at the same time absolutistic view of the Bible."[40] In *A Flying Letter to Nobody Whom Everybody Knows* (1786), Hamann stresses in a Hebraic manner the importance of time and history as they relate to sacred speech. Hamann's sense of history, tradition, and authority are presented in a style that is Biblical and Lutheran. Although it was through Christianity that he began to gnaw upon the bone of speech and develop his fascination for sensuous language, poetry, and those themes which one identifies with the *Sturm und Drang*, few Protestant clergy outside of those identified with the romantic movement were capable of appreciating the all-pervasive and sacramental esteem with which Hamann held natural, everyday speech.

Hamann's Early Life

HAMANN WAS BORN on August 27, 1730 in Königsberg, where his father, a most respected citizen, held the office of chief surgeon, a position which in those days consisted largely of bleeding and the prescription of baths. Hamann's father cherished the title which the citizens had bestowed upon him, "the Old Town Bather"; Walter Lowrie remarked that Hamann said that he "revered his father's bathtub just as Socrates did the stool of his mother, the midwife."[41] At sixteen, Hamann entered the University of Königsberg as a theological student, but as was noted, soon gave that up, giving as a reason the fact that his tongue was too thick for public speaking. He flirted with law, but gave it up as a mere bread-and-butter curriculum, then devoted himself to philosophy and languages for a period of five years, but in the end did not attempt to sit for the Master's degree. His writings abound with references in French, English, Hebrew, Arabic, Greek, and Latin, and he is said to have been able to read Spanish and Italian as well. Between his leaving the university in 1752 and his London religious experience of 1757, Hamann served as tutor to two wealthy families near Riga, where he was exposed to the main tenets of the Enlightenment through his friend Johann Christoph Berens, the son of a wealthy merchant family. He was also close to the estate of his childhood friend Johann Gottlieb Lindner, then Rector of the Gymnasium in Riga. In 1755 the Berens family asked Hamann to represent their interests in London with the hope of his becoming an established and prosperous merchant. He arrived in London on April 17, 1757, and remained there until sometime in June 1758.

This fourteen-month interlude was perhaps the most significant of Hamann's entire life. We know about this period primarily through his notes on the Bible and through a written confession intended originally for his father, brother, and a few close friends. During this time he wrote to few friends, not even Berens. What little we do know about his London sojourn indicates that he was completely discouraged with himself, probably due to the realization that he lacked the qualities which make for a successful businessman. He thereupon led a life of complete debauchery which left him financially destitute and psychologically despondent. In his *Biblical Reflections* he likened his situation in London to that of the Prodigal Son. Like the Prodigal Son, Hamann underwent a spiritual crisis which he described as "the descent into the Hell of self-knowledge." The *Anfechtung* that Hamann experienced parallels in many ways the lengthier periods of searching, struggle, and doubt which marked the lives of Augustine and Luther, with one notable difference. In Hamann's thought, pietistic and Biblistic as it was in 1758, to speak of the workings of the Holy Spirit within a man was to experience the revelation of self-discovery. Admittedly, the divine and human are inseparably connected through natural speech; and yet, unlike Augustine's preoccupation with the predestinarian character of God's guiding hand in the *Confessions* and Luther's remarks about the exclusive role of Grace at the expense of the human condition, in Hamann we detect in outline form already in 1758–59 the basis for a theological doctrine of self-love and self-affirmation. Although self-love is connected with the divine-human encounter, Hamann's vocabulary is strangely unorthodox. Again, the unorthodoxy of his remarks was due to that bone, language, upon which he constantly gnawed. In connection with the theme of self-knowledge, Hamann refers to *homo sum* as the basis of all other relations. In a letter to Kant, July 27, 1759, he wrote, "Just how far man can work in the order of the world is a task for you to determine, which one should not venture to approach, however, unless one understands how our soul works in the system of the little world."

By 1758 one also detects from his *Biblical Reflections* the general principles which Hamann was to adhere to for the remainder of his life. For some of his insights into the significance of Scripture, Hamann was indebted to Johannes Albrecht Bengel, who wrote his *Gnomon* in 1742 and whose influence Hamann first formally acknowledged in his *Aesthetics in a Nutshell* (1762). With Bengel there began within the Evangelical Lutheran Church a grammatical-historical approach to Scripture which stressed eschatological themes inherent in the Bible. Both Bengel and Hamann stressed the Hebraic influences upon the Greek New Testament and based whatever hermeneutic principles they developed upon Luther's statement that "The science of theology is nothing else but grammar, exercised upon the words of the Holy Spirit." It was during 1758 in London that Hamann attempted a more disciplined approach to the reading of Scripture, which he tried to read "as if they were addressed expressly for me." In these notes it is clear that everything he experienced was attributed to the Holy Spirit at work within him. Although the language of the *Biblical Reflections* resembles Luther's, Hamann placed greater stress upon the sacramental character of our natural, imaginative, and poetic powers than was true for Luther at any period during the latter's lifetime. At first glance, the *Biblical Reflections* seem without any unity whatsoever; they are as arbitrary, as unconnected as any set of reflections might conceivably be. And yet there is unity to these reflections if we appreciate the fact that unity for Hamann is the opposite of any form of systematic, methodological unity or logical consistency.

It is evident from his *Socratic Memoirs* that by 1759 Hamann had already begun his attack upon the presuppositions of the Enlightenment, especially upon the defense and respect shown during this period for systems of knowledge. In a letter to Lindner in 1759 he wrote, "I am not equal to choose principles and systems." Twenty-seven years later, in a letter to Jacobi, he repeated this conviction: "System is in itself a hindrance to truth."[42] Hamann preferred to speak of unity rather than system, but by the former he meant the unity, the order which the adept discerns in the regular disorder both in nature and in the Biblical narrative. "In the Bible we find precisely the regular disorder which we discover in nature. All methods are to be regarded as go-carts of reason, and as crutches of the same."[43] Unity for Hamann lies in the unity of the Creation, mediated as it is by the sensuous natural speech of men, or as directly realized in nature itself through God's creative speech, His deeds. Against the background of the breadth of experience revealed in the Creation, Hamann looked upon our cognitive powers of abstraction as "nothing but fragments."[44] What we as creatures of the Creator know is rooted in sensuous personal experience and is therefore always incomplete. We can only know, said Hamann, in part; only the Creator has complete and perfect knowledge of the created realm. Knowledge of the created order from the human standpoint is comparable to the regular disorder apparent in the Bible, which parallels and complements the regular disorder in our own sensuous experience. With each utterance, each word, each new event, a new past is created, a new future anticipated. For Hamann, knowledge lacks the mediating role that his friend Kant had attributed to critical reason; it is direct and rooted in sensory experience. Hence his statement that:

> Our own existence and the existence of things outside us must be believed and can be ascertained in no other way. Therefore what is believed does not need to be proved. And the proposition may be proved incontrovertibly without for this reason being believed. Faith is not the

work of reason. By an attack from this side, therefore, it cannot be overcome, since faith is no more due to reason than is taste or sight.[45]

Faith, like knowledge, was something one tasted by means of the senses rather than something which men apprehended by means of reason. In 1759, when Berens and Kant tried unsuccessfully to win Hamann away from his "regrettable religious exaggeration, superstitions, enthusiasm, praying and folding of hands and confessions," Hamann used the example of Socrates to refute their attempts, since for the latter, truth and meaning were not a matter of cognition divorced from total awareness and involvement as much as they were that "which happened to a whole life committed to a continuity of thinking and action." More than Socrates, however, it was Hume whom Hamann relied upon to refute his opponents.

Hume's Influence on Hamann

AT THE TIME of his answer to Berens and Kant, Hamann happened to read the first version of Hume's *Dialogues on Natural Religion*, which were completed sometime in 1755 and were revised just prior to 1761. Upon finishing them, Hamann exclaimed in a letter, "Yes! that's exactly how it is!" Although Hume had directed these dialogues against traditional forms of belief, Hamann saw in them a witness to his own position, which was violently opposed to abstract speculation, to reasoning completely divorced from the sensuous natural speech. For Hamann, the certitude of faith is completely noncognitive. The Socratic ignorance which he professed was not based upon any abstract principle, but rather upon a "live attitude" (*Empfindung*), a receptivity on the part of the senses toward every form of address from every level of experience. In one essay Hume wrote:

> It seems evident that men are carried, by a natural instinct or prepossession, to repose faith in their senses; and that, without any reason, or even almost before the use of reason, we always suppose an external universe. . . . Even the animal creations are governed by a like opinion and preserve this belief of external objects. But this . . . opinion of all men is soon destroyed by the slightest philosophy which teaches us that nothing can ever be present to the mind but an image of perception.[46]

In a letter dated May 10, 1781, Hamann exclaimed to Herder: "Hume is always my man, because he at least honors the principle of belief and has taken it up into his system. Our countryman (Kant) keeps on chewing the cud of Hume's fury against causality, without taking this matter of belief into account." He reiterated this indebtedness when in a letter to Jacobi (April 23, 1787) he said, "I studied Hume before I wrote my *Socratic Memorabilia* and this is the source to which I am indebted for my doctrine of faith—or belief."[47]

Belief for Hume was associated with sense impressions, ideas, and modes of inference; the first two were of special interest for Hamann, whereas the third was of particular interest to Kant. Hume's notion of belief or fideism represented for Hamann a cornerstone for establishing his sacramental attitude toward the concrete and sensuous. For Kant, Hume's position had just the opposite effect—it constituted a scandal. "It remains a stumbling block to philosophy and to human reason in general that the existence of things outside us . . . must be accepted merely on faith."[48] Hamann's fideism was such that even eating and drinking were operations of belief—in fact, they were much more so than any abstract and therefore, in Hamann's opinion, artificial arguments for God's existence, whether they were intellectual or emotional. Eating and drinking were excellent examples of noncognitive certainty; they were acts of faith.

In a letter to Kant (July 27, 1759), Hamann discussed the limits of Hume's influence when he said, "The Attic philosopher Hume finds faith necessary, if he desires to eat an egg and drink a glass of water. . . . If he finds faith necessary for eating and drinking, why does he deny his own principle, when he judges higher things than sensual eating and drinking?" Schiller, incidentally, ridiculed adherents of this position in his *Theophagites* when he wrote: "All is tasting for them. They eat ideas, and even into the Kingdom of Heaven carry their knives and their forks". The lack of sympathy of a Schiller was offset by Goethe's respect for Hamann's insights, as evidenced by Goethe's insistence that everything we do must be done by the total person; any partial or isolated commitment is reprehensible. This is an appropriate commentary upon Hamann's definition of belief, since eating and drinking, like art, life, and poetry, require total involvement. In this connection, note Goethe's insight into the limited character of prose—one which one can only

conjecture Hamann would certainly have approved—". . . whenever
we use words in prose; words of necessity, are isolated (or partial);
and we cannot express ourselves without becoming, for the moment, one-sided (or partial)."[49] The one-sidedness or partial character of prose as against the power of poetry, life, and art to engage
the total person were for Hamann, as for Goethe, due in part to the
absence of the audible quality in prose, in contrast to the presence
of those sound qualities which accompany other literary forms such
as poetry.

Hamann's Differences with Kant

THE RELATIONSHIP BETWEEN Hamann and Kant was of another sort.
To begin with, not only were they familiar with one another's
writings, but they knew one another personally. Whereas Hume's
fideism was due to his cognitive skepticism, Kant began with the
assumption that we possess nonanalytic, necessary knowledge.
Kant's *Critique of Pure Reason* appeared in 1871 at the same time
that Hamann was translating Hume's *Dialogues on Natural Religion*. Kant attempted to observe the respect which Hume and the
empirical tradition had for rooting synthetic judgments in intuitions
of sensibility; but more importantly, he wished to prevent reason
from being broken up into a series of sense impressions. He achieved
this to his own satisfaction and to Hamann's dissatisfaction by making a strict dichotomy between empirical experience on the
one hand and pure forms of knowledge on the other. He claimed
that our transcendental knowledge does not, however, transcend
experience; rather, it merely deals with the presuppositions, the
categories of experience. While this effort may have pleased those
seeking to reconcile the Cartesian quest for rational certitude with
the empiricists' respect for rooting all knowledge in the concrete, it
shocked Hamann. Because language for Hamann was the Alpha and
Omega, the receptacle and life pulse of all experience and knowledge
about reality, it was ridiculous to suppose that a form of reason
existed that transcended or could be purified of the slightest taint of
experience—*i.e.*, language.

Kant's concern was a simple one: "What and how much can the

understanding and reason know independently of all experience? How much ought I to hope to accomplish with the reason, if all the material and assistance of experience are taken away from me?"[50] Apart from Hamann's feelings about the impossibility of separating reason from experience, he was fearful, and rightly, that were such a venture to succeed, the abstract model of rational certitude would soon become the absolute determinant of all knowledge and meaning, and the arbiter between truth and falsehood. Not only was the model itself to be distrusted, but Hamann's sense of man's place in the Creation was such that he was unwilling to make man, through his reason, the center of the universe, and reason therefore the final measure of all things. In retrospect, Hegel's attack upon Kant in 1802 in *Glaube und Wissen* was directed precisely to this point, although his argument was based on an enlarged cosmicized view of reason, whereas Hamann launched his attack from the standpoint of the Creation and language. Apart from the more familiar portions of his attack on Kant, which were based upon his view of language, Hamann in one place concludes with sentiments that might well have been written by Hegel.

The possibility of human knowledge of objects of experience outside of and before all experience, and after this, the possibility of a sensible intention before all perception of an object, belong to the concealed mysteries, the task of solving which—not to speak of the solution,—has yet to be given to a philosopher. The content and form of a transcendental Doctrine of Elements and Method are based upon this double impossibility and upon the forced distinction between analytic and synthetic judgments; for besides the proper distinction between reason as an object or source, also way of knowledge, there is yet a more universal, sharper and purer distinction, by virtue of which reason serves as the basis of all objects, sources and ways of knowledge, and is itself none of the three, and consequently also has need neither of an empirical or esthetic, nor logical or discussive concept, but consists merely in subjective conditions, under which can be thought everything, something and nothing as object, source or way of knowledge, and as an infinite maximum or minimum, can be given or, if need be, taken as an immediate intuition.[51]

For Hamann, transcendental knowledge creates transcendental man and thereby a form of Platonism which, as in antiquity, would be incapable of taking seriously history, the Incarnation, and the absolute forms of knowledge implicit in the relative deeds of human, fallible creatures. As for Nietzsche and Tennyson, human systems and abstract models were a barrier to truth and understanding. The new model of formal reason purified from the dross of experience was for Hamann like a "wax nose" which could be shaped "according to the contemporary fashion." "Out of words and explanations one can produce neither more nor less than what one wants to put or has put in them."[52]

The brunt of Hamann's attack upon "the magic castle" of Kant's critique and his "old cold prejudice in favor of mathematics" went to the heart of Kant's "Gnostic hatred for matter" and his "mystical love for form." The substance of his argument can be gathered from numerous letters to friends between 1781 and 1784 and in his review of the *Critique of Pure Reason*, which appeared in 1781, and especially in his *Metacritique of the Purism of Reason* (1784). He used "meta" in the title of his essay in the Aristotelian sense of "following upon" Kant's *Critique*. That language was the key to his differences with Kant is clear. "With me the question is not so much: What is reason? but rather: What is Language? and this I presume to be the basis of all paralogisms and antinomies which one blames on the former; therefore, it happens that one takes words for concepts and concepts for the things themselves."[53]

In his *Metacritique* Hamann insists that the real "pure forms *a priori*" are sounds and letters—*i.e.*, language, music, style. "Music was the oldest language, and next to the palpable rhythm of the pulse and breath in the nostril was the original bodily image of all measurements of time and its numerical relations."[54] What we know of time and space, two of Kant's categories of the understanding, we know, insists Hamann "through the universal and continuous influence of the two noblest senses, sight and hearing." "Sensibility and understanding" spring from a common indivisible root—speech. Hence, he asks, "what is the use of such an arbitrary, improper and self-willed divorce of that which nature has joined together?"[55] What Kant wished to achieve in his *Critique* climaxed a series of attempts on the part of numerous philosophers to devaluate human tradition, experience, and finally, everyday, commonsense language itself.

> The first purification of philosophy consisted in the . . . attempt to render reason independent of all traditions and belief in tradition. The second purification is even more transcendental, and results in nothing

less than independence of experience and its everyday induction. The third, chief, as it were empirical purism concerns language, the only, the first and the last instrument and criterion of reason, with no other credentials but tradition and usage.[56]

In language our powers of sense and understanding are involved in a miraculous hypostatic union which embraces "the synthesized mysteries of the two corresponding and contradicting forms of *a priori* and *a posteriori*." In the *Critique*, "Analysis" is but a "cutting-up in line with the fashion, just as synthesis . . . an artificial seam made by a master-tailor." In a letter to Herder dated December 8, 1783, Hamann exclaimed, "My poor head is a broken pot compared with Kant—earthenware against iron. . . . All chatter about reason is pure wind: language is its organ and criterion, as Young says. Tradition is the second element." When comparing Hume with Kant, Hamann declared that "Hume's *Dialogues* end with the Jewish and Platonic hope of a prophet who is to come"; but "Kant is more like a cabbalist who turns an aeon into the godhead, in order to establish mathematical certainty."[57]

Hamann's Later Life

AFTER LEAVING LONDON in June of 1758, Hamann paid a brief visit to his father, by then a widower, and then continued on to Riga, where he was warmly received by all his old friends despite his failure as a merchant. The succeeding years were extremely happy ones for him. It was during this period that he met von Moser, who bestowed upon him the title of "Magus (Magician) of the North" and whom Hamann in turn referred to affectionately as "lay brother." Amid all this his father, then ill, had a servant girl, a nurse, in the house. Of this episode in Hamann's life the late Walter Lowrie wrote: ". . . with astonishing indiscretion he had acquired responsibility for a housewife and four wholesome children," who were at once his joy and his burden.[58] The union was never blessed by the Church, although it was legitimatized by the state, nor did they name godparents or sponsors for their children when baptized. It was von Moser who found a tutor's position for him, which he soon left, proceeding to a position in the office of the Customs Collector in Königsberg as a French translator. In spite of his poverty he was able to maintain close contacts with J. G. Lindner, his disciple Herder, and also with Lavater, Jacobi, and oddly enough, Kant. The story of his later life at Münster in the home of Princess Gallitzin, a Catholic, is a tale in itself. He was buried in her garden in 1788.

Hamann's "Verbalism"

WHEREAS RUDOLF UNGER, hampered by the norms of the scientific linguistics of his time, was unable to discover in Hamann's views of speech anything worthy of scientific respect, recent studies of Hamann have been, on the whole, quite appreciative. Some, indeed, look upon him with the same respect Walter Lowrie bestowed upon Kierkegaard. The American scholar O'Flaherty, for example, has provided us with insights that help penetrate more deeply the essential unity and meaning implicit in Hamann's writings. His study confirms the suggested affinities Hamann had with all those who look upon frail human speech as the most trustworthy of all our human powers.[59] He suggests, for example, that "all the essential ideas of Hamann's thought on the origin of language" is contained in Hamann's statement that:

> Every phenomenon of nature was a word—the sign, symbol, and pledge of a new, inexpressible, but all the more intimate union, communication, and community of divine energy and ideas. Everything that man heard in the beginning, saw with his eyes, contemplated, and his hands touched was a living word. With this word in his mouth and in his heart, the origin of language was as natural, as near, and as easy as child's play.[60]

The reason behind Hamann's respect for poetry is grounded in his insistence that "all mortal creatures are only able to see the truth and the essence of things in parables."[61] For Hamann, "Senses and emotions speak and understand nothing but images. The entire treasury of human knowledge and felicity consists in images."[62] The pre-eminently trustworthy character of symbolic poetic discourse, in contrast to the abstract, artificial configurations of most eighteenth-century philosophers, is based upon his conviction that all knowledge is fundamentally sensory, figurative, and by its very nature lacking in that kind of systematic unity which most philosophers find satisfying. "The scriptures," for Hamann, "cannot speak with us human beings otherwise than in parables, because all our knowledge is sensory, figurative, and because reason makes the images of external things everywhere into signs of more abstract, more intellectual concepts."[63] Although statements like this caused Unger in his time to dismiss Hamann as "the most obscure author of our modern literature," others have recognized that for Hamann the unity, however incomplete, inherent in the created realm (which includes all linguistic experience) is of more significance empirically than is the artificial unity which philosophers extrapolate, in secondhand fashion, from the data of raw speech, from that commonsense experience which is the basic reality within the created order. The ordinary linguistic realm is for Hamann the objective aspect of experience, and the cognitive, which is dependent upon it, the subjective. Objective reality is that speech-invested experience of peoples which the Bible presents. The Creation was essentially a speech event for Hamann; as such, our individual and largely solitary attempts to devise systems of rational unity and logical order became for him subjective and secondhand, artificial creations. Hence, his observation that "a mind that thinks at its own expense will always interfere with language."[64] In an essay written in 1760 he said: "The purity of a language diminishes its riches; a too strict correctness diminishes its strength and manhood."[65] Thought and language are inextricably woven together in such a manner that cognition must take its cue from speech, and not vice versa, as is usually presented. The apparent contradictions which prevail in the realm of speech are resolved by Hamann in much the same way as Nicholas of Cues employed his *principiam coincidentia oppositorum*, and the principle of the *communicatio idiomatum*—i.e., the resolution and true unity implicit in the created experiential realm exists explicitly in the divine source of all reality. Thus, his remark in an essay entitled *The Letter H By Itself:* "Is the famous principle of the *coincidentia oppositorum* entirely unknown to you? It is the spirit which makes alive; the letter is flesh, and your dictionaries are straw."[66] To admit to the apparent disorder in experience and yet to believe nevertheless in its ultimate authenticity and meaningfulness constituted for Hamann an act of faith in the Creator Himself.

It was this conviction which prevented Hamann from seeking a kind of Platonic release from the fetters of experience, as well as from attempting its reshaping in accordance with more rigid and precise canons of logical consistency and philosophical clarity. His confidence, his faith in the sacred character of everyday human speech constituted in his day an unnatural and, from a theological and doctrinal perspective, even a profane outlook. Thus, he found himself alienated from philosophers and theologians alike. A year before his death, he described this polarity and advocated his speech-oriented alternative to Jacobi.

> Idealism and realism—Christianity and Lutheranism. The former two are in my eyes ideal—the latter two, real. Between your two extremes there is lacking a mean, which I might call verbalism. My twins are not extremes, but allies and closely related. I desire to refute the Berlin idealization of Christianity and Lutheranism by means of a historical and physical realism, to oppose experience to pure reason. To straighten out this tangle is precisely the herculean task which I have in mind, because I do not know at which end I should properly attack the matter. . . . Our concepts of things are mutable by means of a new language, by means of new signs, which make us aware of new relations or rather restore the oldest, original true ones.[67]

Hamann's verbalism was offered as the gateway to true philosophy and also as the key to an understanding of God's revelation of Himself to His Creation. He compared his approach to Luther's—all philosophy was a grammar of the Spirit and the Word—a *grammatica in spiritus sancti verbis*. In a letter to Jacobi (1787) he wrote, "Do you understand now . . . my language principle of reason, and that with Luther I make all philosophy grammar, a primer of our knowledge, an algebra and construction according to equations and abstract signs, which signify nothing *per se* and everything possible and real *per analogiam*." Hamann's verbalism is intimately linked with natural language, whose author ultimately is God. Rather than distinguish between natural and supernatural, profane and sacred speech, Hamann insisted that the natural language of experience was both human and divine. This principle was responsible for his attack upon Herder's crediting human reflection (*Besonnenheit*) with the origin of language. For Hamann, Herder not only credited man rather than God with the creation of language, but in so doing Herder rejected the essential unity of divine and human discourse.

Herder's efforts represented an attempt to understand man and human language completely apart from God. Hamann's *Last Will and Testament of the Knight of Rosenkreuz Concerning the Divine and Human Origin of Language* was devoted to a refutation of Herder's position. His attack was founded upon his belief in the "*communicatio* of divine and human *idiomatum*," which for him constituted "a fundamental law and the main key of all our knowledge and of the entire visible economy."[68] Natural language, for Hamann, contained a duality in unity—it was a symbol of the inseparability of the human from the divine. This principle is central for an understanding of Hamann's verbalism and is the basis for his attacks upon friend and foe alike. To admit that his disciple Herder was correct would have constituted an admission that reflective abstract language preceded natural speech. It would also have destroyed, for Hamann, the creational unity of the elements of mind and experience. Such an act was not only false, but irreligious, since it would, in effect, destroy the sacramental quality of natural language which the Creator had bestowed upon it. As noted earlier, this was precisely the basis of his criticism of Kant's *Critique of Pure Reason*. "If," as Hamann asserted in his *Metacritique* against Kant, "sensation and understanding . . . arise from a common, but to us unknown root . . . for what purpose such a violent . . . separation of that which nature had joined together."[69]

Symbolic natural language provides the key to understanding the intimate relationship between thought and reality *per se*. Speech manifests the reflective capacities of the mind; it reflects the empirical world of objects; and, finally, it is a manifestation and reflection of each person's interior world. Relationships between abstract concepts are unreal because they are divorced from natural experience and therefore from reality. Only natural language makes sense, because it alone contains the sensory elements which embrace perception as well as reflection, concrete objects as well as the relationships between real objects. Whatever knowledge we possess is derived ultimately from an external and, for Hamann, divine source. "There is nothing in our understanding," said Hamann, "without it having previously been in our senses."[70] In another connection he argued, "One must begin . . . the matter *a posteriori*, not *a priori*, which is a great mistake of the other philosophers."[71] Our sensory and reflective capacities function together in a mysterious hypostatic union and manifest themselves in parables and other forms of symbolic language. Hence, his various references to language as a "shekinah," a "tabernacle," a "sacrament," and finally a *"koinonia* without transubstantiation—neither body nor shadow, but spirit."[72] Natural speech alone connects and does justice to our reflective and perceptive capacities. Kant's cold prejudice in favor of one's reflective capacities manifests itself in his prejudice in favor of the precise yet abstract language of mathematics. In a similar connection, he said of Spinoza that "The geometrical structure is natural for spiders and their admirer, Spinoza."[73] Where the sacramental unity in duality of Hamann's verbalism is denied, the way is opened for relying upon abstract language, with the result that one might assume that relational concepts are more precious than the concrete speech of natural experience. For Hamann, the world created by abstract language is an unnatural and artificial one. Only natural speech is truly veridical in character, since it alone deals with real relations, real objects, real life. From Hamann's perspective, the cause of Kant's misunderstanding was the latter's worn-out assumption that thinking precedes speaking, that thought is prior to language. The Bible for Hamann embodied the indisputable fact that just the reverse was true—first God spoke, then man came into existence. For Hamann, the act of thinking is the natural result of having first been addressed as God's creature.

If it therefore still remains a principal question as to how the capacity to think is possible . . . no deduction is necessary to establish the genealogical priority of language and its heraldry over the seven sacred functions of logical propositions and conclusions. Not only the entire capacity to think rests on language . . . but language is also the center of the misunderstanding of reason with itself. . . .[74]

The Bible provided Hamann with a normative speech style, one sensitive to the symbolic significance of parables and to the poetic inclinations of many of the Biblical authors. Passionate Biblical speech was a mark, for Hamann, of authentic as against unauthentic speech. Biblical history was not only speech-dominated, but it suggested a framework of reference for the individual which encompassed God, man, and world in such a way as to make the individual ever mindful of his creatureliness, yet also of his ability to create, by means of speech, new times and conditions for himself and his fellowman. Though the human condition be relative and ambiguous, speech remained the absolute and sacred means whereby God's creatures provided meaning and direction for the Creation. Martin Buber's description of Hasidic man as a "partner of God responsible for His fate in the world" is equally appropriate for Hamann. In each instance the relativities and ambiguities of life are offset by a sacred confidence in our natural powers of speech. When one speaks meaningfully, the fate of the Word, of men, and finally, of the world, is at stake.

NOTES

CHAPTER 2

1 Basil Willey, *The Seventeenth Century Background* (New York: Doubleday, 1953), p. 5.
2 *Ibid.*
3 Walter J. Ong, S.J., "System, Space, and Intellect in Renaissance Symbolism," from *The Barbarian Within* (New York: Macmillan, 1962), p. 69 Cf. also: Walter J. Ong, S.J., *In the Human Grain* (New York: Macmillan, 1967).
4 Walter J. Ong, S.J., "Psyche and the Geometers: Aspects of Associationist Critical Theory," *Modern Philology*, XLIX, 1 (August 1951), p. 19.
5 Luigi Pareyson, "The Unity of Philosophy," *Cross Currents*, IV, 1 (Fall 1953), pp. 57–69. The same sentiments are expressed by George Boas: "In fact, one could envision the history of philosophy as a continuous dialogue, with argument, rebuttal, counterargument, rejoinder, and no conclusion." *Dominant Themes of Modern Philosophy* (New York: Ronald Press, 1957), p. 1. Cf. also: Page Smith, *The Historian and History* (New York: Alfred Knopf, 1964), pp. 232–49. This approach also dominates Eugen Rosenstock-Huessy's *Out of Revolution: The Autobiography of Western Man* (New York: William Morrow, 1938) and (New York: Four Wells, 1964).
6 Roy Pascal, *The German Sturm und Drang* (Manchester: Manchester University Press, 1959), p. xvi.
7 W. Schwarz, *Principles and Problems of Biblical Translation*, (Cambridge: Cambridge University Press, 1955), p. 83.
8 Lincoln Barnett, *The Treasure of Our Tongue* (New York: Alfred A. Knopf, 1964), p. 46.
9 *Ibid.*, p. 50.
10 *Ibid.*, p. 49.
11 *Ibid.*, pp. 48–50.
12 *Ibid.*, p. 48.
Martin Buber, *Moses* (London: East & West Library, 1946), p. 40 ff.

13 Franz Rosenzweig, "Die Schrift und das Wort," from Buber-Rosenzweig, *Die Schrift und ihre Verdeutschung* (Berlin: Schocken, 1936), p. 76.

14 A. S. Diamond, *The History and Origin of Language* (London: Methuen, 1959), pp. 162–85; 259–75.

15 Roy Pascal, *op. cit.*, p. xv.

16 *Ibid.*, p. 88.

17 *Ibid.*, p. 94.

18 *Ibid.*, p. 95.

19 *Ibid.*, p. 98.

20 Robert T. Clark, Jr., *Herder: His Life and Thought* (Berkeley: University of California Press, 1955), p. 251.

21 Pascal, *op. cit.*, pp. 99–100.

22 *Ibid.*, p. 104.

23 Statement by J. Sully, 1911. Cited in R. A. Wilson, *The Miraculous Birth of Language* (New York: Philosophical Library, 1948), p. 75.

24 Pascal, *op. cit.*, p. 172.

25 *Ibid.*, p. 174.

26 *Ibid.*, p. 175.

27 J. G. Hamann to F. H. Jacobi, 28 October, 1785.

28 G. W. F. Hegel, *Sämtliche Werke*, ed. Glockner, Vol. 20, 1930.

29 Søren Kierkegaard, *Concluding Unscientific Postscript* (Princeton: Princeton University Press, 1941), p. 224.

30 Walter Lowrie, *Johann Georg Hamann: An Existentialist* (Princeton: Princeton University Press, 1950), p. 4.

31 Friedrich Roth and Gustaf A. Wiener (eds.), *Johann Georg Hamann, Schriften* (Berlin: 1824), Vol. I, p. 281.

32 Ronald Gregor Smith, *J. G. Hamann: A Study in Christian Existence* (London: Collins, 1960), p. 196.

33 *Ibid.*, p. 197. The phrase "Speak that I may see thee" Hamann probably took from Ben Jonson. "Language most shewes a man: speak that I may see thee . . ." Ben Jonson, *Discoveries* (1640), line 2031, from Vives, *De Ratione Dicendi*. Cf. *Ben Jonson*, ed. Herford and Simpson, Vol. VIII (1947), p. 625; and notes in Vol. XI, pp. 270 (citing Vives) and 272 (citing Erasmus).

34 Ronald Gregor Smith, *op. cit.*, p. 197.

35 Francis Bacon, *De Augmentis Scientarium*, II, 13. Cf. Ronald Gregor Smith, *op. cit.*, p. 197.

36 Ronald Gregor Smith, *op. cit.*, p. 197.

37 *Ibid.*, pp. 198–99.

38 *Golgotha und Scheblimini; cf.* Smith, *op. cit.*, p. 225.

39 Roth and Wiener, *op. cit.*, Vol. VII, p. 43.

40 James O'Flaherty, *Unity and Language: A Study in the Philosophy of Johann Georg Hamann* (Chapel Hill: University of North Carolina, 1952), p. 56.

41 Lowrie, *op. cit.*, p. 10.

42 The same point is made in a letter to J. G. Lindner, 12 October, 1759.

"I have no aptitude for truths, principles, systems; but for crumbs, fragments, fancies, sudden inspirations."

43 Roth and Wiener, *op. cit.*, Vol. I, p. 118.

44 In a letter to Herder, 8 May, 1785. Hamann wrote, "Our knowledge is fragmentary; this great truth cannot be rightly felt by any dogmatician, if he is to play his part well; and scepticism itself, following an unavoidable circle of pure reason, becomes dogma."

45 *Socratic Memoirs* (1759); *cf.* Roth and Wiener, *op. cit.*, Vol. II, p. 35.

46 David Hume, *Enquiry Concerning Human Understanding*, 12, 1, p. 151 ff. S-B. Cf. Philip Merlan, "From Hume to Hamann," *The Personalist*, XXXII, 1 (Winter, January 1951), p. 11 ff.

47 Hamann wrote again to Jacobi on April 27, 1787, "I was full of Hume when I was writing my *Socratic Memorabilia* . . . Our own existence and the existence of all things outside of us must be believed in and cannnot be proved in any other way."

48 Immanuel Kant, *Critique of Pure Reason*, tr. Normann Kemp Smith, (London: Macmillan, 1933) 2nd edition, Preface, p. 34.

49 J. W. Goethe, *Dichtung und Wahrheit*, Book 12 (Oxenford tr. 2, p. 106). Note Philip Merlan's comment, "In this last sentence of Goethe we see the seeds of some of the most interesting doctrines of existentialism. All we have to do is add two things: first, the use of words is the essence of communication—both self-communication and intercommunication. Second, the *inevitability* of becoming partial does not diminish the *guilt* of being partial. The tension between the duty to communicate and the guilt incurred by the discharge of this duty is the very essence of man's intellectual life." Cf. Merlan, *op. cit.*, p. 16.

50 Immanuel Kant, *Critique of Pure Reason*, pp. xvii, xiv. Cf. J. G. Hamann, *Werke* (ed. Nadler) Vol. III, p. 277.

51 J. G. Hamann, *Werke*, Vol. III, pp. 283–84. For a fuller discussion of this theme, *cf.* W. M. Alexander, "J. G. Hamann: Metacritic of Kant," *Journal of the History of Ideas* XXVII, 1 (Jan.–March 1966), pp. 137–44.

52 Hamann to Scheffner, 11 February, 1785.

53 Hamann to Jacobi, 14 November, 1784.

54 Ronald Gregor Smith, *op. cit.*, p. 217.

55 *Ibid.*

56 *Ibid.*, p. 215.

57 Hamann to Herder, 10 May, 1781.

58 Lowrie, *op. cit.*, p. 15.

59 O'Flaherty, *op. cit.*

60 *Ibid.*, p. 38. Cf. Roth and Wiener, *op. cit.*, Vol. IV, pp. 33–34.

61 Roth and Wiener, *op. cit.*, Vol. I, p. 88.

62 Hamann, *Aesthetics in a Nutshell; cf.* Ronald Gregor Smith, *op. cit.*, p. 196.

63 Roth and Wiener, *op. cit.*, Vol. II, pp. 131–32.

64 *Ibid.*, Vol. II, p. 259.
65 "Miscellaneous Remarks Concerning Word Order in the French Language" (1760); Roth and Wiener, *op. cit.*, Vol. II, pp. 151–52.
66 Ronald Gregor Smith, *op. cit.*, p. 204.
67 C. H. Gildemeister, *J. G. Hamanns, des Magus im Norden, Leben und Schriften* (Gotha, 1868), Vol. V, p. 495; *cf.* also pp. 195, 199.
68 Roth and Wiener, *op. cit.*, Vol. IV, p. 24.
69 Ronald Gregor Smith, *op. cit.*, p. 210.
70 Roth and Wiener, *op. cit.*, Vol. VI, p. 44.
71 Gildemeister, *op. cit.*, Vol. V, p. 232.
72 *Cf.* O'Flaherty, *op. cit.*, p. 66.
73 Roth and Wiener, *op. cit.*, Vol. III, p. 192.
74 *Ibid.*, Vol. VII, p. 9.

Eugen Rosenstock-Huessy (1888–   ): Speech Is Hierarchical and Determines Social Unity

Speech is known to all and yet a mystery.

—JACOB GRIMM

You know not what damage you do to learning that care not for words but for matter, and so make a divorce betwixt the tongue and the heart. For mark all ages and you shall surely find that when apt and good words are neglected, then also begin ill deeds to spring.

—ROGER ASCHAM

Speech is the body of the spirit.

—EUGEN ROSENSTOCK-HUESSY

I respond *although* I will be changed.

—EUGEN ROSENSTOCK-HUESSY

And this temporal character of my thinking is, in fact, the Alpha and Omega from which I grasp everything afresh. Speech reflects this mode of procedure, even for someone who has been influenced by philosophy. For that reason I prefer to talk about speech rather than about reason.

—EUGEN ROSENSTOCK-HUESSY

J. G. Hamann and Eugen Rosenstock-Huessy: Two "Magicians of the North"

ON THE OCCASION of receiving an honorary doctorate in theology from the University of Münster in 1959, Eugen Rosenstock-Huessy was hailed as the new Magician of the North, the J. G. Hamann of the twentieth century. Eugen Rosenstock-Huessy was born Eugen Rosenstock to a respected German Jewish banker and his wife in

Berlin in 1888, one hundred years after Hamann's death. At sixteen, he became a practicing Christian. Like Hamann, he has gnawed continually upon the bone of language, and is appropriately hailed in Europe as *Der Sprachdenker*—"the Speech Thinker."[1] Although addressing two radically different social and intellectual climates, the similarities in their writings, with respect to their reverence for the sacramental power of speech, are indeed striking.

Compare, for instance, the following statement of Rosenstock-Huessy's with three passages from Hamann.

And this temporal character of my thinking is in fact the Alpha and Omega from which I grasp everything afresh. Speech reflects this mode of procedure, even for someone who has been influenced by philosophy. For that reason I prefer to talk about speech rather than about reason.

And now Hamann's statements:

I too know of no eternal truths save those which are unceasingly temporal.

I speak neither of physics nor of theology; with me language is the mother of reason and revelation, its Alpha and Omega.

With me the question is not so much: What is reason? but rather: What is language?

For each, speech (or as Hamann put it, *verbalism*) constituted the *via media* between the Scylla and Charybdis of philosophical and theological discourse.[2] Each regards speech as sacred and each sees in language the answer to his age's obsession with artificial and abstract languages and systems reminiscent of Enlightenment and nineteenth-century philosophers and their modern heirs. Kantian transcendental idealism, which Hamann attacked for its devaluation of sensuous speech and its rejection of the testimonies of everyday experience, had, together with the contributions of Fichte and Hegel, determined the acceptable religious, ethical, political, and philosophical categories in the nineteenth and early twentieth centuries. What Hamann attacked in its inception had permeated in Rosenstock-Huessy's time every quarter of twentieth-century European intellectual life. In attacking the Enlightenment, Hamann had relied primarily upon sensuous poetic speech modeled upon the time-conditioned and time-oriented view of reality inherent in the Bible. For Hamann, sacred natural speech and poetry were practically synonymous. Hamann's deeply personal, if not individualistic, piety, as well as his earthiness, were shaped by his view of language and his preoccupation with aesthetic and literary themes. In the normal use of the term he was not a *social* thinker. The social significance of the events preceding the French Revolution, which for Rosenstock-Huessy and Franz Rosenzweig anticipated the beginning of the Johannine Age, had little, if any, influence upon Hamann, who by then was an old man. The attempts of certain Enlightenment thinkers to put reason to use in freeing men not only from religious superstitions but also from political and economic subjugation went largely unnoticed by Hamann. Anything done in the name of reason, despite its intent, was from Hamann's standpoint hopelessly unnatural and religiously profane. As is true of so many religious existentialists, their obsession with personal existence often makes them incapable of going beyond the solitary soul in conflict to those larger social conditions affecting the human condition. Preoccupation with the rights of man—with the alleviation of harsh working conditions associated with an industrial, technological society, or those problems now created by an electronically controlled society—was equally beyond Hamann's ken. Although anticipated in Hamann's time, the organization of the social sciences did not take place until the nineteenth century, and then only with the aid of the advocates of positivism and behaviorism. Most of all, the current obsession with the soul viewed from the perspective of applied social and analytical psychology and psychiatry as well as other behavioral perspectives was a phenomenon which aroused the general public only after the assembly line had entered the business of creating new kinds of creatures. Nor had the effects of historicism been felt then as they would be in Rosenstock-Huessy's student days. Equally unknown in Hamann's time were the problems generated by a mobile society, by the atomic age, automation, shorter working hours and increased leisure time, and above all, by major advances in the fields of communication: radio, television, and electronics. The latter have appealed not only to man's visual, but especially to his oral and aural powers in a way totally unknown in earlier periods. Still to come was modern urban life, with its division of life into urban work, suburban play, and car pool limbo. There

was also lacking the recent questioning of the adequacy of traditional forms of institutional religion to speak to man's manysided-
ness, or in Rosenstock-Huessy's words, to *the multiformity of man*.
The modern mind, with all its neuroses, assumptions, needs, value
systems, and sense of estrangement and alienation—its problematic
elements—was as yet unborn in Hamann's lifetime. Were he alive
today it would be interesting to discover the degree of concurrence
which might obtain between these two Magicians of the North who
see in speech the remedy for the needs of their respective societies.

The Word and the Johannine Age

OF THE MANY possible intellectual precursors to Rosenstock-
Huessy's thinking, certainly the names St. John, Saint-Simon, Para-
celsus, Hamann, Jacob Grimm, Wilhelm von Humboldt, Friedrich
von Schlegel, Otto Gierke, B. G. Niebuhr, and William James deserve mention. In his first lecture on the *Philosophy of Life* Schlegel
began by paraphrasing Hamlet: "There are more things in heaven
and earth than are dreamt of in our philosophy." Halfway between
heaven and earth ". . . lies the true road; and the proper region of
philosophy is even that inner spiritual life between heaven and
earth." For Schlegel, the thinking soul was the center of consciousness, and speech was the language of the soul. Many of the themes
dealt with by twentieth-century speech thinkers are contained
within the leaves of Schlegel's *Philosophy of Life, Philosophy of
Language* and his *Lectures on History*. For example, the Gospel of
John is referred to by Schlegel as the *Evangel of Life,* and later on
he extols language as the highest creation of artistic genius. "It is
only . . . in poetry or some other form of language . . . that we meet
with the perfect harmony of a complete and united consciousness,
in which all its faculties work together in combined and living
action."[3] In anticipation of Rosenstock-Huessy's *cross of reality* and
gramatical thinking, Schlegel's observations about the fourfold nature
of man's consciousness, his multiform character, and the equation of
this fourfold structure with grammar are most remarkable. Schlegel's understanding of the hierarchy and complexity of those forces
which operate upon the solitary creature, his convictions about the

inability of reason and its categories to know life *absolutely*, and his insistence that life can only be *lived*, certainly provide a link in the chain between Hamann and Rosenstock-Huessy. When asked in 1949 to mention a precursor whose works would be helpful in understanding his thought, Rosenstock-Huessy immediately mentioned Schlegel, and especially his *Lectures on History*.

Though regarded by Rosenstock-Huessy as one of the devil's many advocates, certainly Hegel's preoccupation with time and history and his insights into the successive ages of the Spirit were familiar to Rosenstock-Huessy, as were the millenarian themes in Schelling's writings. Ludwig Feuerbach's name is also worth mentioning, not so much because of any acknowledged influence upon Rosenstock-Huessy's thinking as because of the task he envisioned for future philosophers. In an early preface to his *Principles of Any Future Philosophy* (1843), Feuerbach discussed the task of his age in a way that helps us appreciate the general setting for Rosenstock-Huessy's own intellectual pilgrimage.

The Philosophy of the Future has the task to lead philosophy from the realm of *departed souls* back into the realm of embodied and living souls; to pull philosophy down from the divine, self-sufficient bliss in the realm of ideas into human fashion will, however, be granted only to future generations. At present the task is not to present man as such, but to pull him out of the mud in which he was embedded. These principles are the fruit of this unsavory work of cleansing.

In the opening sentence of this same work he discussed the future shape of Christianity in a way closely resembling Johannine millenarian thinking and suggestive of the quality it was to take in Rosenstock-Huessy's thinking as outlined in his *Out of Revolution* and *The Christian Future*. Feuerbach proposed that "Protestantism is no longer concerned . . . about what God is in Himself, but rather only about what He is for man."[4] This theme is developed at length in the Johannine focus in Rosenstock-Huessy's thought and is best summed up in *Out of Revolution*, where he discusses a proposed sequel to Michelangelo's painting of God creating Adam, in the Sistine Chapel in Rome. God, in the upper right-hand corner, is shown creating Adam, reclining naked and helpless, in the lower left-hand corner. Rosenstock-Huessy suggests that in the beginning all of God's angels were on God's side, contained in the folds of His robe.

We might conceive of a pendant to this picture; the end of creation, in which all the spirits that had accompanied the Creator should have left him and descended to man, keeping, strengthening, enlarging his being into the divine. In this picture God would be alone, while Adam would have all the Elohim around him as his companions.[5]

This is but one expression of the Johannine millenarian quality which permeates all his writings and which places him in the company of all those who shared John's vision on Patmos of the future ages of the Spirit—*e.g.*, Tertullian, Joachim of Fiore, and more recently, Hegel, Schelling, Feuerbach, Franz Rosenzweig, and Dietrich Bonhoeffer. For Rosenstock-Huessy, we are approaching the conclusion of the second age—the unification of space, both geographical and technological—and are on the threshold of the third, the Johannine Age—the Age of the Spirit, which is dedicated to the task of the creation and preservation of a truly human society. It will be a time thirsted after by Jew and Christian, but also one wherein men will feel incomplete simply as Jew or Christian. It will be a time wherein men will feel the need to live in the Spirit and by and through the Word, now become fully clothed in its creaturely attire. Johannine, for Rosenstock-Huessy, combines the respect of John's sense of the future epochs of the Spirit which he described on Patmos, together with the Incarnational effect of the Word in the Prologue to John's Gospel. If the vision at the end of Revelation meant anything for John, it served as a mark of "the new Jerusalem as a healing of the nations without any visible Church at its center." Early in *The Christian Future* Rosenstock-Huessy elaborates upon John's vision by stating:

All things were made by the Word. In the beginning there was neither mind nor matter. In the beginning was the Word. St. John was properly the first Christian theologian because he was overwhelmed by the spokenness of all meaningful happening.

Thus, the Word and *speech*, the Spirit and *history*, Eternity and *timing* are woven together with that same secret quality that has characterized the confidence of Jew and Christian in the future determination of the Creation. However, as even theologians are now suggesting, the Age of the Spirit may turn out to be a totally a-religious and atheological one. "I believe that in the future, Church and Creed can be given a new lease on life only by services that are nameless and incognito." In another place he states, "In the third

epoch, beginning today, Christians must immigrate *into* our workaday world, there to incarnate the Spirit in unpredictable forms."
Further on he sums up the reasoning behind this, when he states that
". . . *each generation has to act differently precisely in order to
represent the same thing.* Only so can each become a full partner
in the process of Making Man." The inadequacy of the Church in
its present institutional attire is a constant theme, especially in *The
Christian Future.* This does not imply the death or eclipse of God;
rather, it suggests that new forms of spirituality must be discovered
in order for the present eclipse to pass. In this connection, one of his
favorite quotations is that of William James, who in 1903 anticipated our present religious dilemma. "The average church-going
civilizee realizes, one may say, absolutely nothing of the deeper
currents of human nature."[6]

For Rosenstock-Huessy, Incarnational speech, the *grammatical
approach* (which should not be confused with Incarnational *theology*), provides the clue to the secret of the coming age. In *The
Christian Future* this process is defined as *anthropurgy:* the act of
winning "the true stuff of Man out of his coarse physical substance." This represents the final realization of the statement in
Genesis "Let us make man in our own image." The Holy Spirit
henceforth "makes man a partner in his own creation," just as the
early Church Fathers "interpreted human history as a process of
making Man like God"—*e.g.,* anthropurgy.[7] Compare this presentation of man's divine role with Buber's rendition of Hasidic man as a
"partner of God responsible for God's fate in the world."[8] The task
of men living in the Johannine Age is captured in an oft-cited
passage in *Out of Revolution.*

The *Cogito ergo sum,* for its rivalry with theology, was one-sided. We
post-war thinkers are less concerned with the revealed character of the
true God or the true character of nature than with the survival of a truly
human society. In asking for a truly human society we put the question
of truth once more, but our specific endeavor is the living realization of
truth in mankind. Truth is divine and has been divinely revealed—*credo
ut intelligam.* Truth is pure and can be scientifically stated—*cogito
ergo sum.* Truth is vital and must be socially represented—*Respondeo
etsi mutabor* (I respond *although* I will be changed).[9]

While preoccupation with the creation of a truly human society
is the religious concern of many liberals and unorthodox thinkers

today, many orthodox religious thinkers have resisted this emphasis for fear of identifying the sacred with the profane, and thereby diluting the power of the Word. At the same time many religious liberals frequently view history and tradition as a barricade which must be broken down in order for the Spirit to speak freely to men. Rosenstock-Huessy, because of his Johannine orientation, because of his emphasis upon the necessary stages of life through which individuals and societies must pass, and above all, because of his view of the way in which the Word may become the fruit of our lips, has managed to avoid the pitfalls inherent in traditional approaches. More recently, Harvey Cox in *The Secular City* has captured this fine distinction in his discussion of the creative spiritual-temporal process of secularization in contrast to secularism. He defines secularism as "any new closed world-view which functions very much like a new religion."

While secularization finds its roots in the biblical faith itself and is to some extent an authentic outcome of the impact of biblical faith on Western history, this is not the case with secularism. Like any other ism, it menaces the openness and freedom secularization has produced; . . . Secularization arises in large measure from the formative influences of biblical faith on the world, an influence mediated first by the Christian Church and later by movements deriving partly from it.[10]

The path traveled by Rosenstock-Huessy to arrive at these insights was, as with Hamann, an unconventional one. Each has regarded himself an impure thinker and distemporary in terms of traditional ways of thinking.[11] The subtitle of a published autobiographical statement by Rosenstock-Huessy, *The Nine Lives of a Cat*, captures this quality and stresses his insistence that true progress and growth is one involving perpetual death and rebirth, viewed as a continuous defiance and desecration of what many regard as normal or natural existence. His motto "I respond *although* I will be changed" (*Respondeo etsi mutabor*) is an allusion to the fact not only that the social representation of truth involves costly commitment for each individual, but more significantly, that one's corporate community of *named* individuals is more sacred and deserving of concern and obligation than are the antinomies and anxieties surrounding the dark nights and moments of individual souls alienated and estranged from their fellowmen. Society, rather than the

individual, is his main concern. And yet, because of his high regard
for speech, individual needs are not overlooked. They are, however,
met in terms of one's named social existence rather than in any
individualistic or asocial context. William James symbolized for
Rosenstock-Huessy the infinite possibilities for the soul's constant
rebirth and renewal in behalf of "bringing about a growing universe
of free people." The substance of William James' own credo, as
well as Rosenstock-Huessy's, is captured in a letter of Henry James
to William, his son. Rosenstock-Huessy has described it as containing James' "own practical attitude to finite things, to the right name
for God, and to the unity of mankind." It certainly captures many
of Rosenstock-Huessy's own sentiments. The words italicized are
Rosenstock-Huessy's emphasis. Referring to Jesus, the elder James
wrote:

> What a mere obscenity every *great name* in history confesses itself
> beside this spotless Judean youth, who in the thickest night of time—
> unhelped by priest or ruler, by friend or neighbor . . . in fact, if we may
> so consider it, only by the dim *expectant sympathy* of that hungry
> rabble of harlots and outcasts who furnished his inglorious retinue, and
> still further drew upon him the ferocious scorn of all that was devout
> and honourable and powerful in his nation—yet let in eternal daylight
> upon the *soul*, by steadfastly *expanding* in his *private spirit to the
> dimensions of universal humanity*, so bringing for the first time in his-
> tory, the *finite* human bosom into perfect *experimental* accord with the
> *infinite divine love.*

Later on in the letter the father confessed to the son that he found
"the conception of any Divinity superior to this radiant human
form inexpressibly treasonable to my own *manhood*." He went on
to add that:

> I shall always cherish the most hearty and cheerful *atheism* towards
> every *orthodox and popular* conception of Deity but him who has illus-
> trated my own nature with such resplendent power as to make me feel
> that *Man* henceforth is *the only name of honor.*
> . . . Infinite wisdom compassed at length a direct and adequate access
> to the *most finite of intelligences* . . . in Jesus' sublime and steadfast
> *soul*, the divine and the human was at last perfectly consummated.
> Thenceforth, the *infinite* expansion of our nature became the most
> strictly *inevitable*. Ever since, husband and father, lover and friend,
> patriot and citizen, priest and king, have been gradually assuming more

human dimensions, have been gradually *putting on glorified lineaments. The universal heart* of man has been learning to despise and to disown all *absolute* sanctities. . . .[12]

Speech and Scholarship: "The Nine Lives of a Cat"

FOR MOST VISIONARIES, significant intellectual contributions and the events in one's life are almost synonymous. This is especially true in the case of Rosenstock-Huessy, who when asked to write an auto-biographical introduction to his lengthy bibliography, entitled his response *biblionomics*, and began by stating that his "too lengthy bibliography" must be read from the standpoint of inward neces-sity—*i.e.*, "the necessity of remaining sane, or, to be more exact, of recovering sanity. . . . Any author lives in some kind of biblionomi-cal field of force."[13]

His early youth consisted mostly of devouring books, of immers-ing himself in history, learning languages, translating the classics, making indexes, and writing poetry. Even when playing with his collection of tin soldiers he would re-enact famous military battles, assuming the title of Emperor Eugen I of Bergenau and chronicling daily the course of each battle. His doctoral dissertation of 1909 is apt testimony to the incredible learning and disciplining of faculties which had taken place in his youth. Professor Bader, the editor of the *Savigny Zeitschrift,* described his effort as "a good example of nineteenth-century erudition." It was understandable, therefore, that he eventually became a *Privatdozent;* but, indeed, it is amazing that his life is one continuous record of almost Kierkegaardian icon-oclastic attack upon the dryness and irrelevance of those kinds of erudition that many associate with the term. Nevertheless, by 1914, then twenty-six years of age, he had already published three books and five articles, among them his first major contribution in the field of law, *Königshaus und Stämme in Deutschland Zwischen 911 und 1250.* Even at this early stage in his development, he declared to his readers that *law* and *history* are intimately bound up with *speech.* In a lengthy, privately published autobiographical statement (to my mind, one of his most enjoyable and informative essays), he draws the reader's attention to the two mottoes for that work: the first taken from Socrates; the second from Goethe:

Law and right and justice, these are words which sound and echo within me so loudly that I cannot hear anything else over their sound.

The word was so important there, because it was a spoken word.

Of these two statements he writes: "The two mottos which preface a book on jurisprudence will, better than my assertion, prove to the reader that *language*, listening and speaking, have been my A and Ω."[14]

During this period he devoted himself to studying the works and unprinted papers of the historian B. G. Niebuhr, and came under the influence of the great jurisprudent Otto Gierke. His *Von Industrierecht* (1926) was an attempt to do precisely for the field of law what he had contributed in the field of history.

In 1912 he was appointed lecturer in law at Leipzig, and during this period he continued his conversations with Franz Rosenzweig, then a secular Jewish scholar immersed in the study of Hegel, whom he had met in 1910 at a convention of young scholars in Baden-Baden. Their now famous encounter on the evening of July 7, 1913, its effect upon Rosenzweig's own development, and their subsequent exchange of letters in 1916 on *Judaism and Christianity* will be discussed in the next chapter. As far as Rosenstock-Huessy was concerned, the encounter was a *public* declaration to the academic world that a man could be a competent scholar and nevertheless a deeply religious and committed Christian. It was precisely this combination of deep piety and erudition which had attracted Rosenzweig to this unusual and brilliant teacher of law.

Already in Baden-Baden in 1910 those present were acutely aware of an impending world catastrophe of the first order. It was equally apparent to them that the intellectuals in the European universities were so involved in departmental and professional squabbling that they had completely divorced themselves from the real and deeper issues facing their culture. The final outbreak of war convinced Rosenstock-Huessy that the guild system of professional compartmentalization and squabblings was detrimental to the very task for which universities and intellectuals ostensibly existed; ". . . the whole world of the educated was embodying a *spiritual lag*." When he wrote his *Biblionomics* in 1958 he compared the situation in 1914 to our own today:

> When, later, I came to America, I here found the term *cultural lag* in frequent use—unfortunately in the opposite sense. In the United States today, as in Europe in 1914, the alleged custodians of culture are lagging behind the allegedly uneducated masses. Greenwich Village seemed to me to belong to the Stone Age as much as the German Universities during World War One.[15]

Unfortunately, as he noted, this "breakdown of the old standards was communicable to a few friends only." When war broke out and the breakdown in communication was complete, he was commissioned a second lieutenant in the army and spent most of his war years as transportations officer at Verdun. It was during a leave that he married a warm, great, and wonderful woman, Margrit Huessy, and according to Swiss custom, added his wife's name to his own. They had one child, Hans R. Huessy, now a professor of psychiatry in this country. Everyone who knew Margrit Huessy loved her as a tremendously patient and loving individual who experienced deeply the many joys, vicissitudes, and adventures which they as a family were to encounter. Her death in 1959 affected deeply all those who knew her. The simple service held at the local Congregational church in Vermont brought to their home, Four Wells, in Norwich, Vermont, many of those from the different generations who had known, respected, and loved her.

Rosenstock-Huessy's profound preoccupation with speech and communication grew out of the kinds of cultural crises, viewed as speech impasses, which he experienced in the years just prior to the outbreak of World War I. Increasingly, he realized that the few with whom he could converse *must* talk to one another to survive as persons. More significantly, they began to realize that small groups like theirs must assume the responsibility for inspiring the dead branches of society in order that communication could be re-established among them. Through speech, they hoped to heal the social divisions and to overcome the professional rifts which mark social decay and any impending cultural crisis. This kind of remedial speech is sacred for Rosenstock-Huessy because it is the means whereby men are capable of either destroying one another or giving birth to a new and truly human society. Though philosophers like

Heidegger have devoted their lives to existential systems of language
and have often been compared to Rosenstock-Huessy (and vice
versa), they differ dramatically, precisely because, for example, of
the asocial origin of Heidegger's thought as opposed to the sacred
character of speech which men discover together in periods of social crisis. Similarly, each has wound up where he started; Heidegger is read and discussed by existential intellectuals as an intellectual
with little social application, whereas the thrust of Rosenstock-
Huessy's influence has been felt most acutely outside the salon and
the learned journals. His greatest impact has been in the classroom,
in work camps, and in those social situations which cut across disci-
plinary lines and which include members from every section of
society.

As a matter of record, Rosenstock-Huessy's purely academic interest in language is undoubtedly comparable to Heidegger's. In the
lengthy autobiographical statement referred to earlier, he notes that
in the four decades "from 1902 to 1942, *speech* made me the foot-
stool of its new articulation." Subsequently, he wrote: "Since 1902 I
have lived consciously under the banner of *speech*." In retrospect,
that particular aspect of language which he investigated was conditioned by the particular front or linguistic crisis which he himself
was facing at the time. According to his cross of reality, individuals,
societies, and nations are understandable in terms of four fronts or
vectors—*i.e.*, past, future, inner and outer. Thus, his autobiographical statement constitutes, in effect, a fourfold love affair with
speech—*e.g.*, his "love affair with the German tongue, as bridal
tongue, as the tongue of marriage and work." For students interested not only in this subject, but in biography and the history of
ideas, his lengthy account of his own involvements with language is
a fascinating one.

Since 1902 I have lived consciously under the banner of speech. I was
in my fifteenth year, and asked for Kluge's *Etymological Dictionary of
the German Language* as a gift. I myself bought Jakob Grimm's *German
Grammar* of 1819 and his *Legal Antiquities*, in which the Word plays
such an important part. At that time, Hamann's observation caught hold
of me! "Language is the bone upon which I shall gnaw forever." In
addition to the usual languages of the Gymnasium I added Egyptian and
became excited about the highly talented Heinrich Brugsch. Reading of
Carlyle's *Sartor Resartus*, this Song of Songs of speaking, of Bengel and

Chesterton, supported the excessive interest in pure linguistics and philology (for I also at the time wrote dictionaries and made translations from all languages); but of course, the child knew nothing else but that only philologists deal with language. Thus a tension arose between that which I longed for and that which seemed to be the only universally recognized expression of this longing: I wanted to decipher the organization of humanity on the basis of language, and strangely I studied everything philological with a zealous fanaticism and awe, as if this sort of linguistics would lead into the sanctuary. Deepest respect for the German university was beyond question for me. Thus I read every scrap of every acknowledged philologist from Scaliger to Ludwig Traube with devotion. But fortunately I fell in love for the first time in that same year and started to write poetry. Throughout many years, then, I always carried the little paperback containing the works of Hoelderlin around with me. And Nietzsche, Goethe, Homer, Schiller, Lessing, Pindar, and towards the end of the century, Chesterton, built a more genuine empire of language alongside the philological one of the Boeckh, Niebuhr, Grimm, Bopp, Erman, Brugmann.

The study of classical philology under its masters Otto Schroeder, Eduard Meyer, Wilamowitz-Moellendorf, Johannes Vahlen, Hermann Diels, and the study of law which I had undergone "against the longing of my heart" sought after a compromise. I had dreams for a while, of becoming another Ludwig Traube and of co-founding a new western philology for the Middle Ages. My main contribution to this I dedicated in 1912 with great pathos to the "Prince of Philology," Johannes Vahlen. I just was able to go to his funeral when the book was finished.

Two comments have to be made in retrospect about this decade, looking from 1912 back toward 1902. I had learned to mix all the essences and tinctures of philology. I had published papers about lower and higher criticism, had done investigations of diplomatic documents, copied and edited manuscripts, and dealt with stylistic and archival investigations. I had planned dictionaries and grammars, published investigations of liturgical calendars, and I had placed the credibility of B. G. Niebuhr's chronicles in a new light. I had investigated buildings and monuments iconographically; and through it all, I felt that the entire body of classical philology plus Indo-germanic linguistics and Egyptian were walking by my side as a bride. Since then I have followed the developments and ups and downs of these branches of knowledge consistently and constantly; without having any official relationship to them, they remained my home. I kept track of humanism and classicism in their study of antiquity from 1450 until nowadays, with all their splendid achievements. For never have I given up August

Boeckh's wonderful word about philology. "Knowledge of the known" he called his doings. We have added to this only the knowledge that it is not proper to recognize without acknowledging and disallowing.

His early passion for, if not veneration of, formal philosophical studies soon gave way to a disenchantment brought about by his recognition that "Language is wiser than the one who speaks it."[16] It marked the beginning of his public as against private involvement with language; *speech* rather than *language* in the sense of mere philology became, as for Hamann, the bone upon which he gnawed. With this insight, his future had direction; "the cat had been let out of the bag" and he now began to experience each of the cat's nine lives, abridged into the decades beginning with 1902 right up to the publication of his two-volume *Sprachbuch* in 1963 and 1964.

At the heart of his own speech conversion lay not only his awareness that speech is greater and more profound than any speaking individual, but, with von Humboldt, that the key to an individual's speech lies in the language of a people. Thus, in 1912 he wrote:

> . . . the living language of people always overpowers the thinking of individual man who assumes that he could master it; it is wiser than the thinker who assumes that he thinks, whereas he only *speaks* and in so doing faithfully trusts the material of language; it guides his concepts unconsciously, towards an unknown future.[17]

Suddenly, the significance of names, historical and ecclesiastical holidays and calendars, and especially those imperative forms of speech which call people to new powers and actions took on new significance. At the same time, the crisis of his own era, and his reliance upon the stimulation and life which his conversations with his friends produced, made him aware that the fate of his own thinking was intimately tied to those questions which he and his *co-respondents* recognized. He and his friends knew that the times beget that particular question which each must respond to in terms of his particular social role. In the words of a Presbyterian ordination hymn, "Each age its solemn age may claim but once." They were convinced that somehow men are driven together and at the same time driven out of their particular niche in society, precisely in order to survive and respond to those questions which have seized them. Recognition of the historical and temporal factors that condition all real speech and subsequent serious thinking was an insight which distinguished this circle, known as the Patmos group, from those scientists and intellectuals either ignorant of this fact or unwilling or unable to accept its consequences. *This* serious speech about *their* times meant for them that as scholars *their* thinking and research must address itself to those questions which had been raised in *their* time. This insight, incidentally, has been appreciated increasingly in Europe today, in sharp contrast to the obsession by most academicians in our own country, particularly in the social sciences, with value neutrality and scientific objectivity.[18]

The Patmos Circle: 1915–1923

THE NAME PATMOS is particularly appropriate for our interests in speech thinking, since for the members of the Patmos group it combined the significance attached to the Incarnate Word by John in the Prologue to the fourth Gospel with the sense of loneliness and vision of another age felt by the other, or same John, when he wrote Revelation on the island of Patmos. For Rosenstock-Huessy and those associated with the Patmos circle, the problem of their age was, as it had been for St. John in his time, a speech problem. This was their conclusion when they appraised the effect of nineteenth-century idealism, historicism, and positivism upon their generation's culture. In many ways their reaction was similar to that of Hamann and his friends during the *Sturm und Drang* protest against the presuppositions of the Enlightenment. The problem as the Patmos group viewed it was characterized by an absence of real personal encounter, together with a lack of a common language able to bridge the cultural and academic compartmentalization which prevailed not only in academic circles but at every level of European and, especially, German culture. According to Kurt Ballerstedt's comments on the situation: "How can a human being teach credibly of history, society or language in monologues? Only a human being who has lived and experienced the *thou* and the *we* in their fullness can reveal the *secret* of the university."[19] The Patmos circle was founded in response to this dilemma, the name serving as a symbol of their need for a common speech, as well as providing both a sense of the past and a vision of their responsibility to shape a common

future. Rosenstock-Huessy has rather vividly spoken of the significance of Patmos upon his own life on a number of occasions and in
several books and articles. Most recently he stated:

From 1915 to 1923 this group of friends felt as though living on
Patmos. And Patmos we called the publishing house founded in 1919
for the purpose of giving us a first opening into the official world of
books. In the main, we remained extramundane, so to speak. But all the
seed of my later work, and if I may say so, of my peculiar contribution,
stems from this period of total renewal and overhauling. If any period
may be called one of emigration, this was it. When I immigrated into the
United States with my wife in 1933, it was nothing like our inner
immigration upon Patmos achieved after 1915. After that year, we lived
totally unconcerned with the prevalent departments or divisions of existing social order and thought. The niceties of the antitheses faith and
science, capital and labor, object and subject, Protestant and Catholic,
lost their vitality. We entered a much more open situation. I suppose
that any crisis brings this experience. We, however, were dedicated
now to never going back behind it and to devoting the rest of our
lives, instead, of a return to normalcy, to the new norm of this extraordinary experience.[20]

Between 1910, when several from this group met to discuss these
problems, and 1930, when the final issue of the periodical *The Creature* appeared, a number of important works bearing upon speech,
encounter, and communication were published. In addition to
Rosenstock-Huessy, the original members of the Patmos group included Leo Weismantel, Werner Picht, Hans Ehrenberg, and Karl
Barth. While only a few of the authors of *The Creature* were identified with the earlier Patmos group, they nevertheless shared many
of the group's concerns. Rosenstock-Huessy's comments about the
purpose of the editors of *The Creature* captures the spirit which
animated their various responses.

The Creature represented the sum of the struggles of Kierkegaard,
Feuerbach, Dostoevsky, Nietzsche and William James. They had all
discovered, that no one has really anything to say, if they all say the
same thing. The creature does not speak as God does. A husband does
not speak as his wife, nor does a Christian as a Jew, nor a child as a
professor. For that very reason and solely for that reason are they able to
speak to, and must they speak to, one another. . . . What the editors of
The Creature discovered, were the spiritually nourishing processes experienced by genuinely speaking and existentially thinking persons.[21]

In addition to Rosenstock-Huessy, those directly connected with the Patmos group included the editors of *The Creature,* Joseph Wittig, Martin Buber, Victor von Weizsäcker, and also contributors like Franz Rosenzweig, Hans and Rudolf Ehrenberg, Karl Barth, Leo Weismantel, Werner Picht and Nicholas Berdyaev. The works that these men produced during this period were actually responses to the fundamentally human and social issues which they experienced. Hence, Rosenzweig's remark, "The dialogue which these monologues make between one another I consider the whole truth." Similarly, Rosenstock-Huessy stated in the introduction to his first major speech book, *Angewandte Seelenkunde (Applied Psychology)* (1924), that "The occasion for this work is rooted in the association of the author with a small circle of speakers and listeners."[22] Their individual contributions had, therefore, a responsive and dependent quality about them. For example, Rosenzweig was not only indebted to Rosenstock-Huessy's insights into speech, which he had gleaned from a rough draft of *Angewandte Seelenkunde* in 1916, but he actually intended that his *Star of Redemption* (1921) complement it. Other related works produced during this period include Buber's *I and Thou* (1923), Ferdinand Ebner's *The Word and the Spiritual Realities* (1921), Hans Ehrenberg's *Disputation, I, Fichte* (1923), Theodor Litt's *Individuum und Gemeinschaft (Individual and Community)* (1923), Friedrich Gogarten's *Ich glaube an den dreieinigen Gott (I believe in the three-in-one God)* (1926), Karl Löwith's *Das Individuum in der Rolle des Mitmenschen (The Individual in the Role of Fellowman)* (1928), Eberhard Grisebach's *Gegenwart (The Present)* (1928), and lastly, Gabriel Marcel's *Journal metaphysique* (1927). Two additional works which deal with some of these same concerns, but from a nonreligious and more philosophical perspective, are Max Scheler's *Wesen und Formen der Sympathie (The Nature and Forms of Sympathy)* (1923) and Martin Heidegger's *Sein und Zeit (Being and Time)* (1927).

Of all the works cited, Buber's *I and Thou* is undoubtedly the best known. While his name and the term dialogue are practically synonymous, the American Buber scholar, Maurice Friedman, noted that "Those who have arrived at a dialogical or I-Thou philosophy independently of Buber and without influencing him include Ferdinand Ebner, Eberhard Grisebach, Karl Jaspers, Gabriel Marcel,

Eugen Rosenstock-Huessy, Franz Rosenzweig, and Max Scheler."[23]
It is misleading, however, to identify Rosenstock-Huessy's
speech writings with a number of the above, in view of his subsequent open criticism of a number of them—especially Buber's *I-
Thou* approach. The last chapter will discuss various aspects of
these differences. At this juncture it might be helpful, however, to
the reader to state in broad terms areas of basic disagreement. For
example, Buber tended to stress the more personal dimensions of
encounter, while Rosenstock-Huessy emphasized the methodological and social implications of speech insofar as it spans at least two
generations or two social groups.

> Our historical mutability . . . is effective as a mental relation between
> two people, two generations, two times. . . . Insofar as we act or speak,
> we can act or speak meaningfully only between two other generations
> preceding and succeeding us, because we always come too late to our-
> selves.[24]

In contrast to Buber, Rosenstock-Huessy insists that we can only
create and preserve a truly human society if we take seriously the
significance of names, history, time, and tradition. This means that
we must appreciate formal as well as informal speech and the impersonal as well as personal qualities in Western man's autobiography.
Significant or sacramental speech embraces, therefore, for
Rosenstock-Huessy third person *I-It* speech as well as the more
direct *I-Thou* forms of address and encounter. But above all, as will
be indicated, the major difference between Buber's and Rosenstock-
Huessy's stress upon language lies in the latter's insistence that
nouns precede pronouns, that formal impersonal address ultimately
is more decisive for personal and corporate existence than the more
informal and personalist qualities stressed by Martin Buber.

From World War I to Camp William James

WHEN THE WAR ended, three attractive positions were offered to
Rosenstock-Huessy; Breitscheid, Minister of the Interior, invited
him to become his undersecretary and to draft a new constitution
for the Republic; and Karl Muth, the editor of the Roman Catholic

magazine *Hochland,* invited him to become its coeditor. The third offer was from the Law Faculty of Leipzig, to continue his university lecturing with a promotion in status. He rejected all three offers, and in so doing, their implications as well. The first demanded that he become a Marxist, the second that he become a Roman Catholic, and the third that he "fall in line with the agnosticism prevailing in academic circles." He was determined that any commitment he should make would not result in departmentalization—in an isolation of his energies in any single area, whether politics, religion, or scholarship. The time was behind him when he could view life categorically in terms of recognized divisions and compartments. In the trenches he had experienced the breakdown of the civilization that included these three intellectual pillars. To him "the professors seemed as wanting as the princes, the ministers of the Word as secluded as their laity, the makers of political constitutions and of party platforms as unaware of the judgment of God upon our world as the blind masses."[25]

His renunciation of the three offers was countered by the passionate affirmation that labor and labor camps were the means by which he might see unity restored in the postwar era. He first accepted a post with Daimler-Benz as editor of a weekly journal, and while there he developed in detail his views on labor. After this he helped found, and was leader of, the Academy of Labor at Frankfurt for two years. In 1923 he accepted an appointment at Breslau as Professor of the History of Law and Sociology because, as he described it, "no legal basis of existence was open except this academic position."[26] Fortunately, he was able in his spare time to devote his energies to the founding of voluntary work camps, such as the one founded in Löwenberg in Silesia in 1926. It was projected as a *universitas* in the wilderness where farmers, industrial workers, and students attempted through their common labors and conversations to bind together people in that region in a common creative social enterprise. From these projects, various forms of work service spread throughout Germany. However, by 1932 the State had taken control, and the initiative of the student element had been changed from one of freedom to one of regimentation.[27]

He has described his literary production between 1923 and 1933 as three-stranded. *Industrierecht* was a straggler from his prewar campaigns, while *Applied Psychology* (1924), "formulated for

Franz Rosenzweig in a manuscript of 1916," was a product of his
Patmos experience. Although less known than *Applied Psychology*,
he regards his three-volume *The Age of the Church* (1928), written
in conjunction with the Roman Catholic priest Joseph Wittig, as
"the most ambitious and certainly the most unplanned" work during
this period.

In Breslau, the comradeship with Wittig gave me the sense of still
having a foothold on Patmos. As the inspiration of 1914 had allowed me
to penetrate into the eternal origin of States, our *Alter der Kirche* paid
tribute to the role of the Church through the ages.[28]

Their work amounted to a justification and presentation of the
Johannine view of the Church which bound them together in their
Patmos activities. Having been excommunicated for his views, Wittig was restored to membership in the Church some twenty years
later, after Pius XII, upon reading the *Age of the Church*, tele-
grammed Wittig, saying that he had never read anything more
beautiful. Like his earlier dialogue with Rosenzweig, this exchange
was another example of a reliance upon the power of the Spirit
revealed in speech through the creature to his fellow creature. Each
lived off the other's words and letters; the result of their conversations was a work whose insights neither could have fathomed or
discovered alone. In Rosenstock-Huessy's *Biblionomics*, the power
of a true *co-respondent* is eloquently portrayed.

Sound calls forth sound, song calls forth song; and innumerable
books given to friends bear witness by their often lengthy, poetical
inscriptions to this infectious character of confabulation. I mention this
so the reader may see . . . that the printed word was not radically
different to me from the words spoken or written between friends. Fit-
tingly, letters have played an immense role in my life. The letters printed
in Franz Rosenzweig's volume of letters are a good example of their role
in my own existence. Many books got started as letters.[29]

Again, the Patmos reliance upon the miracle of speech was a
living reality which each discovered in the midst of a personal crisis.
The principle which evolved and is stated in countless works was a
product of their common existential crises rather than something
which evolved subsequent to detached speculation.

Rosenstock-Huessy remained at Breslau until February 1, 1933,
when in opposition to Nazism he decided to emigrate to the United

States, having been offered a post at Harvard University. The period
from 1931–38 was devoted to the social problems of revolutions, *Out
of Revolution* (1938) being the product of several revisions beginning with the first German edition which appeared in 1931. (The
latest revised edition appeared in German in 1951.) His calendar
thinking, which influenced Rosenzweig's own *Star of Redemption* so
significantly, is fully developed in this lengthy tome, as are significant insights into his Johannine orientation and speech thinking,
themes which have continued to preoccupy him during his later
years. Like his earlier efforts, his plan for the work on revolutions
was conceived amid crisis and social involvement—in this instance on
the battlefield of Verdun in 1917. The fuller significance of his
calendar thinking will be discussed in connection with his speech
thinking and cross of reality, since these three themes must be
viewed in their interrelatedness in order to do justice to any one of
them.

In 1935 he was appointed Professor of Social Philosophy at Dartmouth College, and in 1940 President Roosevelt invited him to train
leaders for the Civilian Conservation Corps. The training center,
Camp William James, in Tunbridge, Vermont, was created in response to this need. Unfortunately, with the advent of the Second
World War and the draft, most of the active workers were enlisted
for military service, and the CCC movement came to an abrupt
end.

Post-World War II: The Modern Mind Outrun

ALTHOUGH IT RECEIVED little recognition when it first appeared in
this country in 1946, *The Christian Future or The Modern Mind
Outrun* is a bridge book, since it spans the sum of Rosenstock-
Huessy's previous German writings and links them with his subsequent insights into the mysterious interpenetration of Johannine and
speech themes within his cross of reality. At the same time, the
work integrates his experience as a German European in the pre-
Hitler period with his American experience during and after World
War II. It was his first truly postwar proclamation and it has taken
twenty years for it to be accorded the recognition it now begins

to receive. For only recently have problems dealing with hermeneutics and radical religion or post-Christian thinking been receiving not only the serious attention they deserve by all those associated with contemporary religious life, but for the first time, these themes are seen as interrelated, since the problem of language and communication is central to each. With this recognition, commentators on the contemporary religious scene like Martin Marty and Harvey Cox have singled out *The Christian Future* as a truly pioneering work. Actually, the stage arrived at—on the one hand in the field of hermeneutics or interpretation by men like Bultmann, Fuchs, Ebeling, and Wilder; and on the other, in the area of religionless Christianity or radical religion by Bonhoeffer, Bishop J. A. T. Robinson, Paul Tillich, and Harvey Cox—is precisely the stage where *The Christian Future* begins. *Speech-thinking* in a Johannine Age looking desperately for religionless forms of sacred expression geared to the creation and preservation of a truly human and sacred society is the concern not only of theologians, but of men in every field of human endeavor today. The ninth life of this remarkable cat has provided us with an abundant storehouse of insights central to these contemporary concerns. *The Multiformity of Man* (1949), *Der Atem des Geistes* (1951), *Heilkraft und Wahrheit* (1952), his two-volume revised *Sociology* (1956 and 1965), and most recently his two-volume *Sprachbuch* (1963 and 1964) represent the fruit of his lips and help us appreciate the marvelous way in which the themes last in print indeed were the driving power throughout his earlier stages, or eight lives, as he refers to them.[30] It was not until he read Shakespeare in English, after coming to this country, that the meaning of Mercutio's taunting of Tybalt in *Romeo and Juliet* was revealed to him as the secret of his own crises, rebirths, and transformations. "Good king of cats, nothing but one of your nine lives; that I mean to make bold withal, and, as you shall use me hereafter, dry-beat the rest of the eight." He reflected on this passage at the conclusion of his *Biblionomics:* "I . . . before I came to the States, had not heard of the nine lives of the cat. Now it seems to me, that though ignorant of their very existence, I had begun to live them quite a while ago."[31] An awareness that each individual goes through definite stages or lives is essential to an understanding of his insights into speech. The power of words is intimately connected with one's own personal history. Words betray our remembered times and spaces as much as they enable us to overcome previous or unnecessary stages. Hence, this statement:

Man is reverberating the Word. How can he do this if he runs away from the first periods of life, in which he should acquire forever the resounding qualities of obedience, of listening, of singing and of playing? These first periods have made me. From them, the power has sprung of giving the slip to any one outdated later period of style or articulation, and to grow up to one more comprehensive. . . . The best pages of my *Sociology* may be those in which I have vindicated these four chapters of the life of the spirit as creating our true time, our full membership in history.[32]

Herbert Marcuse in his recent work *One Dimensional Man* discussed some tragic obsessions of the modern mind which make it difficult to grasp the subtlety of Rosenstock-Huessy's understanding of man: first, the common assumption that we creatures speak a single language and play a single role; and secondly, that a single linguistic methodology—the language of a single social science—can do justice to our multiformed, multiroled, hierarchical existence. Rosenstock-Huessy's son, the psychiatrist Dr. Hans R. Huessy, has discussed this difficulty in a recent unpublished paper devoted to applications of his father's thought in the field of psychiatry. In discussing the effect of the revolution in the exact sciences, he notes that "it became evident that insights at higher levels along the pyramid were not always derived from the building stones below, but that the new insights at the higher levels required a re-explanation of the lower building stones."[33] He adds that:

The five levels of human functioning described by my father allow an application of this philosophical revolution to the study of man. If we . . . think of a pyramid as five levels, the bottom level of functioning would be physiological and autonomic; the second . . . would deal with eating, sleeping and playing; the third . . . with work; the fourth . . . with love, the re-creation of values; and the fifth . . . with heroism and self-sacrifice.

To treat man adequately requires an understanding of his particular operational level of existence. At the highest level, it may be, for example, that some form of inspiration or confrontation is required "which allows him to rise above his past, and, at times, to overcome his past."

The hallmark of a large percentage of psychiatric patients is their inability to live at all on levels four and five. For these patients (at those levels) the psychological determinism of psychoanalysis would be quite invalid. . . . Events on the upper two levels are almost totally dependent on things having their origin outside the individual and, therefore, will always be unpredictable from a study of mankind.

This hierarchical factor accounts for another difference between Martin Buber and Rosenstock-Huessy with respect to the former's I-Thou formulation, which Rosenstock-Huessy insists must begin with *Thou*, rather than *I*—with forces which originate *outside* the *I*.[34] Hence, the priority of the grammatical second person over the first in Rosenstock-Huessy's grammatical approach. His son has appropriated this in terms of its application to the upper two levels of existence where events

. . . have their origin outside the individual. . . . Our formulation states that there must be a Thou before there can be an I. Support for this formulation is found in the observation that children learn the pronoun "I" last. This demands a 180° shift in our thinking about man. If Thou precedes I, then something outside of man is essential. The first human being had to be addressed as a Thou before he could become an I. This immediately leads to some kind of formulation of God.

In *Liturgical Thinking, Dich und Mich,* and other essays, the father dwelt upon this theme at considerable length. Our *first liturgical* and *grammatical figure* is *Thou*, which is the "health principle of the soul."

The soul must be called Thou before she can ever reply I, before she can ever speak of us and finally it. Through the four figures, Thou, I, We, It, the Word walks through us. The Word must call our name first. We must have listened and obeyed before we can think or command.[35]

For those capable of living at times on all five levels, *speech, encounter, inspiration,* and *social confrontation* may possibly change the configurations of lower levels during those periods when we are operating at the highest level of existence. Furthermore, the *way* we speak our roles and *what* we say at any single level—*e.g.,* as son, husband, father, teacher—is dependent not only upon that particular level, but also upon the outside community, which calls forth each role we play. All of these permutations are possible within a relatively short period of time. Compound this with our various roles during an entire lifetime and one gets some idea of the wide variety of roles, the diverse kinds and qualities of speech, and therefore the mystery, problematic, and speech-dependent character of human existence. During every moment of our lives it is possible for us to live in a wide variety of times and space configurations and transformations. Rosenstock-Huessy's own pilgrimage in language beginning in 1902 is an excellent illustration of this insight as it affects an individual's life. In each decade what he pursued formally in the area of language was determined by the particular front he was fighting on.

In all his writings, Rosenstock-Huessy repeatedly insists that the creaturely existence of a named person is unnatural in contrast to that of those creatures living exclusively on the natural or animal level. For natural man, names that span several generations, history, time, and social groups are meaningless, as are memory, inspiration, and the possibility open to all persons of overcoming one's past and participating in the creation of a new, speech-conditioned future. He deplores the assumption that we develop our natural reason and true powers between fourteen and twenty-five, that this is the normative stage for determining values and meaning in life. Actually, it is but a transient phase, about which he says:

It is the Reason of the classroom student. Greek philosophy, eighteenth-century enlightenment, American common sense or pragmatism, are gigantic superstructures of these uprooted minds and unloved bodies in their in-between age, when one set of names has faded and the new call of love is slow to resound.

The liturgy, the call to be a named, responsible person, the soul's being confronted and its resulting inner dialogue—all contribute to both the uniting of our passions and thoughts and their receiving direction, as well as enabling us to declare to ourselves and to society that certain experiences and questions are more significant than others, that a part of us is now past and a new future and new community await us. Hence his statement, "From the liturgy I have learned to think rightly!" The missionary charge, "Go ye into all the world" demands from the missionary himself a change of his own mind, a price.

True partnership puts my mind at the service of my partner, and his mind at my service. *Our minds work much better for our partners than for ourselves.* The Spirit was not given to man for himself. Self-reliance is an abuse of the greatest gift of the Spirit, or our reason.[36]

The alternative to self-reliance, *i.e.*, the missionary submission to the Word—to those crucial words which call us into responsible action—highlights the risk, possible sacrifice, and above all, the un-naturalness of this kind of response. Dwell on the significance of the *etsi*, the "although" in his motto, "I respond *although* I will be changed." To be a person in this setting means more than simply the fact that we utter many sounds and enact a wide variety of roles; it involves the willingness to take on those forms of responsibility which run counter to our natural inclinations.

As developed in his *Applied Psychology* and later works, our grammatical life is one involving named persons, whose involvement in the modes, tenses, and intonations enable us to experience the rebirth and transformations which the Word makes possible. In *Liturgical Thinking* he notes that before 1500 to be called a person in canon law meant that:

> A person was always responsible for a functioning part of the whole community, he held an office of some kind. The smallest "office holders" were the fathers and mothers who presided over households. We forget too readily that not everybody or anybody was free to marry, but that to establish a home was itself a privilege.[37]

More recently at the University of California he reiterated the fact that our names link us to universes of discourse which go beyond an individual's existence. At the very least, names signify the unity provided by the home, as well as national and historical ties. "House from Moses to Edwards meant that spiritual unity which forges two or three generations and an inner sanctum and some space into a cross of reality whose center is not to be formed in any one person."[38]

In the light of numerous variations upon the theme of modern assembly-line existence, which so many in our society lead, is it not a strange assumption, as is so often asserted, that we are persons by nature? With Kierkegaard, Rosenstock-Huessy would insist that humanity is a task and not a fact. Up until the late Middle Ages, before a monk received his monastic name signifying his responsible entry into a new community, he underwent a previous ceremony during which he formally renounced the name given at birth. He renounced his worldly person by renouncing his worldly name, just as in the ancient world it was believed that one could destroy a man by writing his name on an earthenware jar and then dashing it to the ground to break into pieces. Each decision, each new act, is a unique and irreversible one which announces to those affected that one part of us has died, and another been reborn. It is belittling to the nobility of named persons, as presented by Rosenstock-Huessy, to categorize a richly lived life as merely a form of natural existence. *Persons* are precisely those who, often through costly decisions, have defied the natural laws of determinism.

The Ingredients of "Speech-Thinking"

NAMES ARE IMPORTANT not only as the focuses and standard-bearers of sacred speech, but they are essential for an understanding of the named individual's involvement in history, in the autobiography of Western man. Names are our link with history; this is the theme of *Out of Revolution*. This work helps us realize the significance of Rosenstock-Huessy's calendar thinking referred to earlier, especially as it relates to *speech-thinking* and the cross of reality. Hence his concluding statement in *Out of Revolution:* "Regeneration of Language would be no faulty name for the due process of Revolution. This process was the means of survival during the sixth day of creation."[39] In *Out of Revolution* the calendars of world history and personal biography are wedded as an attempt to "read world history as our own autobiography. The calendar form of thinking accords to time, history and names their proper place in the development of our own autobiographies." Calendar thinking alone does justice also to the historical millenarian emphasis so evident throughout Rosenstock-Huessy's writings. There can be no speech, no time, no history of any consequence, unless all these elements are involved. As Rosenzweig and Rosenstock-Huessy developed it, God, man, and world; creation, revelation, and redemption; together with speech, time, names, and history, are connected in such a way that to omit the influence of any single element lessens our collective human potential and also an understanding of the dynamics involved. *Out of Revolution* is probably the first attempt in recent times to understand European history through a blending of these themes. Calendrical thinking presents this heritage in terms of our festivals, holidays, holy days, and national revolutions. These calendars represent Western man's corporate memory, his determination of what it is that is worth preserving, observing, and remembering.

The holidays which you and I respect are composed of the memories of all the vicissitudes of man. So much then must be said in emphatic defense of the calendar: . . . I . . . have written the history of the last thousand years around the holidays and the calendars instituted during this epoch; and I am sure that this new method places the historian in the center of human history.[40]

The degree to which his entire orientation in every field has been influenced by his respect for and veneration of calendars is captured in a passage from his *Biblionomics*. Referring to the bricks of his "house of history," he writes:

Ever since my lines of Nother and Clodius, and my first printed essay on the Medieval Calendars, research in the calendars of all religions and countries, and in the lives of workers, scientists, saints, revolutionaries, businessmen, etc. has been perpetual. Therefore, if I may say so, *lifetimes* and *holidays* are my bricks of time, although the bibliography does not list more than half a dozen titles in either field.[41]

The central theme in *Out of Revolution* is stated in the Prologue:

Mankind has always, with the ultimate tenacity, cultivated its calendar. One of the innovations of this book in point of method consists in taking the political and ecclesiastical calendar seriously. A day introduced into the calendar or a day stricken out of the calendar, means a real change in the education and tradition of a nation. Mankind writes its own history long before the historians visit its battlefields; days, festivals, holidays, the order of meals; rest, and vacation, together with religiously observed ritual and symbols, are sources of political or economic historians. . . . A holiday is always a political creation and a political instrument.[42]

Earlier, he distinguished between the reasoning mind for whom time is a matter of months, days, and years, and the time sense of the man of faith whose calendar is "independent from nature's mechanism." For the Christian, "from Christmas to Easter, a whole lifetime of thirty years is remembered, and from Pentecost to Advent, the whole experience of mankind through the Old Testament and our whole era is remembered."[43] Any sense of a presence fraught with meaning depends for its content upon the intersection of four of these calendars, each of which should be regarded as essentially a speech event where formal named address, rather than informal pronominal speech, was uttered to give direction to Western man's destiny.

The use of *four* for Rosenstock-Huessy is central to his cross of reality and forms an essential part of his methodological interests. In this instance its application reveals the ingredients of the presentness of a people consisting of the intersection of four speech calendars representing nature, secular history, sacred or Church history, and our own private, uniquely personal calendar. Being confronted and torn in this manner leaves the present, as Homer described it, "as inconvenient to sit on as the blade of a razor." As individuals, we live similarly at the crossroads—"at the juncture of four fronts: backward toward the past, forward into the future, inward among ourselves, our feelings, wishes and dreams, and outward against what we must fight or exploit or come to terms with or ignore."[44] In the discussion which follows, the cross of reality and speech will be presented as the basis for determining those speech forms which determine social health as well as indicate the possibility of social decay.

The significance of the cross of reality and speech can be highlighted by examining Rosenstock-Huessy's methodological insights into speech, as contained in *Applied Psychology* (1924) and subsequent works and essays. *Applied Psychology* is a reworking of a *Sprachbrief* (Speech Letter) addressed to Franz Rosenzweig in 1916; it was offered as a defense against the then prevailing interest in scientific linguistics. It first appeared in print in 1924, and was presented as "an attempt, in the most compact style, to offer for the first time an appropriate *discours de la methode*, a *Sic et Non* for our day."[45] This task, to which the man has devoted his total energies, was outlined in the brief three-page Foreword almost fifty years ago. On the occasion of his seventieth birthday, and more recently in his lectures at Columbia, this devotion was reaffirmed. The appearance of his two-volume *Speechbook* in 1964 represents truly the fruit of his lips, since it contains his own selection of his numerous insights into the sacramental character of speech. In the

following pages an attempt will be made to state briefly and then
indicate applications of the grammatical method; first, to the life of
the individual as it is discussed in the fifth chapter of *Applied Psychology;* secondly, to society as described in the ninth chapter; and
lastly, as it relates to the intimate connection that exists between
these insights and his application of the cross of reality to social
unity, as discussed in his essay *In Defense of the Grammatical
Method,* which first appeared in English in 1955. Though necessarily brief and sketchy, it may be possible both to outline the focus of
his remarks and to give the reader a sense of his style.

The *"Grammatical Method"*: 1916–1964

ONE OF THE clearest statements about the aim and purpose of his
grammatical method appears at the beginning of his essay *In Defense of the 'Grammatical Method* (1955). A comparison of this
with the earlier Foreword to *Applied Psychology* will testify to
Rosenstock-Huessy's faithfulness to his earlier manifesto on this
subject. The essay begins, "Grammar . . . is the future organon of
social research."

In this way, following the astounding developments of dialectics and
mathematics, from ancient analytics and arithmetics, to their modern
standards, grammar, too, will ascend beyond the grammar school, and
become from a dry-as-dust textbook obsession, the open sesame to the
hidden treasures of society.[46]

The complete breakdown of the German language between 1933
and 1939 was, for Rosenstock-Huessy, "one of the speediest and
most radical events of all times in the field of mind and speech."
Reflecting on this breakdown he remains more convinced than ever
that ". . . the science of this lifeblood of society [*i.e.*, language]
should . . . be exalted to the rank of social research."

The originality of social research hinges on the existence of a method
that is neither stolen from theology nor from natural science. We intend
to prove, in the terms of grammar, of theology and of natural philosophy, that such a particular method exists, and that by using it Roman
Catholics and Protestants and Free Thinkers are united in a common

enterprise. Without such a unity, the revolt of the masses must find the various intellectual groups in a helpless division, as helpless as in the new war. . . . We must discover a common basis for social thinking.[47]

It is fascinating to follow Rosenstock-Huessy's development of this methodology in a work like *Applied Psychology*, not only because of the compactness of the argument, but because of the structure of its development, which proceeds from a discussion in the first four chapters about our having substituted the soul for real named persons, to outlining a complex program for co-ordinating art, religion, and law in the ninth chapter. The early chapters reflect his reasons for choosing the title *Applied Psychology*, which he took over from a popular paperback tract on social psychology.Through the deception of having lured a particular audience with a popular title, he hoped to reach those who in his opinion were most in need of hearing such words. The fascination of psychologists in his time for the soul was, from his standpoint, a "de-souling" of people, since it meant that the soul was more important than one's name; hence, of more significance than the creature's link with time, history, and his actual biography. During this period Martin Buber also recognized this danger. In 1930 he gave a lecture entitled "The De-souling of the Soul" (*"Die Entseelung der Seele"*). Descartes' preoccupation with the cogitating mind and his admitted disdain for his own autobiography prior to his vision in a country hut is a good example of the split which such emphases could produce. Actually, Descartes' mind-matter dualism made it theoretically possible, but practically speaking impossible, for either mind or matter to do justice to precisely those aspects of reality which each was ostensibly concerned with. In Descartes' case, he viewed mistakenly his *second mind* as the authoritative. From such a split, the subject-object, inner-outer characterization of reality inevitably follows, with the thinking mind determining the truth and meaning of the concrete experiential world. At the heart of this dilemma lies the mistaken assumption that the soul is an object, a thing.

The fifth chapter is devoted to answering the question of whether or not the soul has its own peculiar grammar. He begins with an attack upon those false grammars which reflect the dominance of the perceiving I—*i.e.* those which begin with the I rather than, as experience tells us, with the Thou. Not *amo, amas, amat*, but rather *amas, amo, amat* is the correct order of our proper grammatical posture. This is confirmed by our responses to external forces and pressures, which address us as they did primitive man, namely as a thou. It is through outside address that we gradually become a person, conscious of our identity—*e.g.*, our name becomes meaningful. During this period we are most aware of imperative and vocative forms of speech—*e.g.*, "Go! Come! Listen!" etc. Similarly, the child's response "No! Yes!" represents an assertion by the child that gradually his identity is being established. In each instance, personality is rooted in the fact that we have a name within a community and are capable of being addressed and responding. This, for Rosenstock-Huessy, is basic to our grammatical life.

It is only after we have utilized the grammatical forms I and Thou that we begin to employ the grammatical third person He, She, or It. Our normal grammatical existence informs us that both the personal as well as the impersonal are integral parts of our vocabulary. The transition from childhood to adulthood is marked by this distinction. While the second person is our primary grammatical form, the complete grammar of the soul is revealed in the changes and transformations resulting from the basic grammatical laws. "Every change in the life of the soul appears as an inflection of its grammatical configurations."[48] The various grammatical moods become the medium through which our grammatical persons are expressed. They constitute, in effect, the particular garb of the soul in each moment of its existence. As with the three grammatical persons, all grammatical moods and tenses manifest the "soul's possibilities." ". . . the soul can swing to the melody of becoming just as it may resound with existence's tune of the rhythm of transformation." Thus love, being *in* love, is the supreme force capable of transforming the I—releasing it from its own thoughts and obsessions with individual freedom. As with Augustine, love surpasses all the pagan virtues, since love alone can bend the I. We can be courageous, temperate, etc., but we cannot *be* love: we are always *in* love. To be *in* love is to admit the priority of the grammatical second person over the first.

Crucial for grammatical existence is the temporal factor of timing. While for many, to quote a popular German song, "Thoughts are free," just the opposite is true of speech, which is the creature of time, bound to various time sequences and yet capable of creating new times and ages. Timing, inspiration, transformation, and speech always go hand in hand with grammatical living.

Rosenstock-Huessy concludes the fifth chapter with the following summation about the grammar of the soul. "It is the theory of the transformation of shapes. Inflection, transformation, changes of time are its contents. Our school grammar speaks of umlauts and ablauts; the Urgrammar of the transformation of shapes."[49]

As indicated earlier, the ninth chapter is the appropriate complement to the fifth in view of its devotion to the social implications of the grammatical method; namely, its concern for the we rather than the I, with community rather than the individual. The we, for Rosenstock-Huessy, is more than merely the total sum of a number of individuals. As he and also Rosenzweig stated it, "The Urgrammar blends God, Man and World in the resounding 'We'." In its grammatical attire the first person plural embraces the world of art— *i.e.*, lyric song, drama, and prose. These are the elements of the aesthetic world that unite us most intensively as a people (*Volk*). The second person plural embraces those legal norms which again define the nature of communal existence, whether they be the laws of the secular or spiritual realm. Finally, the language of the scientific world is subsumed under our grammatical third person plural. In each of the three realms Rosenstock-Huessy has singled out one example as embodying the purest form of that particular grammatical voice. Thus, lyric poetry is the purest example of art, jurisprudence the purest and simplest expression of the social order, and lastly, natural science the purest but also most elementary kind of science.[50] It is noteworthy that religion is discussed not only in connection with lawgiving and lawmaking in the field of jurisprudence and ethics, but also as that vital force which is present when significant personal and collective transformations occur in any of the three realms. Here and in other writings, Rosenstock-Huessy identifies religion and religious experience with that power or force which enables us to speak and respond during any period of our spiritual biographies. These two chapters contribute greatly to an appreciation of the transforming and sacramental powers inherent in speech, as evidenced in his motto, "I respond *although* I will be changed." It also helps us to understand that "Speech is the body of the Spirit."

The "Cross of Reality" and Social Unity

FINALLY, LET US note Rosenstock-Huessy's application of speech as the means whereby social unity is determined by examining his essay *In Defense of the Grammatical Method,* referred to earlier. This essay is particularly relevant inasmuch as it illustrates the inter-relatedness of his grammatical approach and his cross of reality. The unity of speech, both individual and collective, constituting the authentic spiritual biographies of all those involved, can be appreciated at any one moment only in terms of the intersection of at least four vectors which represent the meeting of the spatial and temporal axes within which all life unfolds. In his two-volume *Sociology,* in *Applied Psychology,* and elsewhere, he has reiterated his conviction that dualisms like subject and object never do justice to the complexity of any situation. He has described himself as an impure thinker because of his unwillingness to settle for the normal polarization that typifies most thinking. His use of the four vectors of a cross enables him to give appropriate recognition to the traditional subject-object distinction representing the spatial axis, represented by the two vectors which embrace past and future, traject and preject. The rationale behind this division he explains as follows:

The terms preject and traject above we have chosen out of respect for the inveterate usage which divides the world into mind and body, into subjects and objects. It did not seem wise to by-pass these well-established terms of our tradition in logic. The battle had to be joined on the battlefield defined by the classical tradition; and we tried to make room for two more aspects of the real by introducing the time cup. Of any time cup the subject and the object were fragments because the future was anticipated by the prejective or imperative, the past ascertained by the report or narrative (trajective).[51]

Note his application of the cross of reality when analyzing; first, those evils which destroy unity. It is anarchy that "prevents trans-local units from cooperating"; decadence destroys our sense of future because it means that people "do not have the stamina of converting the next generation to their own aims and ends"; in revolutions men do violence to the past and to the existing order; and it is war that forces a country to "incorporate external territory." Corresponding to his cross, anarchy and war represent the inner and outer "space in society." Thus, he writes:

> We are compelled, by the two facts of anarchy and war, to distinguish between an inner and an outer space in society. The twofold character of space is that, in any society, a border-line . . . cuts the world of space into two parts, one inner, one outer.[52]

Similarly, decadence and revolution destroy the possibility of future and the necessity of past so essential to the growth of any healthy society. Upon such discussions Rosenstock-Huessy bases his claim that this represents "an undebatable basis for the social system." "For the two axes of time and space, with their fronts backward, forward, inward, outward, are not merely verbal definitions of the social order; they are open to a unanimous experience and an identical consciousness of all human beings." These social truths are, he claims, "universally valid as any mathematical and logical truths." It is only when one realizes that we are threatened on any one of our "time or space fronts" that we are compelled to acknowledge the existence of social processes and the need for integration and preservation. The fight to restore social health is akin to that described by William James in his insistence upon the need for a moral equivalent for war. When one front is threatened, we become aware that the "four fronts of life perpetually must be balanced." Where these evils are allowed to continue unchecked, "no social research is meaningful or possible." Corresponding to the four "evils" enumerated above are the tasks confronting social research to restore the perpetual balance vital to a healthy society.

> Social research is imprisoned in a reality, in a cross of reality between four simultaneous tasks to cultivate faith, power, unanimity, respect, all four. Social research is the search for the restoration of the perpetual balance.[53]

Perhaps the only advance made in this most recent presentation of the grammatical method is its relatively striking clarity of style and the concreteness of application. The more theoretical pronouncement of 1924 is enhanced by Rosenstock-Huessy's practical and concise exposition of 1955 and more recently in his *Speechbook* of 1964. His discussion of social evils is an excellent illustration both of his method and of the relevance of speech to it. In short, the above four evils "hurt language," since it is "speech" that defends society against these ills. Thus the heading of his third section: "Society lives by speech, dies without speech." We speak out of need and out of fear; out of fear that decay, anarchy, war, and revolution will destroy the time and space axes of society which "give direction and orientation to all members of society." In order to prevent social disintegration, men reason, pass laws, tell stories, and sing. In so doing, "the external world is reasoned out, the future is ruled, the past is told," and "the unanimity of the inner circle is expressed in song."

Without articulated speech, man has neither direction nor orientation in time and space. Without the signposts of speech, the social beehive would disintegrate immediately. When speech is recognized as curing society from the ills of disharmony and discontinuity in time and space, grammar is the most obvious organon for the teachings of society.[54]

By means of this method, we become conscious of our "place in history (backward), world (outward), society (inward), and destiny (forward)." The grammatical method constitutes "an additional development of speech itself," which fulfills itself in our new powers of "direction and orientation." Thus, he writes that "Grammar is the self-consciousness of language, just as logic is the self-consciousness of thinking." Rosenstock-Huessy's constant use of language as the means of social unity and peace is never stated without reference to the space and time axes of society.

Without common speech, men neither have one time nor mutual respect nor security among themselves. To speak has to do with time and space. Without speech, the phenomenon of time and space cannot be interpreted. Only when we speak to others (or, for that matter, to ourselves), do we delineate an inner space or circle in which we speak, from the outer world about which we speak. . . . And the same is true about the phenomenon of time. Only because we speak, are we able to establish a present moment between past and future.[55]

It is interesting to note his rejection of scientific notions of time and space. "Grammatical time and space precedes the scientific notions of an outer space or of a directed time. For they presuppose an inner space between the scientists and some contemporaneity between them too." The types or forms of speech which are our social watchdogs are, in words resembling Schelling's in his Introduction to his *Weltalter*, "speaking and listening, teaching and studying."

God is "The Power Which Makes Us Speak"

THE TIME SPENT pursuing the various themes in Rosenstock-Huessy's writings is a forceful and imaginative journey into the secrets and mysteries of human meaning. If the cross of reality has any meaning, it must by definition affect every quarter of human existence. No single style can bring life to all others; only a harmonious blending of numerous styles confident in their oral and aural powers can bring about the continued creation and preservation of a truly human society—*i.e.*, complete the envisoned sequel to Michelangelo's painting in the Sistine Chapel. In the concluding pages of *Out of Revolution* this is admirably stated:

> Mankind does not try to speak one language. He does not monotonously speak the same words. But this is because in every dialogue the two partners assume different parts, represent different points of view, use different arguments. Variety is the essence of real speech between men. . . . By the multitude of dialects we are reminded of the innumerable quarrels, dialogues, disputes between the men of the past. But interplay and mutual relation are at the bottom of the tower of Babel which linguists study today by the queer method of approaching each language separately. Each human variety has its particular coagulated speech. Every speech is dissoluble; it is retranslatable into the universal language behind one separate tongue. Through translation, each variety of man remains in contact with all other varieties.[56]

Speech is presented as the means whereby men become conscious of their variety and at the same time aware that it is speech which provides the clue and means to healing the rifts between men and creating a viable, healthy society. In all of this there has been notably little mention of God or use of traditional theological categories. For those readers oriented in traditional forms of Petrine and Pauline Christianity, this presentation will undoubtedly present serious difficulties. They may simply wish to reject these concerns as having nothing to do with religion as they know it. For those willing to submit themselves to a Johannine approach, such a presentation may provide a means of overcoming the difficulties created by those who insist upon rigid, often absolute distinctions between sacred and secular concerns. For such persons, the answer to the question about the place and nature of God within a Johannine setting is a simple one. "The power who puts questions into our mouth and makes us answer them is our God."

The living God thus revealed by Jesus must be forever distinguished from the merely conceptual God of philosophers. Most atheists deny God because they look for Him in the wrong way. He is not an object, but a person, and He has not a concept but a name. To approach Him as an object of theoretical discussion is to defeat the quest from the start. Nobody can look at God as an object. God looks at us and has looked at us before we open our eyes or our mouths. *He is the power which makes us speak. He puts words of life on our lips.*[57]

NOTES

CHAPTER 3

1 Georg Müller, "Der Sprachdenker Eugen Rosenstock-Huessy," *Evangelisches Theologie* (July–August 1954), pp. 314–34. Dr. Müller has written numerous penetrating articles on various aspects of Rosenstock-Huessy's writings.
2 Eugen Rosenstock to Franz Rosenzweig (10/28/1916); J.G. Hamann, *Golgotha und Scheblimini* (1784); Hamann to F. H. Jacobi (1785, 1784, and 1787).
3 Friedrich von Schlegel, *The Philosophy of Life* (London: Henry G. Bohn, 1847), pp. 1–2, 207–8, 387.
4 Ludwig Feuerbach, *Grundsätze der Philosophie der Zukunft* (Zürich: Verlag des litarischen Comptoirs, 1843), pp. iii–iv, 1.
5 Rosenstock-Huessy, *Out of Revolution* (New York: Four Wells, 1964), pp. 727–28.
6 Rosenstock-Huessy, *The Christian Future* (New York: Harper Torchbooks, 1966), pp. 159–60, 129, 127, 130, 2.
7 *Ibid.*, p. 108.
8 Martin Buber, *Mamre* (Melbourne: Melbourne University Press, 1946), p. 70.
9 Rosenstock-Huessy, *Out of Revolution*, pp. 740–41.
10 Harvey Cox, *The Secular City* (New York: Macmillan, 1965), p. 21.
11 Rosenstock-Huessy, "Ich bin ein unreiner Denker," *Neues Abendland*, 8 Jg. (1953).
12 Cited by Eugen Rosenstock-Huessy in a privately printed address entitled "The Soul of William James," delivered at Dartmouth College in 1942.
13 Rosenstock-Huessy, *Bibliography/Biography* (New York: Four Wells, 1959), pp. 13 and 16.
14 From a lengthy privately circulated autobiographical essay, p. 180.
15 Rosenstock-Huessy, *Bibliography/Biography*, p. 17.
16 The preceding citations are all from his privately circulated autobiographical essay, pp. 172–76.

17 *Ostfalens Rechtsliterature unter Friedrich II* (Weimar: H. Bohlans Nf., 1912), p. 144.
18 Cf. for example, the recent exchange at the Weber Centenary Congress in Heidelberg (April 1964) between Professors Herbert Marcuse and Benjamin Nelson. Herbert Marcuse, "Industrialization and Capitalization," *The New Left*, London, No. 31 (May–June 1965); Benjamin Nelson, "Diskussion über Industrialisierung und Kapitalismus," *Max Weber und die Soziologie heute, Verhandlung des 15 deutschen Soziologentages* (Tubingen: J.C.B. Mohr, 1965).
19 *Bibliography/Biography*, p. 36.
20 *Ibid.*, pp. 17–18.
21 Rosenstock-Huessy, "Rückblick auf die *Kreatur*," *Deutsche Beiträge* (Chicago: University of Chicago Press, 1947), pp. 209–10.
22 Eugen Rosenstock, *Angewandte Seelenkunde* (Darmstadt: Roether-Verlag, 1924), p. 8. This work has been republished in Volume One of Rosenstock-Huessy's *Die Sprache des Menschengeschlects* (Heidelberg: Verlag Lambert Schneider, 1963), pp. 739–810.
23 Maurice Friedman, *Martin Buber: The Life of Dialogue* (New York: Harper Torchbooks, 1960), p. 162.
24 *The Christian Future*, p. 222.
25 J. H. Oldham in his "Foreword" to the 1947 English edition of *The Christian Future*, p. viii.
26 *Bibliography/Biography*, p. 18.
27 Dietrich Bonhoeffer's twin sister, Mrs. Sabine Leibholz, has discussed these "universities in the wilderness" in terms of their significance for those who subsequently fought and died in the German Resistance Movement in World War II. Cf. Sabine Leibholz, "Eugen Rosenstock-Huessy and Dietrich Bonhoeffer—Two Witnesses to the Change in our Time," *Universitas*, Volume 8, 3 (1966), pp. 282 ff.
28 *Bibliography/Biography*, p. 19.
29 *Op. cit.*, p. 23.
30 *Bibliography/Biography* contains a complete list of publications up through 1959. Note also: *Die Sprache des Menschengeschlects, I and II* (Heidelberg: Lambert Schneider, 1963 and 1964) and *Judaism Despite Christianity* (University of Alabama, 1968).
31 *Op. cit.*, p. 25.
32 *Ibid.*, pp. 23–24.
33 These remarks are contained in a paper delivered by Dr. Hans R. Huessy at a symposium on Rosenstock-Huessy's thought held at the Miramar Conference Center at Woods Hole, Massachusetts, during July 1965. It was entitled "Some Applications to Psychiatry of the Work of Eugen Rosenstock-Huessy." The citations which follow are from Dr. Huessy's paper.
34 Cf. "Liturgical Thinking" (II), *Orate Fratres* (Collegeville, Minn.: January 1950), pp. 12–13. Cf. also a related essay which deals with his differences with Martin Buber, "Dich und Mich, Lehre oder Mode," *Neues Abendland*, 9 Jg. (November 1954). An account of

his subsequent exchange with Buber is contained in *Philosophical Interrogations* (ed. Sydney and Beatrice Rome) (New York: Holt, Rinehart and Winston, 1964), pp. 31–35.
35 "Liturgical Thinking" (II), p. 12.
36 "Pentecost and Mission," *The Hartford Seminary Foundation Bulletin* (Winter 1954), p. 21.
37 "Liturgical Thinking" (I), *Orate Fratres* (Collegeville, Minn.: November 1949), p. 2.
38 A report in a letter to the author, 12/26/65.
39 *Out of Revolution*, p. 739.
40 *The Christian Future*, p. 209.
41 *Bibliography/Biography*. p. 22.
42 *Out of Revolution*, p. 8.
43 *The Christian Future*, p. 209.
44 *Ibid.*, pp. 167–68.
45 *Angewandte Seelenkunde*, p. 8.
46 "In Defense of the Grammatical Method," (privately printed) p. 1.
47 *Ibid.*, p. 2.
48 *Angewandte Seelenkunde*, p. 27.
49 *Ibid.*, p. 31.
50 *Ibid.*, pp. 51 and 53.
51 "The Individual's Right to Speak and Some Final Terms of Grammar" (privately printed, 1946), p. 25.
52 "In Defense of the Grammatical Method," pp. 2–3.
53 *Ibid.*, p. 3.
54 *Ibid.*, p. 5.
55 *Ibid.*, p. 8.
56 *Out of Revolution*, p. 738.
57 *The Christian Future*, p. 94.

Franz Rosenzweig (1886–1929): Speech Precedes Thought and Needs Time

> My words are too difficult for you;
> Therefore they appear to you as simple.
>
> —JUDAH-HA-LEVI, *The Book of Kuzari*

> Why is truth so woefully
> Removed? To depths of secret banned?
> None perceives in proper time! If we
> But perceived in proper time, how bland
> The truth would be, how fair to see!
> How near and ready to our hand!
>
> —GOETHE, *Westöstlicher Diwan*

In the new thinking, the method of speech replaces the method of thinking maintained in all earlier philosophies. Thinking is timeless and wants to be timeless. . . . Speech is bound to time and nourished by time, and it neither can nor wants to abandon this element. It does not know in advance just where it will end. It takes its cues from others.

—FRANZ ROSENZWEIG

For in the course of a dialogue he who happens to be listening also speaks, and he does not speak merely when he is actually uttering words, not even mainly when he is uttering words, but just as much when through his eager attention, through the assent or dissent expressed in his glance, he conjures words to the lips of the current speaker.

—FRANZ ROSENZWEIG

Franz Rosenzweig: Another Johannine Visionary

ALTHOUGH FRANZ ROSENZWEIG died in 1929, it was not until 1953 that the English-speaking community was permitted to read his *Understanding the Sick and the Healthy* and selections from his essays and letters.[1] One reason behind current interest in Rosenzweig's writings and also those of Rosenstock-Huessy, Buber, and Ebner is the general interest among philosophers and theologians in existentialist concerns touching upon themes like encounter, hermeneutics and communication. Certainly his close association with Martin Buber and their translation of the Hebrew Scriptures into German called attention to Rosenzweig simply by virtue of Buber's current popularity. It is appropriate for many reasons to introduce the reader to Rosenzweig's insights into the sacramental character of speech; it would be appropriate for no other reason than that, along with Martin Buber, he was undoubtedly one of the most profound Jewish religious thinkers of the twentieth century. He and Buber were in basic agreement in many of those areas which touch upon the sacred power of the word, but their differences were nevertheless profoundly sharp, especially when discussing the word as it relates to time, history, and Jewish learning. Although the one was a Jew, the other a Christian, Rosenzweig and Rosenstock-Huessy were undoubtedly much more in sympathy with each other's estimate of the importance of speech as it relates to names, calendars, time, tradition, and history, than was true for Rosenzweig and Buber throughout their close collaborations. With respect to those themes under consideration, it is suggested that Buber and the Austrian Roman Catholic Ebner had much more in common than did Buber and Rosenzweig.

Not only was Rosenzweig known to those associated with the Patmos circle, but as was indicated in the previous chaper, he and Rosenstock-Huessy regarded one another as alter egos, as partners in a common venture in behalf of the word. His concern with speech and the word, as reflected in almost every letter, essay, and book, as well as in his subsequent collaborations with Martin Buber, earn him a position of special prominence in a study of this type. Efforts in this country to draw attention to his writings have been marked first by a profound respect for his personal qualities, and second, by a universal high regard for his scholarship, both as a student of German idealism and as an erudite and creative Jewish sage. Unfortunately, he is recognized in most quarters almost exclusively as a great *Jewish* thinker. This is maintained despite the well-known fact that he was adamant that his great work, *The Star of Redemption*, should not be bought and read simply as a Jewish book, and also despite the presence in his writings of the same Johannine millenarian focus that marks Rosenstock-Huessy's writings. In a letter to Rosenzweig in May 1916, Rosenstock-Huessy described their common interests as ". . . only for the people who had already suffered from philosophy before 1914."[2] After *The Star to Redemption*'s publication, Rosenzweig lamented its reception. "It is above all not a *Jewish book*. . . . Rather it is merely a philosophical system."[3]

I hope that my Jewish friends and colleagues will not object if an attempt is made in these pages to wed these concerns of Rosenzweig's and present him as a Jew who was continually uneasy about his Jewish identity, except it be wedded to a Jewish-Christian partnership devoted to helping usher in the Johannine Age—the Age of the Spirit. The *Letters on Judaism and Christianity* between Rosenzweig and Rosenstock-Huessy (1916) indicate not only how deeply versed and knowledgeable each was about his own tradition, but how each regarded Judaism and Christianity as copartners in the creation of the future Johannine Age. Like Rosenstock-Huessy, he was wedded to his own religious tradition, but was equally unwilling to have his sense of the future condition of all men determined by a single religious tradition. The universalism and catholicity each envisioned was open-ended rather than closed—*i.e.*, open to the possibility of a time when it will be insufficient, when one will feel incomplete as a human being, if one's identity is determined exclusively in either Jewish or Christian terms. To minimize this aspect of their respective longings for the Johannine Age is to do an injustice to the richness of their insights.

From Hegel to Revelation:
Franz Rosenzweig and Eugen Rosenstock-Huessy

BORN IN 1886, Franz Rosenzweig was brought up in a cultured Jewish home in Cassel, Germany. Between 1905 and 1912 he studied medicine, philosophy, history, and theology, and in 1910 began his scholarly two-volume work on Hegel, which eventually was published as his doctoral thesis in 1920 under the title *Hegel und der Staat*. Except for a period of about a year, Rosenzweig had studied history under Friedrich Meinecke in Freiburg from the autumn of 1908 through the summer of 1912. From Meinecke, Rosenzweig appropriated a history-of-ideas approach to history, which enabled him to appreciate the influence of nineteenth-century idealism upon German culture, especially upon her political life. During this period he developed a profound appreciation for philological and empirical evidence, and also from Meinecke, a respect for the dangers inherent in constructing a theory of history in the absence of proper historical data.

In 1912 Rosenzweig and Rosenstock-Huessy met while attending a conference of young philosophers and historians at Baden-Baden. Among those present were cousins of Rosenzweig, the brothers Hans and Rudolf Ehrenberg. Hans Ehrenberg eventually converted and became a Christian pastor, while Rudolf eventually became a biologist at Göttingen. The seeds for the interests and eventual formation of the Patmos circle were already being sown during meetings such as this. When Rosenzweig came to the conference he was rooted solidly in Hegelian thought, but even then he felt that history was something more than Hegel's system made it out to be. History was something one had to act *in* rather than speculate *upon*. In a letter to Hans Ehrenberg (9/26/1910) Rosenzweig's restlessness and religious sensitivities are quite apparent.

> For that reason we also refuse to see 'God *in* history,' because we do not wish to view history [in the religious sense] as a picture, as 'Being'; rather, we disavow God in history in order to restore Him in the Process by which it [history] becomes. . . . 'The battle over history' in the nineteenth-century sense is at the same time for us a battle over 'religion' in the twentieth-century sense.[4]

During these student days he lunched frequently with Eugen Rosenstock-Huessy then a young law professor at Leipzig. What interested Rosenzweig during these many conversations was the fact that anyone in his right mind, much less a brilliant law professor, could be religious—*i.e.*, take the fact of Revelation seriously. At the same time, he had become increasingly uneasy about the completeness and finality of Hegel's system and the inherent relativism he saw in it. His general concern for the problems his generation faced and his respect for the forcefulness of Rosenstock-Huessy's personality and religious position brought about a crisis in his life which came to a head during a heated confrontation with Rosenstock-Huessy on the evening of July 7, 1913. In his discussion of this meeting Alexander Altmann has said that, "It was the most decisive and most far-reaching event in Rosenzweig's inner life. It produced a crisis from which after months of struggle, the new Rosenzweig emerged."[5] The encounter itself is an admirable illustration of the transforming power of the spoken word where both partners allow the other person's speech to sink in and take its toll. It was a model example of the meaning implicit in Rosenstock-Huessy's motto *Respondeo etsi mutabor* (I respond *although* I will be changed). In his excellent discussion of the role of language in Karl Jaspers' thought, the late Fritz Kaufmann said of that evening's "highly charged controversy": "True co-Existenz in the consummation of face-to-face relationships is no less intensive and forceful for being unobtrusive, a model of non-violence." Such is the quality of any "discussion about mankind's great objectives, man's ultimate concerns."[6] When asked later to comment upon that evening, Rosenstock-Huessy stated: ". . . much to their own surprise the two partners found themselves reluctantly put under the compulsion to face up to one another in a struggle with no quarter to be given or asked for. . . . For only in this last extremity of a soul in self-defense is there hope to realize the truth in the questions of life."[7] Some months after their encounter, Rosenzweig described the significance of the evening in a letter to Rudolf Ehrenberg (10/31/1913), a witness to their meeting.

In that night's conversation Rosenstock pushed me step by step out of the last relativist position which I still occupied and forced me to take an absolute standpoint. I was inferior to him from the outset, since I had to recognize for my part too the justice of his attack. If I could then have buttressed my dualism between revelation and the world with a meta-physical dualism between God and the Devil (he meant to say if he could have split himself in half, one half religious, the other worldly) I should have been unassailable. But I was prevented from doing so by the first sentence of the Bible. This piece of common ground forced me to face him. This has remained even afterwards in the weeks which follow the fixed point of departure. Any form of philosophical relativism is now impossible to me.[8]

The change produced in Rosenzweig was that he was no longer a philosopher concerned about reason, but a man of faith, who took Revelation seriously. He was forced to reject a "faith in philoso-phy" and to adopt a "faith based on revelation." The three corner-stones of his *Star of Redemption*—creation, revelation, and redemp-tion—were forged in the course of that evening and in the ensuing days. In two letters to Hans Ehrenberg the change in his outlook was described. Rosenzweig now asserted that the absorption and transformation of creation by revelation means also the absorption of philosophy into revelation and results in the priority of belief over thought. Philosophy is not rejected, but absorbed within the framework of religious history.

Revelation breaks into the world and transforms creation, which is the Alpha of history, into redemption which is the Omega. Philosophy has a pagan quality. It is an expression of the Alpha of creation, of pure nature to which God has given freedom—even against himself. But as revelation comes into the world, it gradually absorbs philosophy, de-prives it of its pagan elements, and illuminates it with its own light. The Omega of history will be realized after the element of creation, the world's freedom has spent itself. Then God, who allowed the world to be the Alpha, will again be the First and the Last, the Alpha and Omega.[9]

The fact that Revelation enters into history and transforms it means that we must see history not as an absolute process, but rather through the eyes of faith. Belief in history had to give way to belief in the God who reveals Himself in history. Thus, Hegel was the "last philosopher," because to Rosenzweig Hegel symbolized the last breath of the pagan philosophical mind. Hegel marked the *finis philosophiae*.

The events surrounding 1800—the French Revolution of 1789; the thinking of Fichte, Hegel, Goethe, and Schelling; and the influ-ence of Rosenstock-Huessy's calendrical thinking—suggested to

Rosenzweig that the Johannine Age had begun. The theme was one familiar to him as it was to anyone immersed in nineteenth-century German idealism. Fichte, Hegel, and especially Schelling in the latter's *Philosophy of Revelation* had developed the millenarian idea of the successive ages of the world—i.e., the Petrine, Pauline, and finally Johannine—to which, for Schelling, corresponded the Christian virtues of love, faith, and hope. The three ages also represented for Schelling the three persons of the Christian Trinity, which corresponded to the three historic forms of Christianity—i.e., the Petrine, Roman Catholicism; the Pauline, Protestantism; and finally the Johannine, which signified the Age of the Spirit and a period marked by an absence of doctrinal and dogmatic concerns. In his *Philosophy of Revelation* Schelling stated, "if I had to build a church in our time, I would dedicate it to Saint John."[10] Johannine for Schelling, as for Rosenstock-Huessy and Rosenzweig, was synonymous with an age ruled by the word wherein traditional sacred-profane barriers would be eliminated. The history of philosophy from Thales to Hegel represented for Rosenzweig the mind's attempt to realize itself fully—independently of revelation.

Subsequent reactions to Hegel, as exemplified in Kierkegaard, Schopenhauer, Feuerbach, and Nietzsche, convinced him that Hegel's grandiose system had failed. Whereas reason had spent itself in Hegel, Rosenzweig recognized that a new age, the Johannine, had begun. It was to be one ruled by the Spirit and the word in the Johannine millenarian sense. In a letter dated March 1916, he wrote, "The idealist movement is both the end of philosophy (that is, of paganism) and the beginning of the Johannine epoch (its patristic age, as it were)."[11] Hegel is therefore the last of the philosophers and the first of the new Church Fathers in the Johannine Age—an age wherein the Church can no longer be identified with the state, nor with any visible ecclesiastical forms, but rather with society directly.[12] It should be noted that the Johannine thinking of the German idealists had also influenced significantly Jewish thinking during the emancipation. In his excellent essay, "Franz Rosenzweig on History," Professor Altmann states: "The messianic fervour which seized the Jewish Reform Movement in the nineteenth century and which is reflected in the philosophical writings of S. Formstecher and S. Hirsch down to Hermann Cohen stems from the idealist concept of Johannine Christianity."[13] While Professor Altmann and I would differ over the particular sources for Rosenzweig's appropriation of the Johannine elements in his thinking, it should be noted that Johannine millenarian concerns had permeated nineteenth-century secular philosophical thinking to a far greater degree than it had Christian theology, which, then as today, was for the most part Petrine or Pauline in both its structure and its preaching.

Following that evening's encounter with Rosenstock-Huessy, Rosenzweig, then steeped in idealism, felt left with no alternative but to become a believing Christian. His only reservation in taking this step was that he affirm Christianity by first rediscovering his Jewish roots, which, prior to that time, he had long since discarded.[14] "I declared," he wrote to Rudolf Ehrenberg (10/31/1913), "that I could turn Christian only *qua* Jew—not through the intermediate stage of paganism."[15] In this letter one gains a valuable insight into his eventual understanding of the rightful relationship between church and synagogue. Those accustomed to viewing Judaism as a socially and temporally dispersed force in the world will be challenged by his insistence that Judaism was essentially an atemporal ahistorical body—"in this world there seemed to me no room for Judaism."

> You know very well what made me not only stand up to him but also submit to him: that I Christianized my view of Judaism, that I shared your faith, or at least thought I did. Consequently I was immediately disarmed by Rosenstock's simple confession of faith, which was only the start of his argument. The fact that a man like Rosenstock was a conscious Christian (in your case these things were still in the liquid state of a problem) at once bowled over my entire conception of Christianity and of religion generally, including my own. I thought I had Christianized my view of Judaism, but in actual fact I had done the opposite: I had "Judaized" my view of Christianity. I had considered the year 313 as the beginning of a falling away from true Christianity, since it opened a path for the Christians in the opposite direction to that opened in the year 70 for the Jews. I had begrudged the church its scepter, realizing that the synagogue bears a broken staff. You saw how, on this assumption, I began to reconstruct my world. In this world (and anything outside the world unrelated to what is inside I did not then nor do I now recognize)—in this world there seemed to me to be no room for Judaism.[16]

Leaving Leipzig, Franz Rosenzweig returned home and told his mother, "There is only one way—Jesus." His mother asked him if he, however, had not been in the synagogue on New Year's Day, to

which Rosenzweig replied that he had, and that ". . . I will go to the
Synagogue on the Day of Atonement, too." His mother's answer
was, "When I come in I will ask them to turn you away. In our
synagogue there is no room for an apostate."[17]

Nevertheless, on October 11 of the same year, Rosenzweig at-
tended the Day of Atonement service. The experience on the Day
of Atonement when the Holy Name is uttered was for him one of
the most moving acts of the liturgy. In that moment, he said that he
had experienced "eternal life." As a result of that moving experience
he declared in a letter to Rudolf Ehrenberg, "I have reversed my
decision. It no longer seems necessary to me, and therefore being
what I am, no longer possible. I will remain a Jew."[18] This decision
in no way constituted a rejection of the force or logic of Rosenstock-Huessy's position. Professor Altmann recognized this when he
stated, "It would be wrong to assume that Rosenzweig's decision to
remain a Jew involved a change in the philosophy to which Rosenstock had converted him."[19] In discussing Rosenzweig's speech
writings, the degree to which Rosenstock-Huessy's influence was
not only present, but frequently acknowledged, will be made
clearly evident.

The Influence of Hermann Cohen
and Friedrich W. J. Schelling

IN 1913, WHILE pursuing Jewish studies in Berlin, he met the neo-
Kantian philosopher and leader of the Marburg School, Hermann
Cohen (1842–1918), whom he later frequently referred to as "The
Philosopher." Cohen was not only an able and eminent philosopher,
but, now in his later years, he represented for Rosenzweig a great
soul, a religious person, a "philosopher and a man." It was an especially propitious meeting for Rosenzweig, inasmuch as Cohen, at
this juncture in his life, had already begun to depart from his earlier
attempts to look upon the principles of Judaism and all other religious and metaphysical categories as "fixed postulates of consciousness." In both his earlier epistemological writings, as well as in his
ethical treatise, the existence of God had merely "the same value as
an idea."[20] For Rosenzweig, Cohen was the new Hegel in the sense

that he had produced a philosophical system which embraced the entire range of human culture. And like both Kant and Hegel, Cohen had written a trilogy of works based on critical idealism.

Until late in life, Jewish faith for Cohen consisted simply in believing in a divinely grounded moral order. The prophets were the carriers of those ideas most essential to the development of an ethic of pure will—namely, "the ideas of humanity, messianism and God." They alone enabled Judaism to shake off its earlier entanglements with mythical thought and establish Judaism as "the religion of ethical sublimity."[21] From 1890 until his death, Cohen's writings were marked not only by an active commitment to Judaism but by his attempt to write a definitive philosophy of religion for Judaism. Both his *The Concept of Religion in the System of Philosophy* (1915) and his posthumously published *Religion of Reason Drawn from the Sources of Judaism* (1919) reflect this specifically religious bent in his thinking. In his earlier system the Marburg neo-Kantian philosopher Cohen had stressed the significance of the elements of flux and becoming. But in his later years Cohen distinguished sharply between God as Being and the world as becoming. The relationship between perfection and imperfection, God and nature, was resolved by virtue of Cohen's stress upon the doctrine of correlation, in which Being and becoming are correlatives of one another. The worlds of becoming, nature, and men have meaning by virtue of their origin in and dependence upon that which "gives power and significance." Within this correlation God needs mankind just as much as men need God; they are correlative—*i.e.*, mutually dependent. "There is no mankind without God, but there can also be no God without mankind." For Cohen, "The basic framework of religious knowledge is established in the correlation of God and man."[22] This dramatic transition from Kantian idealism to his adoption of the principle of correlation marked the religious phase with which Rosenzweig was so familiar. No longer is human reason supreme—anthropocentrism gives way to theocentrism. For Rosenzweig, Cohen had "advanced with a powerful surge far beyond the philosophical movement of the nineteenth century into the philosophical country of the future."[23] The absolute supremacy of the reasoning ego was replaced by the I-Thou language of the correlation between God and man which permeates Rosenzweig's writings. Professor Bergman has suggested a parallel between Kierkegaard and Cohen to the extent that each rebelled against a particular form of idealism, each underwent an ethical phase, and finally each focused upon the concrete individual in his final religious phase. Unlike Kierkegaard, however, the individual has meaning only as man beside fellowman (*Nebenmensch*). "Man is wolf to man" in the natural order; within the divine-human encounter they are destined to become co-partners within the Creation—man becomes a fellowman—a *Mitmensch*. "Nature's creation is . . . broken off in order that man himself may carry it forward and create out of man a fellow man."[24] In addition to the personal attraction of Cohen's deep piety, the religious significance of the principle of correlation in his later writings had a lasting influence upon the shaping of Rosenzweig's own religious development. Cohen, more than any other single person, provided the stimulus which enabled Rosenzweig to discover the same satisfaction in Judaism as his alter ego Rosenstock-Huessy had found in Christianity.

The year 1914 was not only the occasion for Rosenzweig's meeting Hermann Cohen, but it marked his accidental discovery of Schelling's outline of a system of German idealism which until then had been attributed to Hegel. Rosenzweig discovered that the document had simply been copied by Hegel in 1796. This discovery is particularly relevant, since Rosenzweig's plan for Book One of his *Star of Redemption*, as well as his frequent use of terms like substance and elements, was in all probability due to Schelling's influence. The limitation, however, of Elsa Freund's analysis of Rosenzweig's *Star of Redemption* is reflected in her inability to resist giving Schelling the credit for Rosenzweig's insights into *speech-thinking* in Book Two. Apart from a few weak attempts at pointing up occasional references to language in Schelling's writings, she totally missed Rosenzweig's own admitted indebtedness to Rosenstock-Huessy when developing Books Two and Three of *The Star*.[25] Rosenzweig felt a pronounced kinship to Schelling in still another respect. Schelling's *The Ages of the World* helped Rosenzweig escape the relativism of his Hegelian background and assisted in shaping his view of history. This influence is especially evident in Rosenzweig's presentation of the relationship between the spatially oriented pagan mythical world and the "truly historical world of revelation."[26] In passing, it is noteworthy that in *The Ages of the*

World the future philosophy for Schelling will be essentially *narrational* in character.

In his *Philosophy of Revelation* Schelling resisted any moral interpretation of Christianity based on Jesus' teachings because of the tendency in this view to emphasize man's fallen condition, rather than his redeemed estate. What Schelling emphasized was the importance of Christ's entrance into history and the effect of the Incarnation upon human reason and human history. In his excellent analysis of Schelling's philosophy of religion, Emil Fackenheim has shown how against an Incarnational background, Revelation penetrates human reason. There are close parallels to Rosenzweig's own resolution of this problem in his *Star of Redemption*.

Thus, Fackenheim's statement that the content of Schelling's *Philosophy of Revelation* is Revelation:

. . . for if God is wholly other than human reason, then He can be accessible only if He has revealed Himself. But it is nevertheless philosophy: for because of its dialectical relation to the divine, reason can by itself understand the need for revelation, and its meaning if and when it takes place.[27]

Rosenzweig's Correspondence on "Judaism and Christianity" with Eugen Rosenstock-Huessy—1916

In september of 1914 Rosenzweig entered the Red Cross service and in 1915 volunteered for the regular army. As a noncommissioned officer, he was assigned for the remainder of the war to the Balkan front. Writing from the trenches on scraps of paper in May of 1916, he felt the need, this time as a believing Jew and as one whose self-confidence and powers had been strengthened immeasurably since his last encounter with Rosenstock-Huessy, to reestablish contact with his former adversary. During an army leave when he stayed at Rosenzweig's home in Kassal, Rosenstock-Huessy provided the occasion for a response by writing a letter to Rosenzweig, who was then on the Eastern front. Their exchange of letters lasted from May of 1916 through December 24 of that year. From it, Rosenzweig derived further material for his own insights into speech thinking, which he developed in Book Two of *The Star of Redemption,* in his essay *New Thinking,* and in other essays and letters. Their exchange also enabled Rosenzweig to formulate his interpretation of the relationship between church and synagogue. This formulation is set forth both in the correspondence itself, and also in Book Three of *The Star of Redemption.* Rosenzweig's uneasiness over their correspondence is reflected in a letter written in October of that year to Rudolf Ehrenberg:

> I am having a correspondence with Rosenstock which is not an easy thing for me; we have not yet got over the initial state, and it proves to be very bad that since that night's conversation in 1913 . . . I have not really spoken to him; as a matter of fact, I could not have done it, because I had to continue the discussion with his ghost of that night.[28]

Not even the vicissitudes of war, of life in the trenches at the front, could match the inner crisis brought about by his encounter with Rosenstock-Huessy and his subsequent conversion experience.

> The war itself has not caused any break in my inner life. In 1913 I had experienced so much that the year 1914 would have had to produce nothing short of the world's final collapse to make any impression on me. . . . Thus I have not experienced the war. . . . I carry my life through this war like Cervantes his poem.[29]

When their exchange was over, Rosenzweig reiterated the profound significance of this event to Ehrenberg.

> The real adventure and achievement of the last few months was for me my correspondence with Rosenstock. You will read it one day. You know (or should be able to know) that I expected, dreaded, and postponed the inevitable second discussion with him since November 1913. It was to be the test of my new life. . . . Now the task is completed.[30]

Like their earlier encounter in 1913, each realized full well that in committing himself to hear the other's words, the shape and quality of his own convictions would inevitably be affected. In a letter to Rudolf Hallo, Rosenzweig said, "Without Eugen I would never have written *The Star of Redemption.*"[31] When all the pieces belonging to *speech-thinking* are put together and considered, it is apparent that each regarded the other truly as an alter ego, a copartner in a common venture whose outcome left on each partner the indelible marks of the other's thinking. Their respective writings about the methodological implications of the dialogical approach to ultimate problems were based, in fact, upon the fruits of living encounters such as this. They were not responding simply as Jew and Christian, hoping to establish an "ecumenical bridge" between two religious traditions; rather, they were dedicated to the *word*—to a common speech which each viewed as *the* fundamental vehicle for discovering meaning and truth at that moment. Implicit in this dedication was their assumption that doctrinal and theological concerns were meaningful only insofar as each bore them within his soul and on his lips. Thus, the authority of each tradition was represented in and through the named individuals as an ontological reality—as a part of his actual being, rather than as an intellectual system of thought and doctrine which stands over against and judges human deeds. In this manner the authority and the mediation of the Spirit were present in an exchange wherein each partner had committed his person through his words. Professor Altmann summed up the purpose of the correspondence as ". . . not to continue the monologue of dogmatic thought (which was bound up with the need for absorbing pagan philosophy) but to start the dialogue of speech, of personal approach."[32]

Before the correspondence began, Rosenzweig felt that we all were living in a Christian world and that the Church was a living fact. For Rosenzweig their correspondence served as an anvil upon which he could hammer out with Rosenstock-Huessy the role of Israel in a Christian world. He was indebted to the Christian, Rosenstock-Huessy, both for the latter's view that Revelation means direction—*i.e.*, orientation in time and history—and also for an understanding of the function of the Church—namely, "to convert the heathen and to transform the *Alpha* element of *creation*, the world in its raw state, into the *Omega* element of *redemption*—into the *world* as the place of *revelation*."[33] By this time Rosenzweig realized that his thinking had become so Christianized that his position as a Jew was an embarrassment to him. Their eventual solution to the coexistence of Jew and Christian was once summed up by Rosenstock-Huessy when he said that he had learned from "Franz" that "Nothing can be fulfilled that has not been promised." Until this time, in the face of "the sceptre," Christianity, Judaism for

Rosenzweig was "a broken staff and bandages before her eyes." The aloofness of Judaism from the world had been to him a sign of her "hopeless sterility and a lack of meaning and purpose in its continued existence."[34] The meaning of the synagogue gradually became clear. The synagogue's "stern refutation of the pagan world and her uncompromising attitude was the only safeguard for the completion of the work of Revelation and of the church herself."[35]

Just as Israel's problematic status in a Christian world raised serious questions for Rosenzweig, so too, for Rosenstock-Huessy, his own Johannine perspective seemed incompatible with the prevailing Petrine and Pauline forms of Christianity which his age, as ours today, had become so accustomed to. At the same time, he realized that the Johannine Church faced inherent dangers quite apart from its own conflict within the Church with prevailing Christian norms. The encounter between Johannine Christianity and history and the secular world was fraught with difficulties as great as those which it faced on the home front within the Church itself. For example, the Johannine Church in its fight against the pagan remained in constant danger of compromising with the world and its pagan instincts. There was the danger, and still is, that Christianity might be identified with current myths, ideologies, or philosophical systems.

The difficulties which each man had with his own tradition were only resolved after their correspondence was completed. Thus, the existence of the people of Israel served eventually, for both men, as a reminder that Revelation comes from God, not from the natural mind; from the Jews, *not* from the Greeks. In her seclusion from the world in her priestly way of life, in her strict observance of the law, Judaism expresses "the essence of Revelation in an absolute form, unalloyed by any element of paganism."[36] In an undated letter (probably in early October 1916) Rosenzweig asked Rosenstock-Huessy about the meaning of Revelation. ". . . please explain to me your present idea of the relationship between nature and revelation."[37] In his answer Rosenstock-Huessy wrote, "The question you put, *Nature* and *Revelation*, I can only understand as a natural understanding and revelation. Nature and Revelation are not comparable." Rosenstock-Huessy saw them as "the same material, but opposite ways of being exposed to the light." Christ is this Revelation, because "Christ has mediated to us the breaking through into the universe; . . . where hitherto was only Abraham's bosom, is now a living eternity and ascent of spirits from star to star. Revelation means the linking of our consciousness with the union between earth and heaven which transcends the world."[38]

We must no longer stand in space, in the areas conquerable by knowledge, but rather in time, in which we are only sanctifiers of the Sanctified. By standing in time, in the calendar of God's economy of salvation, we sanctify our activities in the world of space. "We must renounce our purely mental approach and speak ". . . from the seat of our passions. The . . . hub of the universe is no longer a matter of natural understanding, but is the means in us which makes revelation to, in, and for us possible."[39] This, for Rosenstock-Huessy, was the meaning of the reconciliation in Christ of the natural mind of the Gentile and of Israel as the preserver of the Promise.

For Rosenzweig, the revelation in Christ preached by the Church to the heathen could only be preserved by the existence of the synagogue. For Christians, Jesus is the only way to this knowledge. For the Jew, Rosenzweig, the way represents the means available to the pagan (pagan from the Latin *paganus* meant originally one who was a civilian rather than a soldier of Christ) to knowledge of the truth which the Jew declared when man was created, and for which both he and the Christian were rejected by the pagan world—namely, the truth that God is One. Rosenzweig's earlier experience in 1913 on the Day of Atonement had, in effect, begun to free him from "the curse of historicity" in the Hegelian sense, and also from the need for the apologetics of the Church.

In the course of their correspondence, both realized that the dissolution, first of the Petrine Christianity of the first millennium, and then the Pauline of the second, had left the Christian in the Johannine Age without any visible means of identification. In living off the word in its Incarnational fleshly attire, the only sustenance and direction for our words can come from the Jew who reminds all mankind that even in the Johannine Age "my kingdom is not of this world." Similarly, Johannine Christianity makes no sense except the Jew's knowledge of eternity be taken seriously. The liturgical calendars of synagogue and *Church*—"two eternal dial plates under the weekly and annual pointer of ever-renewed Time"—need one another if the work of creation, revelation and redemption is to be effected.[40]

The three elements of reality, i.e., God, World, and Man, appear each in three different qualities: God is Creator, Revealer, and Redeemer. Man is a natural being (part of creation); the receiver of Revelation (Priest and Prophet); the agent of Redemption (the holy work of the Saint). The World is Creation (Natural law, *civitas mundi*); the place of Revelation (community of the believers); the place of the accomplished Redemption (Messianic Day, *civitas Dei*).[41]

The task of the Christian is equally clear, providing he recognizes the Jew as his copartner, the Church the complement of the synagogue.

And the church, with unbreakable staff and eyes open to the world, this champion certain of victory, always faces the danger of having the vanquished draw up laws for her: Sent to all men, she must nevertheless not lose herself in what is common to all men. Her word is always to be "foolishness and a stumbling block." . . . Again and again they will ask: why is just *this* word supposed to be the power of God . . . Why just Jesus and not (or at least, not also) Goethe? . . . And when the last Greek has been silenced through the work which the church performed in time, the word of the cross—at the end of time but still included in time—will no longer be foolishness to anyone.[42]

In his celebration of its holy events the Jew retains his contact with eternity and serves as a living symbol to the Christian that we speak in time in order to redeem both time and the world—thereby hastening the Messianic Age. Future, for the Jew, is "eternally on its way," "without ceasing to be future," it "is nevertheless present." It grows in time but is conditioned by eternity. *Ahistorical* and *atemporal* as applied here do not mean that the Jew is unconcerned about time and history; rather, the terms imply that his primary devotion is to eternity. Within his vision of eternity, however, the future must be seized and realized daily.[43] Thus, in Book Three of *The Star* Rosenzweig writes, "Eternity is just this, that time no longer has a right to a place between the present moment and perfection and that the whole future is to be grasped today."[44]

Thus, the historicity of the Jew lies exactly in his *ahistorical* role. Freed from historical obligation and destiny, and living in the vision of eternity, the Jew "must forever remain a strange thing and an annoyance to the State and to world history." The ahistorical role of the Jew begins with the period encompassing the birth of Christ and the destruction of the second temple in 70 A.D. The pre-Christian historical role of Biblical Israel served as a historical witness to the fact that the Messiah was expected. The redemption of the world by Jesus Christ rent the veil of the temple in two, and both Jew and Greek were reconciled in the Second Adam.[45] The distinction between Jew and Greek before Christ rests upon the fact that revelation comes not from the natural mind of the Greeks but from the God of Israel. In the post-Christian era the synagogue, though unable to cope with paganism, stands as a mute admonisher to the Church of the last things, of Eternal Life. Wherever the Church is caught up in the affairs of this world, the Jew is a silent reminder to her of God's promise in his covenant with Noah, and it is toward that fulfillment that she points.

Time, history, and above all, speech are essential in this task—not as ends in themselves but rather as means for ushering in the Kingdom. As Rosenzweig insisted, eternity and the Kingdom have no history but are rather the driving forces behind time, history, and the word. For only in eternity will speech give way to silence; until that time men must live under the spell and power of the word.

In eternity the spoken word fades away into the silence of perfect togetherness—for union occurs in silence only; the word unites, but those who are united fall silent. . . . Liturgy, the reflector which focuses the sunbeams of eternity in the small circle of the year, must introduce man to this silence. But even in liturgy shared silence can come only at the end, and all that goes before is a preparation for this end. In the stage of preparation the word still dominates the scene. The word itself must take man to the point of learning how to share silence. His preparation begins with learning to hear.[46]

It is on "The Word became flesh" that everything depends. "While the word of man must always become a concept and thereby stagnant and degenerate, God speaks to us with the word become Flesh, through the Son." Revelation and the power of speech are inseparable.

And so the Christian revelation is the healing of the Babylonian confusion of tongues, the bursting open of the prison, but also the sign on the new tongues, speech which is now informed in the soul. Since then, it has become worthwhile to think again because thought has a standard outside itself in the visible footsteps of God.[47]

The rending of the veil of the temple is the reconciliation of the world by God's Word become flesh to men. Revelation and word are inseparably united for the redemption of the world, of the natural mind, in order that men may again think out of the speech of the ages. This essentially is the foundation for Rosenzweig's work in *The Star of Redemption*. The priority of belief (*Glauben*) over thought (*Denken*), which for Rosenzweig is the sign of all post-Hegelian thought, and which undergirds the New Thinking, rests upon the union of revelation and speech, as developed by Rosenzweig and Rosenstock-Huessy.

The significance of the correspondence seen as one between Church and synagogue is that both are in constant dialogue with each other. To neglect this underlying theme is to miss the significance of their exchange of letters. Not only do both men encounter one another in dialogue, but their respective historical traditions, by some seen as exclusive of each other, are seen as historical dialogical counterparts of one another. How strange that what theologians refer to as the eschatological tension, wherein history is filled with divine meaning—that this should depend for its realization upon a Jewish-Christian alliance wherein the Jew makes it possible for history to be filled with divine purpose and content by his dedication to an *ahistorical* role! While such an interpretation of the Jew's mission in history might gain the respect of the more orthodox and conservative elements in Judaism because of the implicit recognition in this view of the importance of Jewish tradition and learning, some, within these traditions, would reject the explicit underlying recognition of Jesus and the Church's ministry in the world. Similarly, reformed elements in Judaism would, on the one hand, probably reject the ahistorical role relegated to the Jew, but on the other hand, would explore with an open heart Rosenzweig's and Rosenstock-Huessy's proposed Jewish-Christian copartnership in their recognition of the impingement of eternity in the creation and preservation of a truly human society.

In summary it should be noted that Rosenstock-Huessy's and Rosenzweig's characterization of the shape of spirituality in a "post-Christian" Johannine Age is predicated on a rather unusual relationship between Jew and Christian. It is at this juncture that "post-Christian" and ecumenical considerations are joined. The a-religious quality of the Johannine Age involves Jew and Christian in a partnership based on a mutual recognition of the validity of each other's universal claims. Within this framework the integrity of the Jew's and the Christian's view of reality is legitimated but also viewed as a copartnership. The "stubbornness of the Jew" in the Christian's eyes is a condition for their coexistence. Implicit in this partnership is a rejection by both Jew and Christian of one being the "daughter" religion of the other or of their sharing in a common Judaeo-Christian tradition. The success of their partnership requires that the Jew stubbornly reject the Christian's claim that Jesus is the Messiah; similarly, the Christian no longer needs the Jew's *"Old Testament,"* insamuch as the traditions of the Church—her Councils and her Creeds—have indeed become the Christian's historical past —his own testimony to the fact that Jesus is the Christ. The Jew rests all claims for his uniqueness upon his stubborn insistence that the Jews have known from the beginning that "God is One." For his audacity and his refusal to recognize the Christian claim that Jesus is the Messiah he remains historically rejected and despised.

The Jew lives already *in* the *eschaton*, the end, toward which the Christian strives to direct all history. Thus, the role of the Jew is an ahistorical one—he lives already from and in eternity as a living testimony to those who wrestle within a historical eschatological framework, that history has a goal. The Jew stands already at the end of history, while the Christian is contantly living *in* the world as a mediator to the Gentile of that saving eternal knowledge which the Jew has carried in his heart and for which he has suffered from the beginning of time. That history and mankind have not yet been redeemed needs no apology. Only when that End Time has come will the perversity of the Jew be understood in retrospect by men everywhere as a sign of their own perversity and incompleteness. Were the Jew not to exist despite Christianity, the source of the claim of the Christian to be in and yet not of the world would be forgotten, and the Christian would soon lose himself in the world. Thus, the "stubbornness of the Jew" signifies to the Christian that there is purpose and meaning in history, but also that history is not that purpose, nor can history alone provide an adequate *raison d'être* for living. Although the Johannine Age will be a-religious and post-Christian, new speech patterns can only be redemptive—historically meaningful—if there remains until the "end of time" an ahistorical reference as well as persons committed to the redemption of time and history. Without the word, eternity will not become a universal fact; without the presence of eternity, the word will not become the master and instrument but rather the servant and pawn of "purposeless" historical relativism.

The New Thinking—"Speech-Thinking"

LET US TURN now to an examination of those writings that bear most directly upon Rosenzweig's remarks about sacred speech—*speech-thinking (Sprachdenken)*, as he refers to it in *The Star of Redemption*, in his essay "The New Thinking," in *Understanding the Sick and the Healthy*, and in other works. The terms *speech-thinking* and New Thinking are practically synonymous, since speech is the pre-eminent concern of the new thinking. For Rosenzweig—as for Hamann, Rosenstock-Huessy, and all other speech thinkers—experience, speech, time, and an awareness of the importance of names are man's primary means of discovering life's secrets and of realizing his creaturely potential. Together, the way, the measure, and the rhythm of existence are revealed to those who can truly listen to the "music of existence"; only in this way can thought patterns recover their proper tone and sense of mission. Note also that all those associated with the Patmos group and with *speech-thinking* have taken seriously the reality of history and religious tradition, of creation, revelation, and redemption—without urging upon mankind that the true keys to the kingdom are to be divined by the cloven hooves of theologians. The Johannine setting for the insights of these men appears to have saved them from such tendencies and forced them instead to meet one another under the aegis of the Spirit, of the word—in speech, in their own unique, experiential, and temporal situations. This orientation is apparent from Rosenzweig's account of those who influenced his discovering the new thinking and his writing *The Star of Redemption*. Speaking of the method of speech thinking, he wrote:

Whatever the *Star of Redemption* can do to renew our ways of thinking is concentrated in this method. Ludwig Feuerbach was the first to discover it. Hermann Cohen's posthumous work reintroduced it to philosophy, though the author himself was not aware of its iconoclastic power. When I wrote the *Star of Redemption*, I was already familiar with the pertinent passages in Cohen's book, but their influence was not decisive for the genesis of my own work. The main influence was Eugen Rosenstock; a full year and a half before I began to write I had seen the rough draft of the now published *Angewandte Seelenkunde*. Since then, the new philosophy has been expounded in another work, besides the *Star*, in the first volume of Hans Ehrenberg's *Fichte*, a study of idealism written in the new form of the true, time-requiring dialogue. Victor von Weizsäcker's *Philosophie des Arztes* will appear shortly. Rudolf Ehren-berg's *Theoretische Biologie* is the first work to subordinate the doctrine of organic nature to the law of *real, irreversible time*. Martin Buber in his *I and Thou*, and Ferdinand Ebner in *Das Wort und die geistigen Realitäten*, written at exactly the same time as my book, approached the heart of the new thinking (I dealt with that in the middle section of the *Star*) independently of the aforemen-tioned books, and of each other. The notes to my *Judah ha-Levi* give instructive examples of the practical application of the new thinking. The epochal, largely unpublished works of Florens Christian Rang are founded in a precise and profound knowledge of all this.[48]

Two classic passages from his essay *The New Thinking* describe speech thinking and point up the importance of time and timing as its essential ingredients.

In the new thinking, the method of speech replaces the method of thinking maintained in all earlier philosophies. Thinking is timeless and wants to be timeless. . . . Speech is bound to time and nourished by time, and it neither can nor wants to abandon this element. It does not know in advance just where it will end. It takes its cues from others. In fact, it lives by virtue of another's life, whether that other is the one who listens to a story, answers in the course of a dialogue, or joins in a chorus; while thinking is always a solitary business, even when it is done in common by several who philosophize together.[49]

In real conversation, minds are open and ears willing to allow the mind to be affected by the other's words. Even the initiator of conversation never knows fully in advance what he will actually say until he "sizes up" the situation—literally, plays it "by ear." Quite often the very desire to bridge a gap, to reach the other, will, when two partners meet, establish contact with the other. Meaningful conversation is invariably linked to proper timing; the moment is seized by speech and an event takes place. Similarly, our words are seized, drawn out, created by the moment, as was the case for

David, Jeremiah, and the Gospel dialogues. Just as speech can create a new time sense, create future and meaning, so too, a certain time may elicit verbal responses even against our will or even against our "better judgment." Productive thinking is thinking tied to speaking and timing—it is thinking geared to a mandate, a command, a question, and frequently, merely a glance, a nod, as is the case where one is addressed although no spoken words were uttered. For such speech thinkers, speech precedes thought and needs time: I think because I have been addressed at a certain moment. This is quite the opposite understanding of the relationship between thought and language where language is but an imperfect tool for articulating ideas thought to have been previously conceived in the mind. Reflect for a moment upon the way in which our minds, our thoughts, are really servants of the word, whether it be a letter in the mailbox, a telegram, a remark in the marketplace or classroom, a phone call, an unsolicited confrontation. Schleiermacher in his *Dialektik* remarked that he needed his students and the classroom precisely in order to be able to think. The classroom was not merely a sounding board for ideas; rather, it was the arena of the mind's engagement—its link with its next destiny. As was noted earlier in the case of the Sophists, it was the agony (*agones*), the strife of words, which governed the Sophistic mind; whereas in the case of Plato and Socrates, dialogue was a tool for enabling the mind literally to see the immutable and eternal forms of truth, beauty, goodness, and justice. For Platonists, *mind* is always pitted against *mind*—speech being a poor means for conducting the traffic of ideas. For Homer, for the Israelites, for great Sophists, and for rhetoricians like Isocrates, as for the Christian, the word and timing were the true vehicles of meaning. "The play's the thing wherein I'll catch the conscience of the king" illustrates the way words touch, reach, confront our most private and sacred regions when and only when they are uttered at the right time—a time we never are certain of until the event is actually occurring.

Note that in the next passage, Rosenzweig's term *speech-thinking* is equated with Rosenstock-Huessy's *grammatical* approach. Note also that logical thinking for Rosenzweig is identified with the traditions of the solitary thinker for whom time and timing are nonessential elements. The logical thinker "knows his thoughts in advance, and his expounding them is merely a concession to what he regards as the defectiveness of our means of communication." In actuality this defectiveness is not due to speech but rather to time. "To require time means that we cannot anticipate, that we must wait for everything, that what is ours depends on what is another's."[50] This truth, so basic for the *speech-thinker*, is, for Rosenzweig, beyond the thinking thinker's comprehension.

I use the term "speech thinking" for the new thinking. "Speech thinking" is, of course, still a form of thinking, just as the old thinking that depended solely on thinking could not go on without inner speech. The difference between the old and the new, the "logical" and the "grammatical" thinking, does not lie in the fact that one is silent while the other is audible, but in fact that the latter needs another person, and takes time seriously—actually, these two things are identical. In the old philosophy, "thinking" means thinking for no one else and speaking to no one else (and here, if you prefer, you may substitute "everyone" or the well-known "all the world" for "no one"). But "speaking" means speaking to someone and thinking for someone. And this someone is always a quite definite someone, and he has not merely ears, like "all the world," but also a mouth.[51]

Like Rosenstock-Huessy in his *Angewandte Seelenkunde*, the new thinking was presented as the basis for a scientific methodology which, though subjective and extremely personal, was nevertheless capable of attaining "the objectivity of science." Reminiscent of Hamann's verbalism, it had to be a science capable of avoiding the Scylla and Charybdis of the artificial language of both idealism and theology and yet be rooted in concrete everyday experience. It is for this reason that another term used by Rosenzweig for the new thinking is experiential philosophy (*erfahrende Philosophie*).

The new thinker is one who will "employ the method of sound common sense as a method of scientific thinking." What is it that distinguishes sound from unsound common sense? Again, the answer lies in a sense of time and timing. "Common sense waits, goes on living; it has no fixed ideas; it knows all": but only "in due time." This, asserts Rosenzweig, is the secret of the new thinking; it enables us to grasp the meaning of Goethe's "understanding in time" when he said:

> Why is truth so woefully
> Removed? To depths of secret banned?
> None perceives in proper time! If we

But perceived in proper time, how bland
The truth would be, how fair to see!
How near and ready to our hand![52]

Like Hamann, and also Rosenstock-Huessy, the new thinking must avoid the "mental gymnastics" (*Kopfakrobaten*) of theology, and take speech, revelation, and time seriously. The middle road, the bridge which the new thinking provides is summed up in *The Star* as follows:

Where is the bridge to connect extreme subjectivity, one might even say, deaf and blind subjectivity, with the luminous clearness of infinite objectivity? . . . The theological concept of revelation must provide the bridge from the most subjective to the most objective. Man, as the recipient of revelation, as one who experiences the content of faith, contains both within himself. And whether the new philosophy admits it or not, such a man is the only thinker fit to deal with it.[53]

In order to become scientific, future theologians will have to philosophize adhering at every step to the principles laid down in the new thinking. This occasions a new type of thinker, one who "stands between philosophy and theology."[54] While "theological concerns have assisted the new thinking in coming to the fore," the method and its focus is not with "religious problems," although these are dealt with side by side with "problems of logic, ethics and aesthetics." If one wishes, despite these protestations, to call the method theological, then he insists that it is "no less new as theology than as philosophy." "God did not, after all, create religion; he created only the world."[55] Originally, Judaism and Christianity were something quite a-religious; even after their institutionalization, each realized an "impulse to overcome the fixity of a religious institution, and to return to the open field of reality."[56]

As Hamann attacked Kant's rejection of commonsense experience and time-bound everyday language in favor of the artificial and abstract world of impersonal reason and mathematics, so too, Rosenzweig, like Hamann, asserted that all cognition is time-bound—the product of timing. In *Understanding the Sick and the Healthy*, a popularization of his *Star of Redemption*, Rosenzweig diagnosed the symptoms of the patient as "acute *apoplexia philosophica*," which results from being separated from his proper environment, which is determined by speech and timing. In a hypothetical exchange of letters with a fellow doctor, he discusses possible cures that have been tried—such as the *criticin* vaccination and mystical injections —but rejects them because they have "wrecked so many generations of patients, despite illusory successes in the first stages of treatment."[57] In the first instance, reliance upon Kant's transcendental categories as developed in his *Critique of Pure Reason* (hence, *criticin* vaccination) produced a temporary solution—it freed a man from the oppression of his immediate environment, but offered no ultimate solution for living, because it did not take time seriously. Similarly, mysticism (hence, mystical injections), though enabling one to escape the pressures of everyday existence, was ultimately doomed to failure since it too offered no reconciliation with time, history, and the created order. In the next letter the environmental treatment, primitive as it may be, is suggested, because of his own institution's success with it. Another word for environmental is experiential, which involves all the ingredients outlined in the new thinking. Experience is time- and speech-bound; only this can cure the patient and enable him to see God-man-world in their proper relationships as they are revealed to him by speech and in time. For the trained philosopher and theologian this must seem at first a much too simplistic solution. And yet the new thinking is just that simple! To grasp its truth may, however, require a painful unlearning of that which has been learned; or, it may involve a desire to live rather than read or write, as Rosenzweig concluded at the end of *The Star*. Finally, it may involve a realization that the tenses of reality are not interchangeable. As for Hamann in his discussion of the mysterious thread which unites and gives meaning to the Biblical narrative, so too with Rosenzweig: we take our cue from time, not from thought.

> . . . reality . . . has its present, its past, and its future, without which it cannot be . . . properly known. Reality . . . has its past and its future, an everlasting past and an eternal future. To have cognition of God, the world, and man, is to know what they do or what is done to them in these tenses of reality, and to know what they do to one another or what is done to them by one another.[58]

"The Star of Redemption"

THE FIRST CLUE we creatures have as to time's secrets lies in our understanding of the relationship which must be maintained between human cognition and the human fact of death. The opening note of *The Star of Redemption* states this quite simply. "All knowledge of the Whole (*das All*) has its source in death, in the fear of death." In *Understanding the Sick and the Healthy* the theme is repeated. "Life is not eternal. It flows from birth toward death. . . . Life lives itself toward death."[59] "The dominion of death" is the basis for a fully lived life if we face, rather than discount, death as a life-force. Death is our surety that our minds and their thoughts are neither timeless, eternal, nor absolute. Rosenzweig's attack on philosophical idealism is founded upon this awareness of the finitude and frailty of not only the mind, but of every human power. The mind's desire to shake off the knowledge and fear of death can only lead to the spinning of lifeless intellectual systems, and possibly suicide. Each is an escape from life, a violation of the creature's knowledge that "Man shall not shake off the anguish of earthly life; he shall *remain* in the fear of death." Suicide is a violation of death's ordination vows made with each creature. "The ghastly ability to commit suicide sets man apart from all other beings, known and unknown. It is indeed the index of his stepping out of the natural order."[60] Similarly, idealism cheats a man of life—it defies man because it suggests that man's knowledge contains the secret and mystery of the universe. Infinite mind can, as Hamann suggested in Kant's situation, or as was true for Descartes, delude itself into believing that by shaking off the material body, it has shaken off the last vestige of human finitude.

Yet philosophy cheats him of this imperative by weaving the vapor of its idea of the Whole around earthly existence. . . . For idealism, with its denial of everything that sets the individual apart from the Whole, is philosophy's tool for conditioning rebellious matter until it is no longer able to resist being befogged by the notion of the One-and-the-Whole. . . . And indeed philosophy's final conclusion is that *death is nothing*.[61]

Hegel's suggestion that philosophy was the consummation of what was promised by revelation, that Spirit (*Geist*) confirms the unity of the worlds of thought and being, seemed to put an end to traditional modes of philosophizing. Kierkegaard, however, contested this union by insisting that only the personal, only Søren Kierkegaard—a given name and surname—mattered ultimately. The leap of faith reflected his convictions about his own creatureliness and also the existence of a realm of reality which could not be contained by thought. Similarly, Schopenhauer departed from traditional forms of philosophy by giving up the traditional search after the essence (*das Wesen*) of reality and concentrating upon the value and meaning of life for the individual. The transition was completed in the person of Nietzsche, who until he was insane, maintained the ultimate sacredness of life itself and personal existence. Their common focus upon the individual rooted in time and history meant that living man's mind had finally become merely the frozen breath of his soul. The existing creature, defined by a given name and surname, was henceforth the basis for human philosophizing. In taking time and finitude seriously, in giving up once and for all the quest after a single unifying essence, and in concentrating upon the existing individual with a *name*, Rosenzweig established the foundations for his new thinking. On the basis of common sense, of experience, we know how God, man and world as distinguishable and irreducible elements confront us. It is in time, in everyday experience, that we become aware of our uniqueness as creatures, as well as our partnership with the elements of reality. Each element has its own uniqueness. To reduce God-man-world to a single knowable whole would be to affirm the validity of the presuppositions of traditional modes of philosophizing. The separate existence of the elements is one condition for future philosophizing. Ultimately, however, this "separation is spanned, and what we experience is the experience of the spanning."

God veils himself when we try to grasp him; man, our self, withdraws, and the world becomes a visible enigma. God, man, and the world reveal themselves only in their relations to one another; that is, in *creation*, *revelation*, and *redemption*.[62]

The knowledge of that which is revealed "is a unique act, and has its own method." The material out of which knowledge comes must use the word "and," which is the basic word of experience, a word the philosopher's tongue is not used to—"God *and* the world *and* man." If truth were just one and did not use and, it would be God's knowledge of himself. But as Genesis begins, God created the heavens *and* the earth *and* he created man. We are not God and therefore truth in any absolute sense must be manifold, fragmentary, and partial; furthermore, it must be translated ultimately into our truth. "Thus truth ceases to be what *is* true and becomes a verity that wants to be verified, realized in active life." Both the active quality of all truth and the fact of its manifold character as signified by the we and the our are concretely bound to the time theme, which accounts for and necessitates change and activity. One consequence of this approach is that the syllogism and its law of noncontradiction as the property and tool of the objective thinker divorced from time must give way to the truth which arises out of dialogue, dependent as it is not upon the canons of formal logic, but upon time and the active experience of the we engaged in time requiring dialogue. Older theories of knowledge began with the static truths of mathematics—*e.g.*, two plus two equals four—truths which men could agree upon with a minimum use of their full powers. Higher truths demand rather the response of the whole man standing in dialogue with his fellowmen; truths which a man must be willing to verify, if necessary, with the giving of life. Such truths are those "that cannot be verified until generations upon generations have given up their lives to that end." Whereas traditional ways of knowing begin with timeless abstract mathematical truths, speech thinking begins with man as a finite creature rooted in time.[63]

Martin Buber and Franz Rosenzweig: *Biblical Translation*

THE SUMMARY STATEMENT on speech thinking that appeared in Rosenzweig's essay "The New Thinking" marked the end of systematic interest in speech and also the beginning of the concluding phase of his life, during which the miracle of speech permeated all his efforts, particularly those bearing upon Jewish existence, as well as those related to his translation together with Martin Buber of the Hebrew Scriptures into German (1925–29). Already in 1919, as a result of his conversations with Hermann Cohen, Rosenzweig had indicated that his interests were increasingly preoccupied with matters bearing directly upon Judaism. In 1919 The Academy for the

Science of Judaism was founded, and in 1920 (the year he married Edith Hahn) he was appointed head of the Freies Jüdisches Lehrhaus in Frankfurt. *Hegel und der Staat*, begun in 1910, was also published that year. The principles behind the new thinking, as well as Buber's own dialogical principles, are particularly apparent in their correspondence about general problems involved in translation as well as those pertaining to their actual translation of the Hebrew Scriptures into German. Rosenzweig wrote to Buber that "the creative aspect of translating can only manifest itself in the region of the creative aspect of speech itself." True to the qualities of timing and transformation so central to speech thinking, Rosenzweig insisted that "Whoever has something to say, must say it in a new way. He will create his language, and when he has said his say, the face of the language will have changed."[64] When an "alien voice" has been truly sought out by a people it takes its toll—it changes the quality of that people's speech. This principle undergirded all their deliberations over whether in fact they should undertake the prodigious task of Biblical translation. Was this, in fact, the right time for such an effort? Would and could men listen and allow their own speech patterns to be affected, in view of their conviction that "every great work in one language can be translated into another language only once." We strive timorously and yet hopeful that *this* is the time!

Then, one day, a miracle happens and the spirits of the two languages mate. This does not strike like a bolt out of the blue. The time for such a *hieros gamos,* for such a Holy Wedding, is not ripe until a receptive people reaches out toward the wingbeat of an alien masterpiece with its own yearning and its own utterance, and when its receptiveness is no longer based on curiosity, interest, desire for education, or even aesthetic pleasure, but has become an integral part of the people's historical development.[65]

It is unthinkable, wrote Rosenzweig, "that a language into which Shakespeare, Isaiah, Dante have been faithfully rendered, could have remained unchanged by this contact."[66] Another basic assumption they held was that "all languages are basically one." The renewal of a people's language and culture assumes that they are being addressed by the vastness and the powers of all men from the beginning of the creation. Translation of great epics from our past makes sense only if we accept the fact that basically there is a unity among men's powers of speech which cuts across all local dialects and cultural nuances.

Everyone has his own language, or rather, everyone would have his own language if there were really such a thing as a monologue (such as those logicians, the would-be monologicians, claim for themselves), if all speech were not really dialogue to begin with, and hence translation.[67]

Both Buber and Rosenzweig were, like Luther, inspirationalists in their approach to translation. Timing is a matter of faith; the right word, a sign of grace. "The dictates of faith determine down to the smallest detail any translation of the Scriptures." Like Reuchlin, each felt the peculiar difficulties they faced, in view of the special relationship of the Jew to the Hebrew language. While the Jew may read the Bible in German, he can only truly understand it in Hebrew. Their actual translation is, therefore, not German as much as it is a Hebraised German—a German infected with all the peculiarities of Hebrew—its style, its resonance, its dramatic power, and above all its acutely spoken quality. For the Bible was meant not to be read, but heard, listened to. As noted earlier, the Hebrew, like early man, was dependent primarily upon his oral and aural rather than upon his visual powers. To recover this sense—*i.e.*, the secret of hearing—was their task. Only those capable of suspending their provincialism, their political and philosophical cultural identities, in favor of responding to a new time and speech sense would in the final analysis be the legitimate heirs and leaders of their generation and its new cultural configurations. Poetry and song for the Jew, as for Homer and all speech thinkers, were sacred because they linked a man with his past and with his destiny. The spoken word literally seized a man in a way that the written has usually been incapable of.

The spoken word may be accompanied by the written for centuries, without turning into what we designate, rather strangely, as "literary language." The fact that something is written down gives rise to forms of speech adapted to the exigencies of writing; yet beyond that pole of life governed by the printed word speech remains free and creative. So a child may lose the habit of spontaneous speech while he is in the schoolroom, but chatter freely the moment he reaches home. The vitality of his language will not be yoked until he falls under the spell of reading, and this is likely to happen, at the very latest, when he begins to read the newspapers. From that time on he will require a special stimulus in order not to speak as he, or rather, as everyone, writes.[68]

In discussing Buber's fascination with speech, further reference will be made to their Biblical translation and their common concern for its special spokenness. Considerable attention will also be devoted in a subsequent section to an evaluation of Buber's and Rosenzweig's differences with respect to the significance of the Torah and Jewish learning. Their translating effort, like the exchange between Rosenzweig and Rosenstock-Huessy, was indeed another example of mutual dependence and dialogue. Though lacking the forcefulness of Rosenzweig's earlier encounter with Rosenstock-Huessy, neither Buber nor Rosenzweig alone could have begun, much less consummated, this monumental translation.

Rosenzweig's Illness: 1921–1929

IT WAS IN 1921 that Rosenzweig first noticed symptoms of a serious disease, which in 1922 was diagnosed as "amyotrophic lateral sclerosis with progressive paralysis of the bulla." This led to a gradual paralysis of his limbs and loss of speech. By 1922 he was unable to write, and in 1923 he had lost the ability to speak. In 1922 his notes and translations of the poems of *Judah ha-Levi* were published. From the onset of the paralysis until his death he needed the assistance of his wife and frequently of Margrit Rosenstock in order for his by then inarticulate sounds to be interpreted. A special typewriter was constructed for his use, which enabled him to point to the letters he wished to use. For over four years this remained his only means of communication. Suffering under this handicap, he undertook his Biblical translations; the last book which he completed was Isaiah, in November of 1929. He died on December 10, 1929, his last years being nourished by the 73rd Psalm, which had special meaning for him. According to Nahum Glatzer:

> The burial took place December 12th in the new cemetery of the Jewish community (in Frankfort, Germany). In accordance with Franz Rosenzweig's wish, there was no funeral oration. Martin Buber read Psalm 73, which contains the inscription F.R. chose for his headstone. As the coffin was lowered into the grave, the sun broke through the clouded skies; a majestic rainbow appeared, the ancient token of the covenant between heaven and earth. Three friends were chosen to recite the Kaddish.[69]

NOTES

CHAPTER 4

1 Franz Rosenzweig, *Understanding the Sick and the Healthy* (New York: The Noonday Press, 1953); Nahum N. Glatzer, *Franz Rosenzweig: His Life and Thought* (New York: Schocken, 1953). Cf. also Franz Rosenzweig, "The Way Through Time: Christian History," in David W. McKain (editor), *Christianity: Some Non-Christian Appraisals* (New York: McGraw-Hill, 1964), pp. 191–203.
2 Franz Rosenzweig, *Briefe* (Berlin: Schocken, 1935), p. 642. The correspondence between Rosenzweig and Rosenstock-Huessy in 1916 on "Judaism and Christianity" is contained in an Appendix, pp. 637–720. An English edition of this correspondence, *Judaism Despite Christianity*, will be published in 1968 by The University of Alabama Press, along with several additional relevant essays by Rosenstock-Huessy. Holt, Rinehart and Winston will also publish shortly an English translation of Rosenzweig's *The Star of Redemption*.
3 Franz Rosenzweig, *Kleinere Schriften* (Berlin: Schocken, 1937), p. 374.
4 Rosenzweig, *Briefe*, pp. 53–54.
5 Alexander Altmann, "Franz Rosenzweig and Eugen Rosenstock-Huessy," *Journal of Religion* (October 1944), p. 261.
6 Fritz Kaufmann, "Karl Jaspers and a Philosophy of Communication," *The Philosophy of Karl Jaspers*, ed. Paul Arthur Schlipp (New York: Tudor Publishing, 1957), pp. 214–15.
7 From Eugen Rosenstock-Huessy's introduction to his correspondence with Rosenzweig in the latter's *Briefe*, p. 638.
8 Rosenzweig, *Briefe*, pp. 71–72.
9 Alexander Altmann, *op. cit.*, pp. 261–62.
10 Alexander Altmann, "Franz Rosenzweig on History," in Altmann (ed.), *Between East and West* (London: East and West Library, 1958), p. 196.
11 Rosenzweig, *Briefe*, pp. 91 and 265. Cf. Altmann, *op. cit.*, p. 198.
12 Rosenzweig to Rosenstock-Huessy, 11/30/1916, *Briefe*, pp. 705–10.

Franz Rosenzweig (1886–1929): Speech Precedes Thought   181

13 Altmann, *op. cit.*, p. 197.
14 Rosenzweig, *Briefe*, pp. 341–44.
15 *Ibid.*, p. 72.
16 *Ibid.*, pp. 71–76.
17 Glatzer, *op. cit.*, p. 25.
18 Rosenzweig, *Briefe*, pp. 341–44.
19 Altmann, "Franz Rosenzweig and Eugen Rosenstock-Huessy," *op. cit.*, p. 264.
20 Julius Guttmann, *Philosophies of Judaism* (New York: Holt, Rinehart and Winston, 1964), p. 353 ff.
21 *Ibid.*, p. 361.
22 Hermann Cohen, *Religion der Vernunft*, p. 244. Cited by Samuel Hugo Bergman, "Hermann Cohen," in Altmann (ed.), *Between East and West*, p. 42.
23 Bergman, *op. cit.*, p. 43.
24 *Ibid.*, p. 45.
25 Cf. Elsa Freund, *Die Existenzphilosophie Franz Rosenzweigs* (Leipzig: Felix Meiner, 1933).
26 Altmann, "Franz Rosenzweig on History," *op. cit.*, p. 212.
27 Emil L. Fackenheim, "Schelling's Philosophy of Religion," *Toronto Quarterly*, XXII, 1 (October 1952), p. 15.
28 To Rudolf Ehrenberg, October 1916. Rosenzweig, *Briefe*, p. 121.
29 To Hans Ehrenberg, October 1916. *Ibid.*, p. 123.
30 To Rudolf Ehrenberg, December 24, 1916. *Ibid.*, p. 143.
31 Letter dated February 4, 1923. *Ibid.*, p. 475.
32 Altmann, "Franz Rosenzweig and Eugen Rosenstock-Huessy," *op. cit.*, p. 263.
33 *Ibid.*
34 Rosenzweig, *Briefe*, pp. 71–76; Altmann, "Franz Rosenzweig and Eugen Rosenstock-Huessy," *op. cit.*, p. 263.
35 Altmann, "Franz Rosenzweig and Eugen Rosenstock-Huessy," *op. cit.*, p. 264.
36 *Ibid.*, pp. 264–65.
37 Rosenzweig, *Briefe*, p. 675.
38 Letter dated October 28, 1916. *Briefe*, p. 676.
39 *Ibid.*, p. 677.
40 Altmann, *op. cit.*, p. 268.
41 Rosenzweig to Rudolf Ehrenberg, October 31, 1913. *Briefe*, p. 74.
42 *Ibid.*
43 Rosenzweig, *Der Stern der Erlösung*, II (Frankfurt: Lambert Schneider, 1921), pp. 176–77.
44 *Ibid.*, III, p. 87.
45 Compare: Genesis 3 and I Corinthians 15. The significance of the French Revolution to both Rosenzweig's and Rosenstock-Huessy's millenarian thinking has been treated by Prof. Altmann in "Franz Rosenzweig on History," *op. cit.*, pp. 198–99.
46 Rosenzweig, *Der Stern der Erlösung*, III, p. 61.

47 Rosenstock-Huessy to Rosenzweig, October 28, 1916. Rosenzweig, *Briefe*, p. 679.
48 Rosenzweig, "Das Neue Denken," *Kleinere Schriften*, pp. 387–88.
49 *Ibid.*, pp. 386–87.
50 *Ibid.*, p. 387.
51 *Ibid.*
52 *Ibid.*, p. 384.
53 Rosenzweig, *Der Stern der Erlösung*, II, pp. 23–24.
54 *Ibid.*
55 Rosenzweig, "Das Neue Denken," *op. cit.*, p. 389.
56 *Ibid.*, p. 390.
57 Rosenzweig, *Understanding the Sick and the Healthy*, p. 47.
58 Rosenzweig, "Das Neue Denken," *op. cit.*, pp. 385–86.
59 Rosenzweig, *Understanding the Sick and the Healthy*, p. 89.
60 Rosenzweig, *Der Stern der Erlösung*, I, pp. 7–8.
61 *Ibid.*, I, p. 9.
62 Rosenzweig, "Das Neue Denken," *op. cit.*, p. 386.
63 *Ibid.*, p. 395.
64 From the Epilogue to *Judah ha-Levi*, (Berlin: Lambert Schneider, 1927) pp. 153–55. Cf. Glatzer, *Franz Rosenzweig.* p. 261.
65 *Judah ha-Levi*, pp. 256–57.
66 *Ibid.*, pp. 253–54.
67 *Ibid.*, p. 255.
68 *Ibid.*, pp. 255–56.
69 Glatzer, *Franz Rosenzweig*, pp. 175–76.

Martin Buber (1878–1965): Speech Is Relational

Spirit is the word . . . in actuality speech does not abide in man, but man takes his stand in speech and talks from there; so with every word and every spirit. Spirit is not in the I, but between I and Thou. It is not like the blood that circulates in you, but like the air which you breathe.

—MARTIN BUBER

For the word always arises only between an I and a Thou, and the element from which the we receives its life is speech, the communal speaking that begins in the midst of speaking to one another.

—MARTIN BUBER

The importance of the spoken word . . . is grounded in the fact that it does not want to remain with the speaker. It reaches out toward a hearer, it lays hold of him, it even makes the hearer into a speaker, if perhaps only a soundless one.

—MARTIN BUBER

Human existence, even the most silent, is speech; and speech, whether intentionally or unintentionally, directly or indirectly, along with gaining ground and forcibly penetrating, along with sucking and tasting, along with advancing over untried ways, is always address.

—MARTIN BUBER

Language and the Life of Dialogue

THE DEATH OF Martin Buber marked the end of a life whose entire energies were devoted to explicating the sacredness, the poetry, and the sense of mystery which pervade our creaturely relationships with God, our fellowman, and the universe. It is seldom appreciated by those familiar with the life of dialogue, how greatly Buber revered speech as the key to his personalist orientation—as the primary vehicle for conveying sacred meaning and direction for relational living. Not only had Buber expressed a willingness several years ago to discuss language with Martin Heidegger, but one of his last major essays before his death is entitled "The Word That Is Spoken." His indebtedness to Hamann in this essay, together with his development of the theme that "the fate of being is determined through the speaking of the word," justifies placing him in the company of our previous speech-thinkers, despite obvious differences in emphasis in their respective developments.[1] Quite apart from these recent essays on speech, it should be remembered that Buber, like Rosenzweig, was known to those identified with the Patmos group, and later he became an editor and regular contributor to *The Creature.* These men regarded their own efforts as arising out of a common concern over the decay of vital speech and the absence of communication which preoccupied European intellectuals just prior to the outbreak of World War I.

In 1922, after reading Ebner's *The Word and the Spiritual Realities,* Buber realized "that men of different kinds and traditions had devoted themselves to the search for the buried treasure. Soon I had similar experiences from other directions."[2] The friendships made during this crisis, such as that between Buber and Rosenzweig, were to shape decisively the quality and direction of their respective efforts, the most noteworthy being their translation into German of the Hebrew Scriptures, which was begun in 1920 and carried on by Rosenzweig up to the time of his death, despite the increasing paralysis of his powers during this entire period. Students of Buber would be interested in the fact that in 1914, after reading Rosenstock-Huessy's *Königshaus und Stamme,* Buber wrote and told him how deeply he had been moved by the author's insights into language, and particularly by his adoption for a motto of Goethe's comment about the passage of heavenly speech to earth in its primeval form: "How the word was so important there because it was a spoken word." How interesting that almost fifty years later this passage should occupy a prominent place in Buber's most significant essay on the spoken word![3]

In his discussion of the historical background for his dialogical or

I-Thou principle, Buber makes it clear that he, like Rosenstock-Huessy, had immersed himself deeply in the writings of a number of thinkers, many of whom, like Hamann and Ebner, had dealt with language explicitly, or implicitly, as was true for Jacobi, Lavater, and Feuerbach. The significance of the contributions of these men helped him shape the basis of dialogical principle—*i.e.*, "that the saying of Thou by the I stands in the origin of all individual human becoming." Hence, the importance of statements such as one made in a letter by Jacobi in 1775, "I open eye or ear, or I stretch forth my hand, and feel in the same moment inseparably: Thou and I, I and Thou." Not only did he share Feuerbach's insights in the latter's *Principles of the Philosophy of the Future* (1843) that in the future anthropology rather than theology, the realm of the below rather than the above, would occupy men's energies, but he was greatly influenced by Feuerbach's statements that "the true dialectic is not a monologue of a solitary thinker with himself; it is a dialogue between I and Thou" and, further, that the *real* I is "only the I that stands over against a Thou and that is itself a Thou over against another I."[4]

More than anyone, his teacher, Wilhelm Dilthey, was responsible for Buber's philosophical anthropology. It was almost certain that at some point in his life, Dilthey's influence would be blended with Buber's dialogical insights. Hence, few students of Buber's thought were surprised that his last years were occupied with what is best described as dialogical anthropology, with the revelation of the above as it manifests itself in the below in the life of problematic man.[5]

In addition to Feuerbach, mention should be made of Nietzsche, whom Buber regarded as having been influenced heavily by Feuerbach's almost complete reduction of the human sphere to that of the anthropological. But whereas Feuerbach in his anthropological reductionism had subordinated the role of the individual in favor of the collective—Man—Nietzsche, at least, had endowed "the anthropological question with an unprecedented force and passion."[6] Though perhaps exaggerating the human at the expense of the divine and other elements, Nietzsche, unlike Feuerbach, had at least recognized the fact that man is essentially a problematic creature—*i.e.*, that it is part of the human condition that man can never be fully explained or understood; that mystery, paradox, and ambiguity are basic to his creatureliness.

What Buber particularly admired in Nietzsche was his characterization of man as "an animal that may promise"—*i.e.*, man is capable of treating "the future as something dependent on him, for which he answers." This quality of potential self-determination and creativity which Buber admired is summed up in Nietzsche's statement that "Man is something fleeting and plastic—one can make of him what one will."[7]

If in Nietzsche Buber found a kindred soul sensitive to the dynamic forces operative in the human realm, it was in Kierkegaard that Buber discovered a kindred spirit who appreciated the directness and immediacy of the relationship between God and the solitary soul wrestling meaning out of life. In his essay "The Question to the Single One" (1936), it is clear that Kierkegaard reinforced Buber's conviction that in the divine-human encounter God can only be addressed and responded to, never speculated upon abstractly. The writings of the lonely Dane helped Buber appreciate not only the element of risk involved in each new encounter, but also the need for "becoming a true person before going out to relation . . . the importance of realizing one's belief in one's life."[8] Though indebted to the nineteenth-century existentialist legacy of Nietzsche, Kierkegaard, and also Dostoevski, Buber vigorously attacked the world-renouncing elements in Kierkegaard's writings. Buber described the category of the "Single One" in Kierkegaard as the individual "who is finding himself." To become a single one for Kierkegaard means "to be a single man," which is "to fulfill the first condition of all religiosity." The single one at the same time is "the category through which, from the religious standpoint, time and history and the race must pass." The single one denotes the passage from mere existence as a creature isolated from time, history, and meaning, to participation in that which relates the individual by his participation in the "present being" to "all religious reality." This, asserted Buber, is what Kierkegaard meant when he stated that "the Single One *corresponds* to God," that he "stands alone before God . . . speaking with God."[9] To correspond to God means literally to stand in an intimate relationship of response and address, of hearing and speaking. This is responsible existence for the single one. Most of this Buber could accept and was in agreement with. What was intolerable for Buber was Kierkegaard's stress upon the exclusive quality of the relationship—one which "in virtue of its unique, essential life drives all other relations into the realm of the unessential."[10] It was Kierkegaard's stress upon the fact that the single one "has to do *essentially* . . . *only* with God" which caused Buber to accuse him of contradicting Jesus' insistence that the law of love is fulfilled only in loving *both* God and one's neighbor. In order to become the single one, Kierkegaard saw the Creation and God's creatures as barriers to the religious ideal of a lonely man in love with his God. Hence Kierkegaard "ceased to have common speech" with God's creatures and therefore renounced his love for Regina Olsen as an "object" which had to be "removed," as a hurdle which must be overcome, as part of the price of becoming a single one. Whereas Luther was proud of his marriage to Katherina, Kierkegaard preferred to re-enter the "monastery," the symbol of one historical means of safeguarding the solitary one's essential and exclusive relation with God. Although two years later, in 1843, Kierkegaard confessed in his journal that had he had faith he "would have remained with Regina," the single one at the time symbolized for him the negation of involvement with "politics" and the "crowd"—with anything or anyone having to do with the *polis.* Kierkegaard's refusal to marry Regina Olsen was both an affirmation of the world-renouncing aspect of authentic spirituality as he understood it, and also a further rejection of the Hegelian preoccupation with history, with its identification of the Spirit with political nationalism. Hence his proclamation, "In defiance of the whole nineteenth century, I cannot marry."[11]

By contrast, Buber's single one, as distinct from Kierkegaard's, includes a rejection of the crowd mentality, but has as its ultimate purpose the renewal of the body politic. In the world and yet not of the world, Buber's single one mediates God's love and his speech, which alone serve, for Buber, to bring about the "true community and true commonwealth." Unlike Kierkegaard, Buber affirmed the sacred character of the realm of the below—the Creation—and especially that unique creature one encountered where and whenever meeting takes place. Though rejecting the crowd, Buber regarded the meeting between the human Thou and I as *the* place wherein the Divine Presence was encountered. Buber's socialist background together with his personalism caused him to speak continually in terms of we, rather than utilize the often impersonal vocabulary of political scientists.

One aspect of the narrow ridge which Buber, like Rosenzweig and Rosenstock-Huessy, continually trod was devoted to doing justice to God, man, and world without allowing any single element to be absorbed by the others. In this way Buber was constantly capable of expressing indebtedness to men without identifying with much of their thought. Throughout this formative period he was attracted by a wide variety of insights, such as William James' statement in *The Will to Believe* (1897): "the universe is no longer a mere *It* to us, but a *Thou* if we are religious; and any relation that may be possible from person to person might be possible here."[12]

The Hasidic and Judaic Background

SOMEHOW, THESE VARIOUS influences were blended and nurtured during a two-year period of relatively little scholarly activity which he described as his own spiritual *askesis*. Apart from Descartes' *Discourse on Method*, Buber read no philosophica during this period. Toward the completion of writing *I and Thou* he mentions that he did indulge himself by reading Ebner's *Philosophical Fragments*. The "time of the first World War" was described by Buber as the "Vesuvian hour." "Out of the experience of the Vesuvian hour a strange longing awakens for thinking to do justice to existence itself. This longing even seizes the systematic thinkers."[13] Rarely in history have so many men responded with the same answer when confronted with the problem of thought doing justice to the problem of "authentic existence." Each one of the dozen or more responses between 1910 and 1930 emphasized the need that speech be taken seriously. Buber's life, as was true for the other speech-thinkers, was one of preparation for meeting the demands of "hours of crisis"—whose precise shapes only time would reveal. His own preparation dates from memorable visits in his youth with his grandfather, Solomon Buber, to Hasidic communities in eastern Europe. His preference for the personal, as over against the impersonal, for the encounters between an I and a Thou, for the dynamics which spark a community's existence as over against the difficulties between nations—all of this can be traced to his early fascination with Hasidism and Hasidic literature. Hans Kohn, in an early biography of Buber, said that Buber's preoccupation with Hasidism "was the most decisive encounter of his life."[14] More than any other single influence, Hasidism provides the clues for Buber's interest in the sacramental character of all life and especially speech. It served as a focus for all his subsequent writings, whether on the Bible, law, Judaism, or the life of dialogue. Without wishing to engage in the debate over his interpretation of Hasidism, it is fair to say that whatever Buber read into Hasidism was due to the profound effect it had upon his own life. What in fact began as a scholarly pilgrimage in 1905 turned out to have all the earmarks of a love affair where serious words are exchanged and the personality of each partner is deeply affected. Hence his statement in the *Postscript* to his dialogical principles:

> The question of the possibility and reality of a dialogical relationship between man and God had already accosted me in my youth. This dialogue implies a free partnership of man in a conversation between heaven and earth whose speech in address and answer is the happening itself, the happening from above and the happening from *below*. In particular since the Hasidic tradition had grown for me into the supporting ground of my own thinking, hence since about 1905, that has become an innermost question for me. In the language of the writings on the dialogical principle that arose many years later, it appears emphatically for the first time in the autumn of 1907 in the introduction to my book, *The Legend of the Baal-Shem*.[15]

Though dialogue is always a dominant theme in Buber's writings, it is quite evident from statements such as the preceding one that the possibility of any real dialogue hinges upon the ability of persons not only to employ some form of speech—in the technical sense—but more especially to trust in and place themselves under the spell and power of the word. It is assumed here that silent forms of address and communication, such as a glance, a nod, and bodily responses, are speech forms even though audible address may in fact be totally lacking. The Hasidic adoption of this reverence for all these forms of speech lay at the heart of Hasidic worldly concern, which expressed itself in the theme of the Holiness of God in constant need of man's sanctification and glorification. Hasidism represented an eighteenth-century reaction to the esoteric mysticism of

Kabbalah. It was an attempt to eradicate the Kabbalistic schematization of the *mysterium* and resulted in a sacramental view of reality that became an integral part of Buber's view of Judaism. In Hasidism, the love of God is realized in loving the world in God and loving God in the world. The world is the meeting place between men and God; it is the ground upon which the Holy Spirits go forward in God. The Zaddikim saw in Hasidism a true vision of unity, a passionate asking for wholeness. In contrast to the esoteric cleft between the initiated and the uninitiated in the Kabbalah, Hasidism maintained that "the secret is open to all; God's soul is undivided in His love for His creatures."[16] Over against the *kavanoth*, which could only be known by gnostic acts of penetration, the Hasid knew only the one life-embracing *kavana* of the man who gives himself up to God and his redeeming work "in this lower world, in the world of the body, to let the hidden life of God shine forth."[17] In all of this the theme of the "world as Word" was the link which united the realms of God, man, and world. Indeed, Buber's entire interpretation of Judaism has been influenced by this theme.

Judaism regards speech as a happening which reaches out over the existence of mankind and the world. In contradiction to the static notion of the Logos-idea the word appears here in its full dynamic as that which comes to pass. God's act of creation is speech; but also each lived moment is so. The world is spoken to the human beings who perceive it, and the life of man is itself a dialogue. What happens to a man are the great and small, untransmittable but unmistakable signs of his being addressed; what he does and suffers can be an answer or a failure to answer. And thus the whole history of the world, the hidden, real world history, is a dialogue between God and his creature; a dialogue in which man is a true, legitimate partner, who is entitled and empowered to speak his own independent word from out of his own being.[18]

Hasidism represented more than simply a revolt against the exclusiveness of the gnosticism of Kabbalah. It was also an attempt to make the world of Kabbalah accessible to the masses. In this process many tenets of Kabbalah were preserved and translated so as to appeal to the humble multitude of holy men. One of the most distinctive features of Kabbalah was its high regard for language, which Gershom Scholem has described as "quite unusually positive."

Kabbalists who differ in almost everything else are as one in regarding language as something more precious than an inadequate instrument for contact between human beings. To them Hebrew, the holy tongue, is not simply a means of expressing certain thoughts, born out of a certain convention and having a purely conventional character, in accordance with the theory of language dominant in the Middle Ages. Language in its purest form, that is, Hebrew, according to the Kabbalists, reflects the fundamental spiritual nature of the world; in other words, it has a mystical value. Speech reaches God because it came from God. Man's common language, whose *prima facie* function, indeed, is only of an intellectual nature, reflects the creative language of God. All creation—and this is an important principle of most Kabbalists—is, from the point of view of God, nothing but an expression of His hidden self that begins and ends by giving itself a name, the holy name of God, the perpetual act of creation. All that lives is an expression of God's language—and what is it that Revelation can reveal in the last resort if not the name of God?[19]

So great was the Hasidic influence appropriated by Buber that his relations with representatives of certain traditional forms of Judaism were at times strained ones. This is particularly evident in his discussions with Rosenzweig about Jewish law. The personal word and the sacred were identical for Buber; only that word which affects me personally has meaning and validity. In a letter to Rosenzweig (6/24/1924) Buber wrote,

I do not believe that *revelation* is ever a formulation of law. . . . I cannot admit the law transformed by man into the realm of my will, if I am to hold myself ready for the unmediated word of God directed to a specific hour of life. . . . It is part of my being that I cannot accept both (the law and the word of God) together and I cannot imagine that this position will ever change for me.[20]

In another letter the following month, (7/5/1924) the conflict between word and law is reiterated. ". . . I must ask myself again and again: is this particular law addressed to *me* and rightly so?" A week later in another letter (7/13/1924) he wrote to Rosenzweig, "God is not a law-giver, and therefore the Law has no universal validity for me, but only a personal one." The division between "revelation and law" was for Buber both "a thorn and a trial."[21]

Judaism, for Buber, was essentially the religion of personal address and response, of sacred conversations between God and all his creatures, mediated by the word. In *Hasidism* Buber states that Israel's greatness

> . . . is not so much that it has told mankind of the one, real God, the origin and goal of all that exists, but rather that it has taught men that they can address this God in very reality, that men can say Thou to him, that we human beings can stand face to face with Him, that there is a communion between God and man.[22]

Buber's God is, above all, a speaking God who needs His People just as He requires that they sanctify His Holiness. The unity of Israel is integrally bound up with God's word to His People and their response. The life of Israel is such that their daily conversation serves to remind them that God "is the one who speaks to men."

> God . . . as speaker, the creation as the language, the call into Nothing, and the answer of things through their emergence, the language of creation continued in the life of each created substance, the life of each creature a dialogue, the world as word—to proclaim that was Israel's task. Israel taught and showed: the real God is the God who can be spoken to, because He is the one who speaks to Men.[23]

Although Judaism for Buber is "beyond creed and catechism," containing much that he could not accept, it was in Biblical Judaism, in the "Biblical dialogue between man and God," that he found that which was most "essential" for his own life.[24] When asked in 1957 about the significant sources for his interest in speech, Buber replied, "Hamann had some influence on them in my youth, but the decisive factors were my own dialogue experiences and my Biblical studies."[25] Thus, Buber's Judaism is a blending of Hasidic and Biblical elements interwoven with those convictions derived from his own intensely personal encounters and dialogues with the word. His entire life was, as Arthur Cohen put it in his study of Buber, a constant "pursuit of the Holy."[26]

Sacrament, Symbol, Myth, and Legend

BUBER'S PREFERENCE FOR the term "sacrament" as against "symbol" is particularly helpful to those accustomed to discussing language as a symbolic form of expression. Discussions of the latter kind may be carried on endlessly without involving religious or dialogical considerations. By contrast, in a sacramental act as defined by Buber, such as the making or "cutting" of a covenant, two forces are at work. In Hasidic terms, the *above* binds itself to the *below* and vice versa. A sacramental act involves an action whereby the divine Thou and I alternate their roles of addresser and addressed in the making and renewing of a covenant. The meaning of a sacramental deed is determined by what happens in the dialogue between God and man.

Sacramental existence is, for Buber, "The most dynamic of all ritual forms," since one does not merely perform or experience something, but rather "the core of one's wholeness is laid hold of."[27] The Hasidic understanding of sacrament is therefore an act whereby human and divine join without merging themselves in each other. The fact that speech is the vehicle for the realization of sacramental existence helps preserve the distinctive uniqueness of the personalities involved. Similarly, there can be no union of persons, nor is there room for the "absorption" of one partner by another, since this would nullify speech and substitute a mystical union for the dynamic communion so central to Hasidic sacramentalism. The discovery of the sacramental knows no specific hour, no appointed or foreordained time within the calendar of the community. The discovery occurs most frequently where "the world threatens to become neutralized, and to deny itself to the holy contact."[28] The Zaddikim assiduously avoided any objective safeguards which might be distinguished as holy as opposed to profane and thereby offering a false sense of security to the faithful. They were ever aware of the mandate confronting every Messianic-conscious Jew which requires of him a potentially sacramental view of everything in order "to allow the messianic time . . . to receive what rightfully falls to it."[29] Note again the stress in this context upon the concrete everyday speech associated with human actions, as against the ever-present tendency to retreat to realms of critical and abstract discourse whenever symbolism is discussed.

Similarly in his use of the terms genuine myth and legend Buber strove to avoid any usage which would deprive the words of their summoning and evocative powers. He described legend as "the myth of I and Thou, of the summoner and the summoned."[30] As recently as 1950 Buber described real myth as "the expression, not

of an imaginative state of mind or of mere feeling, but of a real
meeting between two Realities."[31] Against this background the aim
of Hasidism was to release genuine myth from its intellectual
shackles. Buber singled out his introduction to *The Legend of the
Baal-Shem* (1908) as embodying his first efforts at formulating his
dialogical principle, which is presented within the context of his
distinction between legend and a "narrow" view of myth. Note the
degree to which this discussion is rooted in genuine oral and aural
encounter.

> The legend is the myth of the calling. In pure myth there is no
> difference of being. . . . Even the hero only stands on another rung than
> the god, not over against him: they are not the I and the Thou. . . . The
> god of pure myth does not call, he begets; he sends forth the begotten,
> the hero. The god of the legend calls, he calls the son of man: the
> prophets, the saints. . . . The legend of the myth of I and Thou, of caller
> and called, of the finite that enters into the infinite and of the infinite
> that needs the finite.[32]

Speech plays a particularly important role in Buber's discussion of
the power of signs as against symbols. A sign, for Buber, means
incarnation. When man asks God for a sign, he is, in effect, asking
that God's Spirit become incarnate—*i.e.*, corporeal, concrete. The
spoken word "completes itself in the sign and becomes corporeal."[33] The spoken word belongs to the sign; it is a part of the
concretization of the sign, a mark of its incarnation. He who does
not receive God's signs is guilty of a lack of faith: he shuts off his
awareness of God's address—"for He who speaks in the signs is the
'Lord of the Voice,' the eternal Thou."[34] Buber's insistence upon
the spoken word being supplemented by signs is an injunction to
make man mindful of the fact that effective speech must arise out of
the depths of authentic existence where man is most conscious of his
role as *imago dei*, as God incarnate. Signs are reminders of man's
dependence upon Him who invests man with the power to speak;
they give life to the spoken word.

> The spoken word alone cannot . . . satisfy the determining power of
> the moment. In order to be equal to it . . . the spoken word needs to be
> supplemented by the power of the attitude and action of significant
> signs. Only together with this is it possible for the spoken word to be
> present and to invoke the power of determination. Not the word by itself

has effect on reality, only the word set into the whole existence of a human being.[35]

Buber, like Abraham Joshua Heschel, believes that "symbols dwell in the world of 'I-It' "—of the subject-object relationship. His apprehension over speaking about symbolic language is that it often represents either pictorially or otherwise a "stand-in" or static substitute for the dynamics of an encounter. At the same time, he admits that there are "genuine" symbols which do not "hover timelessly over concrete actualities." Such symbols derive their power, however, from the concrete event. A true symbol is like a covenant cut between God and man, which has power only insofar as it continues to invest life with meaning. Living speech, as the vehicle for God's revealing word and man's response, prevents men from lapsing into the abstract because it is bound by the presentness of the encounter. Buber's disdain for symbolic language and his preference for the living language of sacramental existence is another example of his rootedness in a concrete Biblical realism.

The Theater as a Dialogical Source

As EVIDENCE OF Buber's appreciation for the spoken word it should be remembered that during his Hasidic studies in Italy in 1905–06 he spent a good deal of time in the theater and wrote several essays about the power of the spoken word in this medium, especially where it involved the performances of Eleanora Duse. After one performance he said of the theater as an art form that "It is the representation of the word as that which alternates between beings [it is] the mystery of word and answer."[36] This experience was especially meaningful for Buber since it preceded the years devoted to reflecting upon the dilemma of the solitary I in a completely nonacademic setting—almost completely devoid of philosophica. In a later essay, *Drama and Theatre*, Buber wrote:

If the play as poetry is thus grounded in the fact that man seeks to communicate to men through speaking, and across all barriers of individuation actually succeeds in communication, if only in tension, the play as theatre production belongs to a more natural level. It originates

in the elemental impulse to leap through transformation over the abyss
between I and Thou that is bridged through speech.[37]

The stage was more than a replica of the personal for Buber; it
was concrete embodiment of all that is revealed in a genuine dialogue. Through drama and the stage, Buber experienced most of the
elements later associated with relation and distance, his terms for
defining through the words and expressions he uttered in response
to his protagonist. All this took place and was made possible by the
mysterious qualities inherent in the word.

The theatre can take part in this work first of all through submitting
itself to the command of the *word*. The word that convulses through the
whole body of the speaker, the word that serves all gestures in order that
all plasticity of the stage constructs and reconstructs itself as a frame,
the stern over-againstness of I and Thou, overarched by the wonder of
speech, that governs all the play of transformation, weaving the mystery
of the spirit into every element.[38]

Earlier in this essay he wrote:

Drama is therefore the formation of the *word* as something that moves
between beings, the mystery of word and answer. Essential to it is the
fact of the *tension* between word and answer; the fact, namely that two
men never mean the same things by the words that they use; that there
is, therefore, no pure reply; that at each point of the conversation . . .
understanding and misunderstanding are interwoven; from which comes
then the interplay of openness and closedness, expression and reserve.[39]

The word which Buber experienced had all the qualities inherent
in the Biblical notion of *davar*. It was a vehicle of revelation among
men which provided a setting within which each partner in the
dialogue or conversation was changed in the encounter without loss
of his individual freedom. Speech in the dramatic medium was
capable of embodying all the give-and-take, the conflict, and the
strife which we commonly associate with genuine conversation at
a deep level. Of this period in his development, Paul Pfeutze has
remarked, "This experience in the theatre confirmed his studies in
the life of Baal-Shem: Man and God face each other in dialogue."[40]

From "Daniel" to "I and Thou"

DANIEL (1913) WAS Buber's earliest major effort after his Hasidic studies to embody many of these and other dialogical themes which were increasingly occupying his thoughts. The book consists of a series of dialogues between Leonard and a number of friends and focuses upon the actualizing power of the dramatic medium— namely, the realm of the word, of speech and its effect upon the great actor. However, he adds that not only drama, but poetry and lyrical composition must be seen as a medium in which all feeling and action are manifest as conversation. The playwright gives the actor the power to speak; to communicate through gesture and movement. Speech is not limited to vocal expression; there can also be a sacred silence wherein meaningful communication takes place. To enter into the spirit of an event depends, however, upon our "power to enter into relation." For Buber, relation, whether articulate or not, is a sign of fulfilled speech, since that which is spoken can be conveyed in silence, in gesture, in poetry, in song and dance.

All poetry tends towards drama. Every lyrical work is a conversation wherein the partner speaks in a more than human language; what he says is the poet's secret. Every epic work is a conversation, wherein the *moires* (fates) converse with one another; the task of the poet is to provide meaning through their replies. Drama is pure conversation: all feeling and all that happens becomes conversation. It stands on the boundary of its art and in its fulfillment and suspension points to every other in which the conversation is spoken.[41]

In *Daniel* one also notes for the first time Buber's distinction between *orientation* and *realization*—between an "objectifying basic attitude" and a subjective "making present one." Both terms are forerunners to his I-It, I-Thou distinction, which appears in its more mature form in *I and Thou* (1923), where is also the notable introduction of the realm of the *there-in-between*, the interhuman, which replaced the earlier emphasis in *Daniel* upon subjectivity. Of this new emphasis upon the interhuman, Buber wrote, "This is the decisive transformation that took place in a series of spirits in the time of the First World War."[42] It is another example of the way in which the quality and direction of individual thinking can be shaped by significant historical events and the revelations which these crises bring about. Much of modern man's eclipse of God is due to an inability to become a listener and hearer of the word revealed amid such profane crises. His preference for more traditional categories of the sacred have the effect of often effecting a barrier, rather than constituting a bridge, for sacred awareness. In a section of his essay "Dialogue," Buber states that "True address from God directs man into the place of lived speech, where the voices of the creatures grope past one another, and in their very missing of one another succeed in reaching the eternal partner."[43]

For many people *I and Thou* is Buber's greatest contribution; it and the terms "dialogue," "I-It," and "I-Thou" are practically synonymous. And yet, among the countless readers of this great work, relatively few have noted the degree to which Buber explicitly hinges the "life of dialogue" upon speech—upon the word which has penetrated our being and lies upon our lips. It is suggested that *I and Thou* be read in the light of its word and speech-conditioned foundation as revealed in two central passages, and in the light of Buber's general emphasis upon the potentially sacred character of the below.

Spirit in its human manifestation is a response of man to his Thou. Man speaks with many tongues, tongues of language, of art, of action; but the spirit is one, the response to the *Thou* which appears and addresses him out of the mystery. *Spirit is the Word.* And just as talk in a language may well first take the form of words in the brain of the man, and then sound in his throat, and yet both are merely refractions of the true event, *for in actuality speech does not abide in man, but man takes his stand in speech and talks from there;* so with every word and every spirit. Spirit is not in the *I,* but between *I and Thou. It is not like the blood that circulates in you, but like the air in which you breathe.* Man lives in the spirit, if he is able to respond to his *Thou.* He is able to, if he enters into relation with his whole being. Only in virtue of his power to enter into relation is he able to live.[44]

The tone of this paragraph is reflected in the opening lines of *I and Thou,* where Buber says that man's twofold attitude toward the world is defined in terms of two primary words, which bring about relations and relationships when they are spoken. The main distinction in the first edition between the primary words is that "I-Thou can be spoken only with the whole being," while "I-It can never be spoken with the whole being." And yet in each instance the quality of the personality of the I is literally spoken into existence. "The existence of *I* and the speaking of *I* are one and the same thing. When a primary word is spoken the speaker enters the word and takes his stand in it."[45]

Against this background, language is more than merely a means of defining and objectivizing the "symbolic" world about us; it is the perennial stuff of human existence by which destinies are determined and life created. The fact of the priority of this linguistic universe over the subject-object world of the perceiving, sensing, feeling, thinking I is fundamental to the dialogical approach, and is stated at the outset in *I and Thou*. The "*Thou* has no bounds." When it is uttered, the speaker has nothing in the sense in which he has the blood that circulates within him. The I which experiences the world and things for its own sake can be said to have knowledge, but this, for Buber, is comparable to the mere accumulation of information. "It, always It!"[46]

Buber gives further insight into the particulars of his application of speech to our dialogical situation in his description of the spheres in which the world of relation arises. His first statement about standing-within-speech has undergone no major change since the appearance of the first edition. However, with respect to the character of these spheres, especially the second, Buber has clarified in the *Postscript* to the second edition that which was for some only implicit rather than explicit in the earlier edition. Before dealing with these spheres individually, note their general context.

The spheres in which the speech-conditioned world of relation arises are three.

First, our life with nature. There the relation sways in gloom, beneath the level of speech. Creatures live and move over against us, but words cannot come to us, and when we address them as *Thou*, our words cling to the threshold of speech.

Second, our life with men. There the relation is open and in the form of speech. We can give and accept the *Thou*.

Third, our life with intelligible forms. There the relation is clouded, yet it discloses itself; it does not use speech, yet begets it. We perceive no *Thou*, but none the less we feel we are addressed and we answer—forming, thinking, acting. We speak the primary word with our being, though we cannot utter *Thou* with our lips.[47]

Note how determinative speech is and how without it the relational character of existence on every level would be nonexistent. The first of these spheres, "our life with nature," is "beneath the level of speech" and yet is defined in terms of a linguistic frame of reference. One does not have to go beyond Buber's Biblical and Hasidic sacramental view of reality to appreciate that aspect of the Creation with which it deals. On this level creatures cannot respond with *Thou* although they have indeed been addressed. Buber writes: ". . . our words cling to the threshold of speech," or as in the *Postscript*, "to the threshold of mutuality."[48] Within this sphere Buber distinguishes between animals, from whom we are often able to win an "astonishingly active response," and "plants," for example, which are incapable of response. And yet, as in the case of the tree, this does not mean that "we are given simply no reciprocity at all." When we utter *Thou* to a tree, "something lights up and approaches from the course of being."

That living wholeness and unity of the tree, which denies itself to the sharpest glance of the mere investigator and discloses itself to the glance of one who says *Thou*, is there when he, the sayer of *Thou*, is there: it is he who vouchsafes to the tree that it manifests this unity and wholeness; and now the tree which is in being manifests them.[49]

The "*Postscript*" to "*I and Thou*"

GRANTED THE SEEMINGLY mystical quality of mutuality which clothes Buber's words, we are left with no alternative but to accept them at face value and to recognize this "stage" within the first sphere which stretches "from stones to stars, as that of the pre-threshold or preliminal" stage. Buber has clarified the first sphere in his *Postscript* by distinguishing between creatures such as animals capable of response as being on the "threshold of mutuality" and another stage or level below that, the "pre-threshold," which includes those substances incapable of the spontaneity which we share with animals.

Omitting for a moment mention of the second sphere, let us proceed to the third, that of "our life with intelligible forms." In the third sphere the relation "is clouded, yet it discloses itself; it does not use speech, yet begets it." Although we "perceive no Thou," nevertheless we sense that we are "addressed and we answer—forming, thinking, acting." In this sphere the primary word is uttered with our whole being, despite the fact that we are unable to utter *Thou* with our lips. Buber has referred to this third sphere as "above the threshold," and as with the first sphere, has affirmed in the *Postscript* that it is capable of a twofold division. In the *Postscript* Buber distinguishes between "what of the spirit has already entered the world and can be perceived in it by means of our senses," and "what has not yet entered the world but is ready to do so, and becomes present to us."[50]

Buber has treated this division in the third sphere in another connection as that between what is "at hand" and what is "not at hand." What is "at hand" has to do with the world of form and order. That which is "not at hand" arises out of meeting the word, the Spirit. Such a meeting arises not out of man's world, but arises from this world's meeting with that of the Spirit, "which blows around us and in us." In the realm of the "not at hand" one can never determine the origin or cause of the Spirit. "He is . . . disloyal when he ascribes the gift to himself." In its presence, one can only offer his humble thanksgiving.[51]

Prior to the appearance of the *Postscript* to the second edition, some scholars questioned the possibility of an I-Thou relation of extended duration within the spatiotemporal experiential framework. The apparently momentary and fleeting character of Buber's earlier use of "meeting" as forever dissolving into an I-It relationship with the passage of time seems to have undergone substantial revision since the first edition appeared in 1923. This assumption is offset, however, by Buber's statements in *Dialogue* (1929) and *Education* (1926) wherein his recognition of the temporal and ongoing character of growth and creativity is discussed in detail. Quite apart from this, it should not be forgotten that Buber's earlier Zionist activities represented his own way at that particular period in his life of taking history, time, and cultural crises seriously.

In the *Postscript* Buber reserves his discussion of the second sphere, the important area of "our life with men" until last. This is due, perhaps, to the significance which he attached in later years to the implications of the "life of dialogue" for anthropology. This is the sphere of mutuality and reciprocity; "the relation is open in the form of speech. We can give and accept the *Thou*"; mutuality presents "itself as the door into our existence." Here Buber considers the extent and nature of the speech-conditioned and speech-created relations between men and has singled out this sphere for special consideration.

Of the three spheres, one, our life with men, is marked out. Here language is consummated as a sequence, in speech and counter-speech. Here alone does the word that is formed in language meet its response. Only here does the primal word go backwards and forwards in the same form, the word of address and the word of response live in the one language, *I* and *Thou* take their stand not merely in relation, but also in the solid give-and-take of talk. The moments of relation are here, and only here, bound together by means of the element of the speech in which they are immersed. Here what confronts us has blossomed into the full reality of the *Thou*. Here alone, then, as reality that cannot be lost, are gazing and being gazed upon, knowing and being known, loving and being loved.

This is the main portal, into whose opening the two side-gates lead, and in which they are included.

The relation with man is the real simile of the relation with God; in it true address receives true response; except that in God's response everything, the universe, is made manifest as language.[52]

Buber and Rosenzweig: Biblical Translation

THERE ARE TWO more aspects of Buber's interest in speech which deserve our attention. The first concerns his interest in language in connection with his and Rosenzweig's translation of the Hebrew Scriptures into German. The second is concerned with speech as it manifests itself in his later writings on dialogical anthropology—particularly in two essays, *What Is Common to All* and *The Word That Is Spoken*.

After Buber and Rosenzweig had convinced themselves that they should and could undertake the monumental task of translating, they were in fundamental agreement that the spoken and evocative quality of every word of Holy Writ should be recaptured and stressed in their joint effort. Only in this manner could the dialogical style of Scripture be preserved, thereby making it possible for men once again to rediscover in the word the secret to understanding not only the historical Biblical divine-human encounter, but also the secret whereby today God and all his creatures are able to know one another's will through Holy conversations. The justification for their efforts as translators was based on the conviction stated by Rosenzweig, namely that there has always existed an essential oneness amid the varieties of languages, as well as a "command from that oneness that there shall be communication among all men."[53] As noted in the preceding chapter, they were keenly aware that their own method and approach to these ends required that each look upon the other as his alter ego, his sounding board. Their desire that the Bible be read as a spoken, ongoing holy dialogue required that they themselves submit to the word in order to discover its proper style for their time. Thus, they accepted the principle that they, like the early Hebrews, were essentially ear men rather than eye men. In an early essay, *Art and Judaism* (1903), Buber stated that "the Jew of antiquity was more acoustically oriented (*Ohren mensch*) than spatially (*Raummensch*). Of all his senses, he relied most heavily upon his *hearing* when forming his picture of the universe."[54] Note, incidentally, the parallel between this statement and Hamann's remark "Speak that I may see thee!" Both translators accepted unquestionably the truth signified in the liturgy when it is proclaimed: "Hear, O Israel, The Lord Thy God is One!"—*i.e.*, the Jew knows through hearing. This fact was closely related to one of the chief reservations they shared when their initial discussions took place. Was it possible for modern man once again to trust his oral and aural powers in a time dominated by the quantitative and visually oriented approaches to truth and meaning? The Jesuit scholar Walter J. Ong has remarked that the radical change which occurred in the West when knowledge was no longer conceived in terms of discourse, hearing, and persons, but rather in terms of observations, sight, and objects "dominates all other [changes] in Western intellectual history, and as compared to it, the supposed shift from deductive to an inductive method pales into insignificance."[55] For both men the problem of knowing God was contingent upon modern man's ability to recover the primordial fact that address and hearing are our chief means of access to certain intense and unique forms of truth and knowledge. Thus, modern man's eclipse of God is intimately bound up with the eclipse of his own ability to be both a hearer and listener of the word. In accepting the challenge presented them, they accepted not only the philological scholarly difficulties, but also the task of recapturing the original audible dialogical quality of the Scriptures. Thus, they attempted to preserve the original rhythmic breathing pauses in Scriptural style, which are particularly evident in the Psalms. In other ways they tried to preserve the sense of being-in-the-presence of God by inserting the pronouns I and My where God speaks, You and Your where He is addressed, and He and His where God is referred to or spoken of. The Holy Name, God, originated, Buber contends, as an elemental cry, completely oral and evocative in character; His response and address is always directed to concrete moments. That which man receive is therefore not a specific content but a presence, "a Presence as Power." The speaker of power is none other than the Lord of the Voice. God's revelation of Himself as address-in-the-present, as a power and force with little else as a surety or sign, is supported by the passage in Deuteronomy (4:12) where it is announced, "Then the Lord spoke to you out of the midst of the fire; you heard the sounds of words, but saw no form; there was only a voice!" The ability to hear and then trust a felt presence in the midst of our everyday life, oftentimes without any accompanying signs or guarantees, is a risk and venture that few people standing within traditional forms of religion seem prepared to take. For Buber, our role as partners of God responsible for His fate in the world is dependent upon such risks and the responses following upon them if the eclipse of God is ever to pass.

This is the eternal revelation that is present here and now. I know of no revelation and believe in none whose primal phenomenon is not precisely this. I do not believe in a self-naming of God, a self definition of God before men. . . . That which reveals is that which reveals. . . . The eternal contact persists, the eternal voice sounds forth, and nothing more.[56]

Buber's Last Period: Dialogical Anthropology

THE TWELVE-YEAR interval between Buber's seventy-third and eighty-fifth birthdays was taken up with the implications of the life of dialogue for his thoughts on philosophical or dialogical anthropology. For this stage the early influence of his teacher Dilthey was incorporated with elements from his Biblical and dialogical experiences. His writings during this last period represent an elaboration upon those themes dealt with in his presentation of the sphere of the between and the problematic in man as they were developed in his essay *What is Man?* They might properly be regarded as an attempt at a social complement to the more personalist I-Thou writings which preceded them. In *Distance and Relation, Elements of the Interhuman,* and especially *What Is Common to All* and *The Word That Is Spoken,* one discovers Buber's answer to the way in which the word as speech is the flame that sparks men's lives as a we rather than simply as an I. Because of our interest in speech it is appropriate to concentrate upon the latter two essays, which are also his more explicitly anthropological as against psychological writings.

The importance of the problematic element in his anthropology is an attempt to do justice to that element in human existence that may not be reduced to rational, natural, or exclusively human factors, as Kant, Feuerbach, and Nietzsche had attempted. In emphasizing the problematic, Buber insisted that any consideration of the anthropological question must include an admission that man also "faces a being that is not human," and further, that he is constantly overwhelmed by the fact that he often faces "an inhuman fate."[57] The disciplines of the social sciences can contribute significantly to our understanding of the human situation insofar as they acknowledge the problematic in man, which is also an admission that no single discipline can deal exclusively and adequately with man's many-sided problematic character. A viable anthropology for Buber is one therefore which is cognizant of the problematic as it manifests itself in "the life of men together in all its forms and actions." The task of a legitimate philosophical anthropology is that it "must know that there is not merely a human species but also peoples, not merely a human soul, but stages in life." It is "only from the systematic comprehension of these and of all other differences, from the recognition of the dynamic that exerts power within every particular reality and between them" that men can "come to see the wholeness of man."[58]

In *Distance and Relation* Buber developed his basic "twofold principle of human life" upon which his anthropology is based—namely the twofold ability of men, first, to distance themselves from things and objects, and secondly, to establish personal relations with that which encounters one. He calls this twofold process "synthesizing apperception" and states that the universal act of distancing enables us to answer the question, "How is man possible," while the personal act of entering into relations helps us answer the question, "How is human life realized."

In these essays, speech is the fiber which gives meaning to this double process, inasmuch as speech is "the great characteristic of men's life with one another." Human speech is fundamentally different from that of animals, despite their common ability to "call out to others." The uniquely human ability to "speak to others . . . is based on the establishment and acknowledgment of the independent otherness of the other with whom one fosters relation, addressing and being addressed on this very basis."[59] Although Buber consistently prefers pronouns to nouns and proper names, he admits that originally an individual's name may have represented "the situations for those who had to be informed." At one time the name may have been man's sole means for bridging the distance between men and informing the other "that his presence, and none other, was needed in a given situation." Thus, for Buber the "holophrase" as well as the "name" are "signals" as well as "words." But speech also enables man to store up his signals, to give them distance and independence so that like tools they remain available for subsequent use. In this instance, it is in speech that

the addressing of another as it were cancels out, it is neutralized—but in order to come again and again to life, not indeed in those popular discussions which misuse the reality of speech, but in genuine conversation. If we ever reach the stage of making ourselves understood only by means of the dictograph that is, without contact with one another, the chance of human growth would be indefinitely lost.

Genuine conversation, and therefore every actual fulfillment of relation between men, means acceptance of otherness.[60]

The element of acceptance of the other over against one is often presented in terms of genuine listening or a turning or giving of one's entire being to the one's partner. Though often a silent giving of oneself, Buber regards it as "the hidden accompaniment to the conversation itself." The truth revealed in a conversation is imbedded in the fact that men "communicate themselves to one another as what they are."[61] The authenticity of any conversation is dependent upon this surrendering, this giving up of a part of oneself in much the same way as genuine response for Rosenstock-Huessy involves the *etsi*—"*Although* I will be changed, I nevertheless respond!" In such situations of mutual giving, "Speech arises between us," and consciously or unconsciously, men have admitted the truth that real being and becoming involves a submission to a force larger than ourselves—in this instance, Spirit as word as the heart of the interhuman or the realm of the there-in-between. Submission to speech is a risk inasmuch as we neither know what we will utter in advance, nor can we anticipate its final effect upon our person. ". . . the course is of the spirit, and some discover what they have to say only when they catch the call of the spirit."[62] In an earlier passage Buber reiterates the fact that man alone has his personality determined by the ability of the Spirit to share decisively in its shaping. Letting the word as speech arise in the interhuman and take its toll is indeed work, since at times we are forced to utter words, and therefore create new situations of truth and meaning, as if the words, the truth, were wrenched from us. The effect, however, of being possessed by speech is that "where it appears dialogically, in the climate of great faithfulness, it has to fulfill ever anew the unity of the two."[63] Even the harsh effect of words and the truth which they reveal carries with it a promise that the possibility of richer personal authenticity and meaning lies before us.

Buber and Heracleitus: "What Is Common to All"

BUBER'S ESSAY *What is Common to All* discusses the importance of Heracleitus' use of *logos* and *cosmos* as they bear upon the social dialogical life of the we. It is a particularly significant essay, not only as it bears upon Buber's basic differences with Freud, Jung, and

Carl Rogers, but more especially because of the creative importance
for personality which Buber attaches to our social speech-filled existence, as against the solitary silent conversations which the I carries on within itself while asleep. Hence Buber's emphasis upon
Heracleitus' statement that "the waking have a single cosmos in
common." For Heracleitus as for Buber, the common is "the sustaining category"; it enables man, despite his "want of understanding—so painfully suffered and so fiercely reproved by him—to
grasp and confirm as a spiritual reality their togetherness, the full
mutuality of human being."[64] In contrast to the traditional emphasis by psychoanalysts upon sleep and dreams, Buber wishes to regard
waking and sleeping as "pairs of opposites in which the unity of
being fulfills itself."[65] To minimize the influence of our speech-filled
waking hours is, in effect, to deny that men have obligations to accept responsibly "the task of establishing in common a common
reality." Note again the similarity in emphasis to Rosenstock-
Huessy's insistence that taking speech seriously obligates us to partake in the "creation and preservation of a truly human society."
Note also the similarities between these sentiments and Buber's
earlier fascination for the Hasidic view of man as God's partner,
responsible for His fate in the world. For the Hasid as for Buber,
Heracleitus, and Rosenstock-Huessy, the word, speech, is the sacred
vehicle for transforming the world, its times, and its spaces. Buber
contrasts his emphasis in this essay upon the primary world of we
with the preference in Eastern teachings—*e.g.*, those of Tao and the
early Upanishads—for the passive realm, for the "teaching of dream
sleep and deep sleep." Thus, of the teachings of the Upanishads he
says:

> According to them, the existence of a man in the world is the exist-
> ence of a world of appearance, a magical deception. But since the
> identity of the self can be reached only in an absolute solitude, such as
> deep sleep, the existence between man and man is also ultimately only
> appearance and illusion.[66]

The same applies for the fascination of men like Aldous Huxley
with the effects of mescaline intoxication. They seek refuge in a
special sphere set apart from the everyday, "from the existential
claim and the person who must verify himself in We." Such escapes
are fundamentally flights from responsible speech—"from the au-

thentic spokenness of speech in whose realm a response is demanded, and response is responsibility." This common task is one which men contribute to even while asleep.

Even in sleep . . . —no matter though each is submerged in his private sphere—they are still as individuals, workers, and co-workers in the world-happening, passive workers. This means that there is no state in which the individual merely leads his own existence without contributing his part, just through living in this state, to the life of his human environment and to the world in general. But working men add in common to the world-shape itself. . . . They associate with one another in the world, helping one another through the power of the logos to grasp the world as a world order, without which ordering grasp it is not and cannot be a world. They can only do this . . . if they do not sleep while working and spin dreamlike illusions which they call their own insight—if they exist in common.[67]

Only by mutual speaking and listening, accompanied as it is by all the ambiguities and frailities of the human situation, can men discover, as mouthpieces of the word, the logos, the truth which the logos would have revealed at that time. Truth and meaning do not transcend the flux of reality in any Platonic sense; rather, as with ancient rhetoricians like Isocrates, truth is discovered amid the agony and strife of contending speech. Amid humanity's antiphonous vocal setting, civilization's tone is struck. Thinking has its proper place within this setting, but it takes its cue from the "communality in which we participate" rather than in a solitude withdrawn from or above the real world of mutually lived speech. In addition to Feuerbach and those cited earlier, Hamann and Heracleitus were protectors, for Buber, of the sacredness of our frail everyday sensuous speech. In *Man and His Image Work* Buber insisted that "the path of our question must begin in the sphere in which the life of the human senses dwell," and in this connection he cited Hamann as one who "stirred up the revolt of living speech against routine" and helped create a climate of appreciation for art, poetry, and creativity. Of Heracleitus, Buber said that he

always remained in accord with the thoroughly sensuous living speech of his time. For this reason the logos, even in its highest sublimation, does not cease to be for him the sensuous, meaningful word, the human talk which contains the meaning of the true. Meaning can be in the word because it is in being. . . . It stirs deep in the soul which becomes aware of the meaning; it grows in it and develops out of it to a voice which speaks to fellow souls and is heard by them, often, to be sure, without this hearing becoming a real receiving. And like the logos, so also the cosmos belongs to the common as to that in which men participate as in a common work.[68]

Buber and *"The Word That Is Spoken"*

IN ONE OF his last major essays, *The Word That Is Spoken* (1960), Buber further emphasized the fact that meaning is tied to the lived sensuous speech between men, and that by its very nature, authentic living speech must be both ambiguous and problematic. Along with Hamann and Rosenzweig, Buber insists that unproblematic speech such as that which reflects neat systems of thought not only came later, but stands in sharp contrast to the quality of speech identified with the Biblical presentation of God's literally speaking that which exists into being and His giving man the power to name the animals and lesser beings. In earliest times language arose out of address—"it could become monologue only after dialogue broke off or broke down."[69] Just as man must always remain for the sake of his authenticity a problematic creature, so too, authentic speech must remain problematic, inasmuch as "the mystery of the coming-to-be of language and that of the coming-to-be of man are one."[70] As stated later on in this essay, ". . . the fate of being is determined through the speaking of the word."[71] Given the blurred, concealed, and ambiguous setting within which truths are revealed, speech forms such as poetry, for example, are essential types, since they are often capable of imparting "to us a truth which cannot come to words in any other manner than in this one." The poet, like the listener and speaker, takes his cue from that which addresses him, whether from without or within, since he, like all who live off the word, is incapable of distinguishing in any precise fashion subject from object—outer from inner.

This essay is particularly helpful for our purposes since it helps us appreciate Buber's attitude toward the relationship of speech to history. Because of his continued emphasis upon presentness Buber has oftentimes been severely criticized for not taking history, tradition, and names seriously. Before discussing his exchange of views on various aspects of these themes with Rosenstock-Huessy and Franz Rosenzweig, it is well first to understand Buber's stress upon speech as the ontological ground for history, as it is presented in this next to last of his major writings.

At the outset, he states that there are "three modes-of-being" with respect to the effect of language upon human life. He defines these as present continuance, potential possession, and finally, actual occurrence. The last of these reflects actual speaking with nothing else presupposed "than man's will to communicate as a will capable of being realized," which in turn "originates in man's turning to one another."[72] Actual occurrence is the linguistic equivalent of presence and presentness, which traditionally has been a main theme throughout Buber's dialogical writings. This third mode, presentness, would be shorn of all meaning, however, without due consideration being given to the first two modes, continuing and possessed speech. These last two, Buber insists, are servants of present spokenness, which is that speech which occurs at a given moment in time. Though servants, the first two may not be separated from the third. What they represent in this instance is crucial not only to Buber's views on language, but to all that is permeated by speech—which for Buber is everything we call reality. The first, present continuance, cannot be understood "detached from the context of its actual speakers." Present continuance refers to "the totality of what can be said in a certain realm of language in a certain segment of time," regarded from the viewpoint of the speaker. All the possible thoughts of those involved in and conditioned by their particular and unique speech-laden meeting are referred to here. Whereas the first refers to all the possibilities of speech-conditioned thinking, the second mode, potential possession, covers "the totality of what has ever been uttered in a certain realm of language," insofar as it limits itself to "what can still here and today be lifted by a living speaker into the sphere of the living word."[73] This last limitation which Buber places upon the second mode is decisive for appreciating how vital speech conditions his principle of historical bias and selectivity. The eyeglasses through which he views history are colored by the objective word, which determines in actual speech situations what it is that shall be deemed meaningful and relevant and vice versa from among our common past. Hence his statement:

No matter how fundamentally the philologist or the historian of literature can objectively apprehend it, even this mode-of-being of language, apparently unfolded in pure objectivity, cannot be detached in its dynamic facticity from the actuality of the word.[74]

Thus, the first two modes of existence and possession "presuppose a historical acquisition," which is an intimate part and comes through in the actual turning, the listening and speaking covered by the third mode in an actual conversation. The degree of significance of the exchange naturally determines whether or not, as well as how much of, history shall be present in any one encounter. History for Buber, like every aspect of his Jewish tradition, is ontologically grounded and conditioned by the word which is present where serious speech and genuine encounters occur. While one may disagree with the adequacy of his personalist approach to history, Buber does, on the basis of his own view of the word and speech, take history and tradition seriously. His continual concern for presence includes the presence of all those portions of time, history, and tradition which are capable of being brought to any event and shaping the destinies of those involved. Sacred speech is the means whereby past and future meet in eternal presence, thereby raising the possibility that God's creatures may, through the word, create new futures and new paths for themselves and their children.

NOTES

CHAPTER 5

1 Martin Buber, "The Word That Is Spoken," in *The Knowledge of Man* (New York: Harper & Row, 1965), p. 119.
2 Martin Buber, *Die Schriften über das dialogische Prinzip* (Heidelberg: Lambert Schneider, 1954), p. 295.
3 Buber, "The Word That Is Spoken," *op. cit.*, p. 111.
4 Buber, *Die Schriften über das dialogische Prinzip*, p. 287 ff.
5 *Cf.* Maurice Friedman's Introduction to *The Knowledge of Man*, pp. 11–58.
6 Martin Buber, *Between Man and Man* (London: Routledge & Kegan Paul, 1954), p. 148.
7 *Ibid.*, p. 149.
8 Maurice Friedman, *Martin Buber: The Life of Dialogue* (New York: Harper & Row), p. 35.
9 Buber, *Between Man and Man*, p. 65 ff.
10 *Ibid.*, p. 73.
11 *Ibid.*, p. 58.
12 Buber, *Die Schriften über das dialogische Prinzip*, p. 290.
13 *Ibid.*
14 *Cf.* Hans Kohn, *Martin Buber* (Hellerau: Jakob Hegner, 1930), pp. 68–136.
15 Buber, *Die Schriften über das dialogische Prinzip*, pp. 292–93.
16 Martin Buber, *Mamre* (Melbourne: Melbourne University Press, 1946), p. 138.
17 *Ibid.*, p. 144.
18 *Ibid.*, p. 4.
19 Gershom G. Scholem, *Major Trends in Jewish Mysticism* (New York: Schocken, 1941), p. 17.
20 Nahum Glatzer (editor), *Franz Rosenzweig: On Jewish Learning* (New York: Schocken, 1955), p. 112.
21 *Ibid.*, pp. 114–15.
22 *Ibid.*

23 *Ibid.*
24 Friedman, *Martin Buber: The Life of Dialogue*, p. 257.
25 From a letter to the author, April 21, 1957.
26 Arthur A. Cohen, *Martin Buber* (New York: Hillary House, 1957).
27 Buber, *Hasidism* (New York: Philosophical Library, 1948), pp. 129–31.
28 *Ibid.*, p. 131.
29 *Ibid.*, p. 136.
30 Martin Buber, *Die Legende des Baalschem* (Berlin: Schocken, 1922), pp. 11–12.
31 Martin Buber, "Myth in Judaism," *Commentary*, IX, 6 (June 1950), pp. 562–66.
32 Buber, *Die Legende des Baalschem*, pp. 11–12.
33 Friedman, *Martin Buber: The Life of Dialogue*, p. 90.
34 Buber, *Hasidism*, pp. 124–25.
35 Maurice Friedman, "Religious Symbolism and 'Universal' Religion," *Journal of Religion*, XXXVIII, 4 (October 1958), p. 224.
36 Kohn, *Martin Buber*, p. 72.
37 Martin Buber, *Pointing the Way* (New York: Harper & Row, 1957), p. 64.
38 *Ibid.*, p. 66.
39 *Ibid.*, p. 63.
40 Paul E. Pfeutze, *The Social Self* (New York: Bookman Associates, 1954), p. 132.
41 Martin Buber, *Daniel* (New York: Holt, Rinehart and Winston, 1964), pp. 120–21.
42 Buber, *Die Schriften über das dialogische Prinzip*, p. 295.
43 Buber, *Between Man and Man*, p. 15.
44 Martin Buber, *I and Thou*, second edition (New York: Scribner's, 1958), p. 39.
45 *Ibid.*, p. 4.
46 *Ibid.*, p. 5.
47 *Ibid.*, p. 6.
48 *Ibid.*, p. 126.
49 *Ibid.*, p. 125.
50 *Ibid.*, p. 127.
51 *Ibid.*, pp. 129–30.
52 *Ibid.*, p. 103.
53 Franz Rosenzweig, *Kleinere Schriften*, p. 203.
54 Martin Buber, *Die Jüdische Bewegung* (Berlin: Lüdischer Verlag, 1920), p. 245.
55 Walter J. Ong, S.J., *The Barbarian Within* (New York: Macmillan, 1963), p. 70. Cf. also, by the same author, *In the Human Grain* (New York: Macmillan, 1967).
56 Buber, *I and Thou*, pp. 111–12.
57 Buber, *Between Man and Man*, p. 146.
58 *Ibid.*, p. 123.

59 Buber, *The Knowledge of Man*, p. 68.
60 *Ibid.*, pp. 68–69.
61 *Ibid.*, pp. 75–85.
62 *Ibid.*, p. 87.
63 *Ibid.*, p. 86.
64 *Ibid.*, p. 90.
65 *Ibid.*, p. 91.
66 *Ibid.*, p. 95. Cf. also pp. 106–8.
67 *Ibid.*, pp. 90–91.
68 *Ibid.*, p. 98.
69 *Ibid.*, p. 115.
70 *Ibid.*, p. 117.
71 *Ibid.*, p. 119.
72 *Ibid.*, p. 111.
73 *Ibid.*
74 *Ibid.*

Ferdinand Ebner (1882–1931): Speech Is Personal

There is nothing except I and Thou: and if the two of us are not, then God is no more and the heavens collapse.

—ANGELUS SILESIUS

The monological I is a misconception which shattered and had to shatter the entire I philosophy. The I exists in dialogue.

—FERDINAND EBNER

Good words have their own . . . vibrations, which are audible only to musical ears. The meaning of a word is not rendered in a single tone, but rather in an entire chord. Even here the Word of the Gospel is valid: He who has ears to hear, let him listen. To use the same metaphor, the Word without resonance is the Word which has failed to find its Thou.

—FERDINAND EBNER

This book showed me, as no other book since has done, in places with an almost uncanny insight, that in this age of ours men of different kinds and traditions had committed themselves to the search for the same buried treasure.

—MARTIN BUBER's comments after reading
Ebner's *The Word and the Spiritual Realities*

Ebner and the Dialogical Movement

As EARLY AS 1933 the names Martin Buber and Ferdinand Ebner were singled out because of their use of the I-Thou terminology and its bearing upon the cultural crisis they and other Europeans felt in the second and third decades of this century. In that year, John Cullberg in his classic work *The Thou and Reality* stated that both attacked the tradition of the solitary thinker which underlay philosophical idealism in the twentieth century in much the same manner as had Kierkegaard, Feuerbach, and the lesser-known Swedish philosopher Erik Gustaf Geijer in the nineteenth century.

During the general cultural crisis following the World War, and in connection with a general critical coming to grips with the basic ideas of the past, the idealism of the 19th century was put on trial; and now it became evident that once again the problem of the Thou tended to move into the center of all problems.

The beginning was modest. It consisted of two writings which originally found little or no attention in the circles of the professional philosophers: but, which, nevertheless, contained sufficiently explosive material and at the same time determined in certain ways the direction of later development, theological as well as the philosophical.[1]

Cullberg was referring to Buber's *I and Thou* (1923) and Ebner's *The Word and the Spiritual Realities* (1921).[2] Unfortunately, the English-speaking world has had almost no access to the thought of the Austrian Roman Catholic schoolteacher Ferdinand Ebner, except through praises in his behalf by Emil Brunner in *Man in Revolt* (English translation 1939) and *The Divine Human Encounter* (English translation 1943).[3] In *Man in Revolt*, Brunner praised Ebner's insights into the relational quality of human existence, which he contrasted with the notion that humans have a "solitary rational existence quite independently of one another."[4] In a number of passages he also expressed his indebtedness to Ebner's portrayal of the drama of the Incarnation in terms of human speech. As a *human*, man is the being who "can and does speak; the being who not only maintains his own physical existence, but creates and shapes culture and civilization."[5] Despite Brunner's high esteem for Ebner's magnum opus, *The Word and the Spiritual Realities*, nothing except for a brief passage from his writings has appeared in English. It is hardly accidental, however, that it was the Buber scholar, Maurice Friedman, who saw fit to include a translation of a passage from Ebner's writings in his recent work, *The Worlds of Existentialism*.[6] Of all those treated thus far, certainly Ebner's writings bear the closest resemblance to Buber's I-Thou formulation, and in another context, to the thought of the father of modern religious existentialism, Søren Kierkegaard. Ebner's similarities and differences with Buber and Kierkegaard provide a convenient vehicle for introducing the reader to Ebner's thought. Mindful of our earlier presentation of Buber's evaluation of Kierkegaard in his essay *The Question*

to the Single One, it is hoped that the reader's general familiarity
with Buber and Kierkegaard will enable him to grasp more rapidly
the salient themes which pervade Ebner's aphoristic, poetic style.
Although many have regarded Ebner as the Roman Catholic equivalent to Buber, it is well, at the outset, to define their similarities as
well as their marked differences. Ebner's diaries are rich in insights
that parallel Buber's in *I and Thou*.

The Word is the bond between I and Thou.
The true I in Man is his innermost ear which admits the Word.
Spirit is present everywhere, where something happens between an I
and a Thou.
Every relationship involving two people with one another, which sig-
nifies a relation of I to Thou, partakes in the Eternal.
The warranty for the spiritual immortality of Man lies in the relation
of his I to his Thou.[7]

In a curious way Ebner's writings reflect a blending of the salient
aspects of both Buber's and Kierkegaard's insights into authentic
spirituality. First, though a Roman Catholic, Ebner shared their respective difficulties with religion in its various institutional guises.
Like them, he rejected any absolute distinctions between the realms
of sacred and profane. For each, the personal and concrete relationship between I and Thou was the sole means of access to spiritual
existence. Secondly, and related to this, Ebner shared an inability
to look upon the hard speech of politics and social involvement as
bearing directly and significantly upon the language of sacramental
living. Though not as world-renouncing as Kierkegaard—Ebner did
marry and have a family—the path he trod to this decision was
anything but easy. Buber, in fact, has described Ebner as one who
even more than Kierkegaard was unable to discover the Thou
among his fellowmen.[8] One factor in this was that problems bearing
upon sexuality and identity were almost pathological obsessions
with Ebner throughout his life. Along with Kierkegaard, Ebner's
existence was marked by constant inner conflict, indecision, and
anxiety. Third, and despite his declared pacifism and concern for
the social welfare of his fellowmen, Ebner's lifelong search for religious peace—for an encounter with the divine Thou—overshad-
owed all his dealings with mortal Thous. With but few qualifica-
tions, the divine Thou was all that really mattered for both Ebner
and Kierkegaard. In retrospect those few intimate friendships which

Ebner enjoyed were, at best, vehicles, sounding boards, during his intensely personal quest for that succor and peace which only the divine Thou could provide. Fourth and lastly, Ebner may be considered the Martin Buber of Roman Catholicism only if one discounts the radical difference in their respective use of I-Thou terminology. Though some may disagree with this point, what is at issue here is the substance and object of their religious personalism. While each distinguishes sharply between the divine and human Thou, the thrust in Ebner's writings is upward toward God, while in Buber's the Divine Thou can more often best be discovered in the realm of the there-in-between man and man just as easily and meaningfully as in the direct and open discourse between God and his creatures. Each, in Hamann's sense, gnawed upon the word—upon the bone of language—but the effect of their respective formulations is marked with important distinctions and relative degrees of emphasis on crucial points. Having made these observations about Ebner's general orientation with respect to his religious personalism, let us turn now to the man himself, his culture, and his time. From this perspective, it is understandable how men like Brunner, Buber and Rosenzweig should have recognized Ebner as a kindred spirit.

At the outset, it should be noted that prior to the appearance of *The Word and The Spiritual Realities* Ebner was almost completely unknown to those personalities already discussed. Although some may have read with interest portions of this work, which appeared as *Spiritual Fragments* in the periodical *Der Brenner*, it was not until the appearance of the entire work in 1921 under the title *The Word and the Spiritual Realities* that contact was established with Buber, Rosenzweig, and members of the Patmos circle. Despite mixed reviews which the work received, it was immediately recognized as a monumental work by Rosenzweig and his cousin, Hans Ehrenberg. Rosenzweig responded by sending Ebner a copy of his *Star of Redemption*, which had been published earlier that year. Ehrenberg responded by sending Ebner a copy of Feuerbach's *Principles of Any Future Philosophy*, which Ehrenberg had been instrumental in having republished by the Frommann press. Ehrenberg called Ebner's attention to Feuerbach as the "discoverer of I and Thou," but added in a letter that Ebner had significantly enlarged upon this theme. He later developed this point in two reviews in the *Frankfurter Tageszeitung*.[9] In an essay recounting the "History of the

Fragments," Ebner pointed out that Buber, whose *I and Thou* appeared in 1923, was apparently acquainted with *Der Brenner* and had sent a copy of his own work to Carl Dallagos, who was not only a regular contributor to *Der Brenner* but, as it later developed, one of Ebner's severest critics. In fact, at one point, Dallagos' negative reaction practically destroyed any future that *Der Brenner*'s publisher, Ludwig Ficker, envisioned for his journal. Significantly for students of Buber and those interested in dialogical themes, Ebner stated that Buber sent a copy of *I and Thou* to Dallagos *because* of the latter's interest in the Tao-te-king and Eastern thought.[10] Despite Taoist themes in Part Two of *I and Thou*, Ebner evidently regarded Buber's *I and Thou* as a kind of Jewish mysticism which evidenced certain similarities with Eastern mysticism but also, by virtue of Ebner's comments, reflected a form of mysticism which, despite its preoccupation with I and Thou themes, was fundamentally different from Ebner's own development. At this point, it should be stated that I doubt seriously whether the christological factor in Ebner's thought adequately accounts for these differences. For one thing, certainly Buber's Hasidic *this worldly* emphasis was devoid of the Platonic dualistic overtones apparent especially in Ebner's comments about the dichotomy between flesh and spirit. Although Ebner may have drawn certain conclusions from his concern for the word and speech which differed from those of writings already discussed, he nevertheless shared their common convictions about the cultural and spiritual crisis they were experiencing, with respect to both cause and remedy. For each, as we have noted, speech, communication, and the word bore upon the problems they shared and provided the means for addressing themselves positively to these concerns. Naturally, their responses were indeed varied. Consider for a moment the fact that in 1921 not only Rosenzweig's *Star of Redemption* and Ebner's *The Word and the Spiritual Realities* appeared, but, quite significantly, also the major work of another fellow Austrian, Ludwig Wittgenstein. Though hardly recognized today as one identified with the general orientations of Ebner or the members of the Patmos circle, some have regarded Wittgenstein's *Tractatus Logico-philophicus* as another, though quite different, response to the cultural crisis which prevailed between the two World Wars. For example, *Der Brenner* was in many respects to Ebner and his Austrian confreres what *Die Kreatur* was to Buber, Rosenzweig, and Rosenstock-Huessy. Bear in mind that the publisher of *Der Brenner*, Ludwig von Ficker, played an important role in the publication of not only Ebner's and Wittgenstein's works, but also those of the Kierkegaard scholars, Theodor Haecker and Wilhelm Kutemeyer. Karl Kraus, long a student of language, was another figure regularly identified with Ficker's interests. In a recent evaluation of the contributions of *Der Brenner* to Austrian and European culture between 1910 and 1954, mention was made of both Ebner's and Wittgenstein's concern over whether in fact there was a bridge, any connection, between speech and existence, "between the 'mystical,' which only 'indicates' itself, and that which can be formulated. . . ."

Just as, according to Rilke's intuitive prophecy, in Trakl's poetic works the togetherness of language and muteness finds expression, so too, Ebner, as well as Wittgenstein, asked the decisive question whether or not there is a bridge between existing and speaking, between the "mystical" which only "indicates" itself and that which can be formulated. Over against Wittgenstein's apodictic saying: "Whereof one cannot speak, thereof one must be silent," Ebner recognized the principal ability of man to find verbal expression even for the unspeakable of his spiritual life. In these opposing views lies the basic dissimilarity between both attempts; which, nevertheless, because of their preoccupation with thoughts about language, move close to one another.[11]

Although in the fifties few students in either linguistic camp were even barely able to tolerate one another's views, recent developments in linguistic analysis, such as the "theory of games," concern for ordinary language, and discussions about objectivity, relativity, and methodology, indicate possible areas of rapprochement. While the historical links can best be dealt with by cultural historians more qualified than I, the interests today of the heirs of both camps are such that it may be possible in the next few years for students to examine more closely one another's contributions. Even then, however, discussions will probably be limited to areas having little bearing upon speech as a sacramental force and power. One wonders what Wittgenstein himself would say, were he alive today, about the limited appropriation and application of but a portion of his writings.

If the mystical, Platonic, and poetic elements in Wittgenstein have been largely overlooked by his philosophical admirers, these

elements certainly mark one's memory of the writings of Ferdinand
Ebner. The monumental editing and publishing effort undertaken
by Dr. Franz Seyr in conjunction with the Kösel Verlag in making
available in three volumes Ebner's collected letters and writings
lightens considerably the task faced when attempting to introduce
Ebner's insights to an English-speaking audience.

Ebner's Early Development: 1882–1912

EBNER WAS BORN in Vienna-Neustadt on January 31, 1882, the
youngest of seven children (two died in infancy) of Johanna Ebner
and his wife. The father, age 62 when the son was born, was an
unsuccessful farmer and butcher who throughout most of his life
was heavily in debt. Although the family was devoutly Roman
Catholic and it was mandatory that he attend church regularly,
young Ferdinand was unable throughout most of his life to accept
the dogmatic and institutional aspects of religion. Friction soon developed between father and son when the father, having given up
farming, began to attend mass daily and encouraged his family to
follow his example. Their religious differences only accentuated the
strain between them, inasmuch as the son, by this time, already
regarded his father as a strange and overbearing individual.

During most of his youth, Ebner regarded the crucifix not as a
symbol of deliverance and redemption but rather as the symbol of
a man beaten and tortured by those about him. He often likened his
own existence to that of his pet black squirrel, whose freedom was
artificial, limited as it was by the bars of the cage and the treadmill
which never went anywhere. Ebner's attempt to simulate nature by
inserting a branch in the squirrel's cage could not alter his conviction that the life that each led was nothing more than an appearance
of freedom. Real existence rooted in freedom was for both nothing
more than simulation—a mere illusion.

From his earliest school years, Ebner experienced poor health,
periods of depression and anxiety, and a tendency to phantasize.
These qualities intensified and plagued him in later life. He began
his teacher training studies during a period of unresolved sexual
problems, which resulted in a series of traumatic love affairs with

numerous women. The obligation in the midst of this to attend confession, receive the sacrament regularly, and attend religious instruction was particularly unpleasant. Regarding himself more as an atheist and materialist, he was aware that he lived the religious life as a "big lie." As a student, Ebner just got by in most of his subjects, although he did reasonably well in the more abstract disciplines. His school days were filled with apprehension lest he possibly fail a subject, fearing the consequences at home. On one occasion early in his youth, upon receiving word that he had passed his subjects, he ran filled with joy into the street only to collide with another youth, causing the boy a severe brain concussion. His personal guilt and sorrow over the accident immediately doused his spirits. He quickly grew accustomed to expecting that each piece of good news would be followed by some kind of catastrophe. As a result, he did not expect much from life in the way of joy and satisfaction and probably settled for considerably less than he was capable of receiving.

His sister Josephine, whom he had been especially fond of, died when Ebner was eighteen. Following that he was hospitalized for a lung condition. It was in his eighteenth year that Ebner began a relationship with Frau Luise Karpischek, a friend of his sister Mitzis and ten years his senior. It was perhaps the most intense and lasting relationship which Ebner experienced. It lasted more than twenty-five years, during which time they exchanged more than a thousand pieces of correspondence. Though he addressed her alternately as "Dear Aunt Luise" or "Dear Mrs. Luise," she has been described by one commentator as Ebner's *Diotima*. She not only revered and nourished his artistic and poetic tendencies, but provided the warmth and encouragement he sought and needed when his spirits were low. In one passage he even described her as his beloved, Platonic bride and spoke of their relationship as a marriage. Later in life he admitted on one occasion that in retrospect their relationship had been "psychologically unhealthy" and a "mistake." One writer said that, "She personified for him the concrete human *Thou*, which he has in mind when he speaks of the Thou in the *Spiritual Fragments*."[12]

After graduation Ebner accepted a teaching position at a school in Waldegg. During this period he steeped himself in the classics, both ancient and modern, and devoted his energies to poetry. Like

Hamann, he was convinced that man truly becomes a creature as a poet. These tendencies were encouraged not only by Luise Karpis-chek but also by his literary mentor, Edward Bauer. His poetic activity reached its peak during 1903–4 but gradually declined after 1908. Though Ebner never achieved much recognition for his poetic efforts, one wonders whether, as in Hamann's case, the real fruits of this period were not to be realized when he began later on to wrestle in earnest with the problem of word and of speech.

When Ebner was twenty-one his father died, at the age of eighty-three. It was a traumatic event in his life. He discussed its signifi-cance in his last poem, "Golgotha." During 1907–8, Ebner realized that his preoccupation with poetry was steadily giving way to an interest in a program of readings in philosophy beginning with Plato, followed by Nietzsche and Kant. By 1910 the transition of his interests from poetry to philosophy was completed. The discernible Platonic elements in his writings are confirmed by a glance at his monthly reading schedule, which nearly always included one of Plato's dialogues. Also included in this program were the works of Freud, and related essays devoted to psychiatry, psychopathology, and neuropsychiatry, as well as a wide variety of works dealing primarily with sexual motifs. In addition he steeped himself in the writings of religious mystics and existentialists.[13] His entries in his diaries during this period provide us with a thread of continuity for a program which most would regard as a prodigious undertaking, but nevertheless one lacking a systematic disciplined approach. It is interesting, given the fact that subject-object distinctions are gen-erally maligned by our speech thinkers, that Ebner's penciled com-ments in the margins and other glosses represented his *subjective* diaries in contrast to a separate set of *objective* diaries and note-books. He began these objective entries during the period of his transition to philosophy in March of 1908. Written as aphorisms, they were subsequently published through the efforts of his devoted admirer, Hildegard Jone, in *Wort und Liebe* in 1935, and reflect his interests between 1909 and 1926.[14] Although bookworm, poet, and philosopher by temperament, the *Chinese wall* which he expe-rienced as a lonely and isolated creature was really a product of the frustration and disappointment he felt as a result of his constant longing for an authentic and satisfying I-Thou encounter. What he sought was neither philosophical discussion nor congenial socializing, but rather encounters comparable to that with Luise Karpis-chek; relationships capable of liberating the I from the *wall* that increasingly threatened his existence and freedom.

The summer of 1912 was a particularly pleasant period in his life. He left Waldegg and accepted a new post at Gablitz, where he was able to complete his *Ethics and Life,* which was inspired largely through his study of the works of Henri Bergson. *Ethics and Life* is a collection of five hundred fifty-six diary entries between 1911 and 1912 and reflects his own formulation of a metaphysical treatment of biological motifs that bear directly upon the problem of the freedom of the individual. In them, one notes his frequent use of I-Thou polarization developed in terms of the *Thou* of God as the dynamic force that makes human freedom possible. When these entries were made his spiritual pilgrimage had still not found its fulfillment in a renewed and reconstructed form of Christian personalism.

World War I and Ebner's Religious Conversion

THESE GOOD DAYS were quickly shattered when war broke out, and he wrote that he then lived his life as in a stupor. "My thoughts were so much a part of what was happening in the war, as one who was participating even though a civilian in the hinterland. That I declared myself a pacifist is all the less surprising since it was so entirely understandable and natural."[15] In a later essay Ebner discoursed at length not only upon the evils of war, but upon the way in which patriotism and the notion of "a Christian people" had become synonymous.

> *Christian* peoples were the ones who fought this war. In *Christian* churches prayers for victory were offered and processions with miraculous pictures of Mary were conducted. But a prayer for the victory of the just cause—even if this meant the victory of the enemy—would have been condemned as unpatriotic. . . . *Christian* peoples were the ones who fought this war. Therefore, it was impossible during this period to avoid a confrontation with the Sermon on the Mount.[16]

Jesus' radical demands for a life *in* and yet not *of* the world were in Ebner's day dismissed as sheer rhetoric, wholly lacking in a proper respect for the niceties of casuistry. Jesus' verbal excesses could hardly be condoned by any right-thinking individual. Given Ebner's respect for emotive language, it is understandable how deeply offended he was by one newspaper journalist's characterization of the shortcomings of Jesus' proclamations. "Christ speaks as a rhetorician and not as a casuist. Part of his figures of speech are rhetorical exaggerations and drastic phrases and these are understood by every reasonable person."[17]

Ebner's conclusion was a simple one: "Amid the noise of war the Word was forgotten."[18] Long before Ebner developed his Christian personalism, the war had convinced him that whatever Jesus as the Word meant, it must never be identified with institutions, whether religious or secular. For him the institutional Church was as corrupt as the state. Both represented the privileged classes and both were protests against the social revolutions he longed for. "On Shrove Tuesday of the year 1929 a ceremonious alliance was formed between the Pope and Mussolini." Fascism, for Ebner, "has grown in size due to nothing else than the fear of the privileged classes of society about the threatening social revolution."[19]

After completing *Ethics and Life,* Ebner again reverted to a period of intense reading, which included the works of Sophocles, Homer, Goethe, Shakespeare, Rilke, Mann, Ibsen, Strindberg, Tolstoi and Dostoevsky. He continued his interests in dream analysis and in the writings of Bergson and through the translations of Theodor Haecker, he discovered Søren Kierkegaard. His first mention of Kierkegaard was in an entry dated September 1914. He mentions having read Kierkegaard's *Fear and Trembling, Philosophical Fragments, Concluding Unscientific Postscript,* and the *Concept of Dread.* In addition to Kant's *Critique of Pure Reason* and Descartes' *Discourse on Method,* he also read many of the writings of Hamann, Scheler, and Pascal. Through regular readings of Scripture, he claimed to have discovered the God proclaimed by Jesus of Nazareth. With such a galaxy of religious and existentialist influences, it is not surprising that he was about to enter upon a new period of writing which was to reflect many of the themes developed in the writings of these personalities.

The religious turning point in Ebner's life lacked the marks of a definite conversion experience comparable to that recorded, for example, by Augustine. Even the approximate date is difficult to determine. However, in 1931, shortly before his death, he undertook a revision of a fragment written in 1916, declaring in a postscript that his philosophical endeavors had by that time led him up a blind alley. Ebner's transition from a philosophical to a religious stage is markedly similar to Kierkegaard's own development between 1847 and 1848, when Kierkegaard announced to the world that he had to surrender the indirect for the direct style. On Wednesday in Holy Week, 1848, Kierkegaard wrote in his *Journal,* "My whole nature is changed. My closeness and reservedness are broken—*I must speak.*"[20] This meant that he must no longer write using the pseudonymn Johannes Climacus but write as Søren Kierkegaard.

By 1917, as evidenced from his letters to Luise Karpischek and his entries in his diaries, Ebner's religious breakthrough had been achieved. His despair over the tragedy of war, which reflected itself in every encounter, certainly was a significant factor in this development. Undoubtedly his mixed feelings over his relationship to his deceased father was another factor in his conversion. He noted in a diary entry this change in his life. "In the middle of the war—I was in my thirty-fifth year—I began the important turning to Christianity."[21] His conversion would by many be considered a limited or partial one, since he, like Kierkegaard, retained his anti-institutional, anticlerical convictions. Franz Seyr states it quite well when he discusses Ebner's conversion.

But this does not mean for him a step toward the Catholic Church. On the contrary: precisely at this time he even considers a complete break with her, and in 1919 he asks himself seriously whether *anticlericalism* would not be the primary requirement of true religiosity; he even answers this question in the affirmative, but he concedes that the naïve believer who is loyal to the Church can have truly religious essence—being.[22]

Ebner's Most Productive Period: 1916-1923

THE PERIOD FROM 1916 to 1923 was an especially productive one for Ebner in terms of his literary activity. Whereas between 1909 and 1916 he had filled two diaries with some one hundred sixty pages of comments and four notebooks consisting of five hundred

pages, the entries beginning in 1916 and ending in 1923 filled some
ten diaries and eight notebooks amounting to twenty-five hundred
pages written in a small, tight style. All this was accomplished despite poor health and the effects of the war years. The food scarcity
during the war years further affected his frail constitution. Of what
little food was allotted him, he gave much to others, especially
children. Despite these conditions it was in the winter following the
armistice that he began to draft his *spiritual fragments*.

Although afflicted with jaundice in the early spring, he completed a first draft by April 1, 1919. Through the offices of his
friend Bauer, he then began a search for a publisher and offered the
last of his family inheritance as an inducement to any interested
firm. In May of 1919, after several contacts had failed, he sent the
manuscript to Theodor Haecker in Munich. In August he received
an enthusiastic response from Haecker, who asked permission to
send it to Ludwig von Ficker, publisher of the Brenner Press and
the periodical *Der Brenner*. When financial difficulties prevented its
immediate publication, Haecker proposed that portions, single
fragments, be published regularly in *Der Brenner*. Between 1919 and
1920 six of the fragments appeared in various issues, and finally in
1921, they appeared in their entirety in book form under the title
The Word and the Spiritual Realities. As might be expected, the
book received mixed reviews, one of the most critical being that by
Carl Dallagos, one of the oldest contributors to *Der Brenner*.
Steeped in oriental thought, especially that of Lao-tze, Dallagos
identified his own brand of Christianity with that of a religion of
pure love. Despite Ebner's personalist anticlerical orientation, Dallagos attacked him vehemently as a "captive of dogma." Such was
the furor this rift caused within the offices of *Der Brenner* that its
future as a leading periodical was threatened with extinction. During the entire controversy, Haecker, who had sponsored Ebner,
refused to come to his defense. If Dallagos' review was critical,
those of the professional philosophers were even more devastating.
Steeped as they were in German idealism, they regarded the work
not only as unphilosophical in its development, but resented on
religious grounds its attack upon the very foundations of the heirs
of Kant and Hegel. Though differing in approach and vocabulary,
Ebner, like Rosenstock-Huessy, had declared himself a religious believer and had cast his lot with those who took Revelation seriously,

as against those whose religious orientation was founded upon some variation of eighteenth- and nineteenth-century "philosophy of religion." How could any self-respecting philosopher and academician take seriously pneumatology? Was this anything more than a *flatus vocis?* Besides, wasn't it quite apparent from the frequent autobiographical references that the man was mentally ill and needed help? But worse than this was the author's assumption that it was proper to include personal references in any kind of scientific treatise. The difficulty was indeed a real one, inasmuch as Ebner was writing about themes bearing upon his own and others' existences. In addition his frequent allusions to his own problems often, and understandably so, tended to erect a barrier between author and reader.

It is quite correct to inquire about the value of a work which is largely a projection of an individual's personal situation. The works of Pascal, Kierkegaard, and Sartre also fall into this category. It must be assumed, however, that Ebner, like the above-mentioned, viewed his pneumatological (or spiritual) fragments as reflecting a way of life founded upon certain fundamental assumptions and relationships which he recommended for the consideration of others. To achieve this end, he regarded poetry or his own style—*i.e.*, *existence-communication*—as valid means. Ebner's requirement that personal existence be treated concretely—*i.e.*, in biographical or autobiographical terms as the case may be—created difficulties normally lacking in those efforts where greater distance between author and subject matter is possible. His task was understandably a difficult and unenviable one. His sin of excessive subjectivity was probably no worse in his day, however, than were the artificial and in the final analysis equally subjective and excessive claims made by his philosophical critics in behalf of scientific objectivity and value neutrality. If one understands his purpose in the fragments, Ebner was not attempting to outline a marketable existential or dialogical philosophy or system, an exhaustive "philosophy of the word," much less a general *Sprachphilosophie* based upon human as against divine discourse. Rather, he was speaking out of the richness of his own existence to the problem of achieving what he still longed for, namely an existence which could find its fulfillment in God's love mediated by the word. The fragments might well be regarded as a practical exercise in spirituality, presented not in the traditional

manner of the mystics—whether it be John of the Cross or the life
portrayed in *Tales of a Russian Pilgrim*—but rather against a personalist spirituality, pneumatology, or phenomenology, influenced
by elements from Kierkegaard, Hamann, and Scheler. Like Kierkegaard, in order to be effective—*i.e.*, to emphasize the limitations of
our minds when discussing matters of the Spirit—the appropriate
style must remain fragmentary and aphoristic. Whether one could
achieve the desired end under these circumstances was indeed questionable. Is it possible to speak from deep within one's soul and
succeed in communicating with another person? Can one avoid
those artificial abstractions which mark systematic treatises about
the spiritual life and which actually prevent communication? Isn't
the whole notion of a pneumatology doomed to failure under any
circumstances? In a letter to Luise Karpischek (12/20/1917) Ebner
recognized the difficulties inherent in his own efforts.

> As a matter of fact, I consider the *pneumatology* to be quite useless,
> even harmful—being an abstract doctrine of the spirit, which precisely
> in its abstractness has nothing to do with the concrete reality of the
> spiritual life. And yet, most of my notes do not have any other meaning
> than to be thoughts, aphorisms, fragments of the pneumatology.[23]

Ebner's Foreword to *The Word and the Spiritual Realities* contains an acknowledgment of the validity of most of the criticisms
and shortcomings alluded to, but also a defense of the validity of
such an undertaking despite these limitations. For example, Ebner
begins his Foreword by quoting a lengthy, severely critical evaluation of the work made by a Viennese philosophy professor at the
request of a Viennese publisher who had considered the manuscript
for publication before Ludwig von Ficker accepted it. The opinion
attacked the book on the grounds alluded to above—*i.e.*, its unphilosophical and unscientific qualities, and its repeated references
to aspects of the author's obviously psychologically unbalanced
condition. These charges—all of them—Ebner accepted and acknowledged as a sign of the times. The book's content and tone
reflected not only his own existential dilemma, but the dilemma of
academia and European culture as well. Moreover, he insisted that
these characteristics could not be separated. If the world outlook
and norms of the university professors were the generally accepted
ones, as appeared to be the case, then sensitive religious souls were

bound to be crushed and overwhelmed by a sense of alienation and estrangement.

For Ebner the best and most obvious reflection of the soul's interiority was speech, whether spoken or written, depending on the circumstances. Understandably, the quality of a man is normally more easily detected from the voice tone and inflection than from the written word. Ebner's aphoristic style, together with its intensely subjective and autobiographical qualities, reflects his attempt to convey the soul's condition through the written word with the same power and effectiveness as is possible through the spoken word.

Turn for a moment to Ebner's use of *subjective* and *objective* with respect to his diaries and notebooks. It is evident that the two terms are ontologically grounded—*i.e.*, that they reflect from two perspectives the quality of an individual's existence. In line with these distinctions it is suggested that *The Word and the Spiritual Realities* represents Ebner's objective reflection upon his subjective existential situation. As such, it did not and could not, from Ebner's standpoint, do justice to the subjective dimension of existence. He acknowledged this shortcoming when he stated in the Foreword that, with the possible exception of Theodor Haecker, few could appreciate the contradiction inherent in the work—a contradiction which must remain because of the impossibility of any writing *about* life, of capturing the existential quality of the lived existence itself. As with Kierkegaard, Ebner's use of the subjective-objective categories, as well as his aphoristic and fragmentary style, suggested that the deeper truths in life be only partially and inadequately expressed. From an objective perspective, the unity and plan of the work must be but an abstraction of reality.

The attempt to express these realities—*i.e.*, to outline a pneumatology in terms of certain abstract categories—represented a feeble attempt at expressing a truth which could only be lived rather than described. Systematic expression and rational development remained for Ebner a secondary rather than primary mode of expression, an indicator and pointer rather than a reflector of *lived* life *per se*. Though unhappy with the limitations inherent in his pneumatology, Ebner, like Kierkegaard and Buber, affirmed that man, if his authentic creatureliness is to be preserved, must forever remain problematic—even in the face of the most severe and intense self-examination.

In 1922, 1926, and 1928, Ebner wrote four articles dealing with the implications of his pneumatology—*i.e.*, with the relationship between Christ the Word and human speech. These all appeared in separate issues of *Der Brenner*.[24] By 1923 his depressions were not only more frequent but more severe. At age forty-two he was appointed provisional director of the school at Gablitz. On October 7, 1923, he married, and on November 1 of that year gave up for good his twenty-one-year teaching career in favor of devoting his energies to poetry, music, and writing and editing the Gablitz school chronicle. Shortly thereafter a son, Walther, was born to Ebner and his wife. Despite intermittent periods of seeming good health, he became bedridden in the spring of 1931. He died on October 17, 1931, after receiving the last rites of the Church. During his lifetime altogether some twenty-three essays, along with *The Word and the Spiritual Realities*, appeared in print. After his death and through the efforts mainly of Hildegard Jone, his son, Walther F. Ebner, Franz Seyr, Eberhard Steinacker, and other devoted friends and students of his thought, another dozen publications appeared, consisting mostly of letters, excerpts from his diaries, and aphorisms. Since his death more than one hundred and eighty books and articles have appeared dealing with various aspects of his life and thought.

Ebner's Pneumatology: The Word and the Spiritual Realities

EBNER'S THOUGHTS AS represented in *The Word and the Spiritual Realities* and in other essays are worthy of examination because of the light they shed upon the importance of the word and human speech for spiritual (pneumatological) living. As was stated earlier, Ebner, like Kierkegaard, never intended in his writings to develop a system which might have the quality of an *ism*. Like the Dane, he was concerned with a particular existing human being rather than with formulating still another philosophy of existence.

Professor Lowrie's discussions of existence as understood by Kierkegaard and Sartre is significant at this juncture. Lowrie distinguishes sharply between Kierkegaard's existing and subjective creature who exists and thinks *sub specie aeternitatis* and the speculative emphasis of Sartre and Heidegger upon philosophies of existence which, for Lowrie, result in the dilemma that subjective "existence is left hanging in the air."

Ebner and Kierkegaard both emphasized the fact that the subjective existing creature is always in the act of the process of becoming that person which God has called him to become. Thus, Lowrie's statement, "In the first place, he is in process of *becoming*, he is constantly *striving*, and this movement is prompted by *passion*— that is, by imagination and feeling, rather than by thinking. All these traits are existential because they eventuate in a transformation of a man's exisence."[25]

There is no fixed, preconceived goal in this kind of striving. For Kierkegaard, "the existing subjective thinker is constantly occupied in striving. . . . He strives infinitely, is constantly in process of becoming."[26] Earlier in the *Postscript* Kierkegaard wrote: "Since the existing subject is occupied in existing (and this is the common lot of all men; except those who, being objective, have pure being to live in), it follows that he is in process of becoming."[27]

Ebner's concern is with praxis rather than theory—with what both Ebner and Kierkegaard referred to as passionate striving, which is never capable of complete achievement or expression. Like Kierkegaard, Ebner's writings reflect the pathos and loneliness of this quest, the almost pathological obsession with a self-fulfillment realizable only in terms of a divine-human encounter. For both, this striving was an intensely personal one which could only take place within a relationship between persons—in this instance, between the divine Thou and the human I. Although Kierkegaard seldom expresses this in I-Thou terms, when using the pseudonymn Johannes Climacus he alludes to the personal quality of all authentic truth by dwelling on the distinction between interest and disinterest or reflection.[28]

Earlier it was noted that during his prereligious period Kierkegaard preferred to write under a pseudonymn—*i.e.*, Johannes Climacus—and referred to his style during this interval as indirect or maieutic. He chose this mode of expression because he found it was most suitable for expressing truths about the inwardness of the soul. Truths which interest us are those which we have not merely

reflected upon, but have appropriated in such a way as to affect the
· shape and quality of personal living. Double reflection is the term
Kierkegaard used to characterize the steps involved in transforming
the apprehension of truth into a new working force in one's life.
Many of these elements, especially Kierkegaard's principle of double reflection, are evident implicitly and explicitly in Ebner's writings.

Ebner differs in his writings from Kierkegaard most noticeably in
his preoccupation with the word as the key to the quest for authentic spiritual existence. In the Foreword to his spiritual fragments, the word constitutes the link, the relationship with the spiritual realm.

> It [*i.e.*, the spiritual *in* man] is essentially determined by the fact that
> it is basically oriented toward a relationship with some spiritual reality
> *through* which it exists. An 'objectively' comprehensible expression . . .
> for this orientation . . . can be found in the fact that man is a being
> capable of *speaking*, that he "has the word." However, he does not have
> the word because of either natural or social considerations. Sociality in
> the human realm is not the presupposition of language; rather sociality
> requires that language, the word being placed *in* man "I," and the one
> *outside* of him, in relationship toward which the I exists, "Thou," then
> we have to consider that this I and this Thou are given to us precisely
> *through* the word and in it, in its "inwardness"; [they are] not, however,
> [given to us] as "empty" words, in which no relationship toward a
> reality inheres—as they do, indeed, appear in their abstract, substan-
> tivized, and substantiated usage—but rather they are given to us as word
> which, in the concreteness and actuality of its being spoken, "recupli-
> cates" its "content" and reality in the situation which is created by
> speaking. This, in brief, is the basic idea.[29]

With Buber, Ebner would agree that "Spirit is the Word," that it
is not like the blood which circulates within us but is rather like the
air which we breathe. This identification of Spirit and word is fundamental to Ebner's pneumatology, and it helps one appreciate the
way in which the Divine Word assumes its incarnate and personalist
shape in human speech. It also enables one to understand how God's
creatures are immersed in the Spirit, in the word, and yet do not
possess it in any total or absolute sense. Just as the word is in us and
we are in the word, so too, our words are in the word and the word
is in our words and on our lips. This identification is made possible

by Ebner's conviction that speech is the medium wherein the divine-human encounter occurs. This for Ebner is the meaning of the Prologue to John's Gospel and is an indication of the specifically Johannine Incarnational emphasis which permeates Ebner's writings. Only the word is capable of shattering the self-imposed Chinese wall that imprisons most men's spirits, and can liberate them for responsible life as God's creatures who live in and by His Love and His Word.

These two themes, the interpenetration of Divine Word and Divine Love in a Platonic Johannine sense, were for Ebner the basis for a rich spiritual existence. The way in which Ebner developed these themes in his writings and showed at every stage their effect upon human existence caused Theodor Steinbüchel in 1936 to describe *The Word and the Spiritual Realities* as the basis for a "revolution in thinking."[30]

Although Steinbüchel and most of Ebner's admirers have identified his contribution as Christian in a Johannine Trinitarian sense, one discerns in his writings a frequent reliance upon neo-Platonic dualistic categories. Previously, we ascribed to Johannine thought a millenarian, this-worldly temporal emphasis which differs sharply from the dualistic elements so evident in Ebner's writings. At the same time there is also a certain pantheistic quality in his thought similar in many respects to neo-Platonic philosophers and religious mystics in Western thought. The universal significance that Ebner ascribes to the word is quite close at many points to the role played by reason in both Aristotle's and Hegel's thought, and also Being and Eros in Plato's writings. With respect to the Platonic and neo-Platonic strains in Ebner's thought, bear in mind that Ebner always contended that while Plato may have appreciated the objective significance of the word, he never understood its subjective power in anything but a pejorative sense.[31] Consider for a moment the following statement of Ebner's in the light of these observations. It is apparent that Ebner attaches considerably more importance to the Word than he does to human speech—*i.e.*, the word embraces both that which can be uttered as well as that which is unutterable. On the other hand, and from a Biblical perspective, does not the Word of God have this wide range of power *whenever* its force is described? Isn't it also true that Buber in identifying word with Spirit also states that the word embraces every threshold of being and reality, that it embraces that which is below and above the threshold of speech as well as the realm of speech between man and man?

Despite these considerations, Ebner and Rosenstock-Huessy, for example, would probably differ in their use of the term Johannine by virtue of the latter's millenarian historical emphasis, which is almost totally lacking in Ebner's writings. At the same time, given the attention which Ebner devotes to John 1.1, there can be no doubt that he regarded his interpretation of the word as consistent with the author of John 1.1.[32] Remember also that Ebner did not feel a complete kinship of mind with Hamann, despite Ebner's frequent citations from Hamann's writings and his acknowledged respect for his insights into the word. Specifically, Ebner regarded Hamann as being too prone to doctrinal and theological considerations. He also criticized Hamann for minimizing love as the word's complement. Consider, for a moment, his characterization of the intimate and all-encompassing bond between love and the word in his *Aphorisms:*

> The Word embraces and carries language—not only language, but the whole man, and not only man, but the being of the whole world—and therefore it is more than language, more than our spoken words. It embraces everything which we cannot express, for which our language does not have the right word. It embraces God, because God embraces the Word. And it embraces *Love.*[33]

Rightly or wrongly, Ebner insisted that his Johannine emphasis differed from various forms of Platonism by virtue of his own stress upon the need for love and the word being fulfilled by the human I in its relationship with the divine Thou. If one minimized Ebner's preoccupation with the I-Thou, personalist human-divine encounter, his writings would long ago have been dismissed as but another expression of Christian Platonism.

> The word of man should proceed from his being silent before God and from the fullness of his life in God. This fullness of life is love, otherwise one does not understand it in its deepest essence. The *thinkers* about the word must be *philologists,* they must love the word. But also one must illumine love from the essential meaning of the word—otherwise one understands and misunderstands it only as self-love and self-will, as covetousness and greediness, or, at best, as the *eros* of Plato's philosophy. But genuine love is more, it is something quite different

from Platonic love. It is—like the word—the realization of the relationship toward the Thou, of the relationship toward man and toward God.[34]

There is abundant evidence that Ebner, like Hamann, viewed philology not only as an indispensable tool to discover the meaning of Scripture, but also as a more appropriate term than theology to employ when describing the ingredients of his pneumatological enterprise. In the above passage the philologist, in order to complete his task, must be a lover of the word. He must take his cue from the word, and above all be a bearer of and doer through the word.

The interpretation of the Johannine Logos may be the last goal of that true philology which honors the secret of the Spirit and his revelation in the Word, something of which mere readers of the dead letter who are philologists for the sake of having a job, who have not been called by the Word and are incapable of becoming "hearers of the Word," naturally know nothing.[35]

For Ebner, both human speech as well as human reason (*Vernunft*) are affected and embraced by the word.

The logos of the Johannine Gospel is . . . not the logos of the philosophers, which is an object and a monster of metaphysical speculation, but it is literally the Word, the object of faith, the Word in its true spiritual actuality. *Logos* means discourse, Word, but also reason; it means both because in the Word is reason, and Word is in reason. Reason is the inward sense of man for the Word, it is that in him which advances toward the Word and its meaning, as the living eye advances toward the light.[36]

In light of the above statement, it would be unfair to describe Ebner's regard for the potentially sacred quality of human speech as a purely emotive one devoid of rational content or consideration. Rather, it is a matter of priority, of a relationship wherein human reason has no direction, unless it first listens to the Word which is mediated through speaking and hearing creatures. Ebner continually defines the role of reason (*Vernunft*) as related to and dependent upon that perception which comes through hearing (*vernehmen*). Truth, meaning, and understanding are for Ebner relationally grounded and conditioned by our ability to perceive by hearing and listening—a trait which he suggests is denied to animals, having been reserved by God for those creatures created *imago Dei*, in His

Image. In the passage just quoted Ebner cited the story in Mark 7 where Jesus healed the deaf and dumb man after having touched his ears and tongue and, while looking up to heaven, proclaimed, *"Epheta!"* ("Be opened.")

> Epheta—that is the meaning of the Word of God which speaks to man. And it is the meaning of the word in general. The consciousness of the animal is closed for the word, as the ear of the deaf is closed for language.[37]

In sharp contrast to Buber's three spheres of speech which are permeated by the word, Ebner restricts the power of the word to human relationships. Although there can be genuine love and affection between an animal and his master, the animal's absence of the power to speak (in the human sense) limits the quality of the relationship.

> All things were made through the Word. . . . This proposition is the strongest and most comprehensive expression of faith in the Word. Only for man, not for the animal, can his origin in the "Word" become conscious, can it become the content of his consciousness through which it has a relationship toward a different being outside of itself—a relationship toward a higher being without which it would have to collapse into nothingness (Franz von Baader). Only man, not the animal, has the Word—because God is the object of man and only of man, not of the animal (Feuerbach). But God is man's "object," because man has the word—not as his own human invention, but from God.[38]

Both Ebner and Hamann are in agreement over the question of the divine origin of language. Similarly, each defends this position on grounds involving personal inner religious conviction as well as relying upon the authority of the Prologue to John's Gospel. So deep was their conviction on this matter that neither seemed interested in alternate theories about the origin of language except where a scholar—*e.g.*, Herder—offered arguments which either directly or indirectly challenged their convictions.

Only the objective word (*logos*) can free subjective man from the loneliness and solitude of his self-imposed Chinese wall of isolation, because the word to be perceived requires that men break through their isolation and become vehicles of the word—*i.e.*, allow themselves to be addressed and to respond as co-respondents in the Word. Ebner's frequent allusion to the fact that man has the word is similar to Heidegger's reference in *Being and Time* to Aristotle's definition of man as an "animal possessing speech." This makes sense providing one realizes that, for Ebner, a man can only have or possess the word as sacred personal speech if he himself is first possessed by the word. Having the word does not mean possessing it "in the solitude of consciousness, but rather in the mutuality of the I with the Thou."[39] In the same essay and in a Hamannian vein, Ebner suggests that the thinker overwhelmed by the power of the word might choose to express his thoughts in poetry rather than in terms of neat, well-organized philosophical systems.

In Biblical and Christian theological terms the Incarnational effect of the word is determinative of all spiritual existence. "The Word was and is the composition of all spiritual existence."[40] Prior to that he stated, "Creation through the Word was at the same time revelation, but revelation in the Word is creation, the potentiality and actuality of rebirth in the spirit."[41] Christ's words, his speech, like the Word of God, can best be appreciated in their spokenness, in their generative capacity for transforming life. The Word of God must change and transform lives, and through the speech of such regenerated souls, transform the very shape of reality. In this way the Kingdom of God is ushered in. In a tone resembling Professor Wilder's in *The Language of the Gospels*, Ebner discusses the word as revealing its meaning primarily in its spokenness.

If one places the word of Christ back into the personal actuality of its being spoken (by making oneself the person to whom it speaks immediately, whom it concerns personally—which is the way in which it wants to be taken, according to its essence and meaning), that is, if one understands it in its "generative" significance for the spiritual life of man (in the actuality of ideas it would have only "maieutic" significance), then the human-spiritual reality of Christ becomes visible.[42]

The Pauline paradox of being free by being a slave of Christ, which Luther adopts as the textual basis for his treatise *On Christian Liberty*, is analogous to Ebner's presentation of a man having the spirit, possessing the word, only if he be first possessed by, and subservient to, the Word.

In the Word is the grace, but also the freedom of spiritual life. Through the Word man comes of age before God. It was also Ludwig Feuerbach who saw in speaking an act of freedom; he said that the

Word itself is freedom. Before the Word, man is free—in the sense that he has the choice of choosing well or badly, the right or the wrong word. If he chooses well, then he stays within the freedom of the Word, that is in the freedom of the spirit. . . . But if he chooses badly, then his existence will succumb to the power of the wrong word.[43]

In effect, Ebner presents two conditions of man; in one the I is its own prisoner, in the other—in authentic spiritual existence—the I is the prisoner of the Thou. The latter is the true I, whose existence is relationally conditioned by the address and response of its alter ego in dialogue—*i.e.*, the objective divine Thou, the Word Incarnate. "The monological I is a misconception which shattered and had to shatter the entire I-philosophy. The I exists in dialogue."[44]

Ebner's preoccupation with the encounter between the divine Thou and the human I is due to his conviction that only through that particular encounter can the world and the rest of God's creatures become incorporated within the word and share its powers. In a Hasidic sense, man is the vehicle of the word, and through men's speech, the world as word is effected.

The world exists—if not for the animal, then at least for man— through the Word: not in the solitude of the I of human consciousness, but rather in the "relationship of the I to the Thou . . . whose expression and objective vehicle is the Word."[45]

So intense is the drama of creation through speech that all our relationships are inescapably affected by it. It accounts not only for the quality of our speech, but also provides a clue to the selective principle we employ when determining to what or whom we wish to address our concern, as well as how this can be accomplished. What one sees and how one views it is a reflection of one aspect of Ebner's pneumatological existence. The Word is the continuing objective referent that provides from both Hamann's and Ebner's perspective meaning and continuity, albeit many of our subjective situations might appear to contradict one another. The Word remained for both Ebner and Hamann the clue to the riddle inherent in the mystery and ambiguity of human actions. Within the context of the Word, terms like subjective and relative, when applied to human speech, are no longer terms to be distrusted because of their frailty and incompleteness. Rather, they enable us to discern the kind of objectivity which, under certain conditions, is permissible to us mortals.

Some Basic Problems in Ebner's Pneumatology

HAVING NOTED THE salient features of Ebner's pneumatology, a few remarks are in order about those areas where he appears to differ markedly from Hamann and Buber with respect to his regard for the spoken word. While there are passages in Ebner's writings which suggest that human speech is at least potentially sacred, his chief concern is primarily with Christ as the Word who dwells within us and enables us to speak and break through our self-imposed Chinese walls of solitude and speculation. This christological fascination includes a recurrent use of dualisms like eternity and time, and spirit and nature. His use of these dualisms in his christology give his writings a Platonic quality which makes one wonder whether in fact, human speech can ever, for Ebner, have that potentially sacramental quality which we've noted in the preceding chapters. Admittedly, Ebner has disavowed any Platonic influence in view of the centrality of the I-Thou personalist relational categories for his pneumatology. Time and again he notes the absence of these considerations as well as any genuine appreciation for the subjective realm in Platonic thought. At the same time a careful reading of Ebner's writings, particularly the *spiritual fragments*, the seven *Brenner* essays, and lastly, the eleven essays grouped under the heading *On the Problem of Speech and the Word*, suggests that Ebner's use of the I-Thou relationship between man and God plays a role parallel to Socrates' maieutic regard for dialogue in the Platonic dialogues.[46] In each instance the give-and-take between the persons involved is the means whereby men transcend their earthly condition and arrive at, or perceive, the highest reality—for Ebner, the Word; for Socrates, the eternal forms. In each instance, speech is an instrument for some kind of self-transcendence of mind or spirit rather than a means whereby reality and culture are given new shapes and meanings, as exists, for example, in a Johannine millenarian perspective. Put more simply, Ebner utilizes human speech more as a means for arriving at the nonhuman eternal Word (in an almost Barthian sense) than he regards human speech as a sacred vehicle for sanctifying time and history—for creating new times and a new sacred sense of history. His Johannine emphasis is more of an upward striving than it is an outward shaping of the reality about us. Except for terminology, the release of the I from its self-imposed finitude differs little from the manner whereby the individual in Plato's and Aristotle's writings is released from the chains of human finitude by the power of either Eros or Reason. (At least in Plato's and Aristotle's writings it is possible to have some kind of positive and creative relationship to the state.) Because of Ebner's other-worldly christological emphasis he shows little appreciation for the social implications of spirituality, except for frequent allusions to his utopian, ideal state. The crucial factor in this evaluation is whether indeed Ebner regards human speech as potentially sacred in and of itself. Can speech be more than simply a vehicle for obtaining that knowledge about salvation which only the eternal Word, Jesus the Christ, can provide? It would appear that Ebner does not have the same high regard for human language as one finds in the writings of those previously considered. In his *Brenner* essay "The Christ Question" Ebner distinguished sharply between the divine Word and human speech:

> Man has the true relationship to God in the Word: It consists in the "relationship of the I to the Thou," and the "objective vehicle" of this relationship is the Word. The Word is the Divine; language which man speaks because he "has the Word," and which also Christ has spoken, is something human.[47]

For Ebner, Christ the Word is the "provoker" of spirituality in men in much the same way that the infinite is present in the finite in much of Western Neo-Platonism. "The Word of Christ, in its personality and its faith-claiming actuality, wakens the spirituality in man from its slumber. . . . It provokes in man the knowledge of God."[48] Although Ebner insists that his own stress upon the significance of the divine Thou-human I relationship distinguishes his own position from those mystics for whom all human discourse belongs in the differentiated as against undifferentiated realm—*e.g.*, Dionysius the Aeropagite—the same upward movement of return and reunion is present in both styles. The fact that Ebner can converse with his God, whereas the mystic often cannot, is of little consequence when considered from the perspective of Ebner's apparent lack of genuine appreciation for the social and historical dimensions of human relationships. Where Ebner does refer to the spiritual dimension in human relationships, he does so very often at the expense of the *whole* man—e.g., the Spirit is sexually neutral. Whereas Hamann could sign his name "pan" and often employed sexual metaphors in describing spirituality, Ebner states emphatically in fragment 16 that the categories of I and Thou are, as in their grammatical forms, genderless. "The I and the Thou are, not only as pronouns, without a gender. If one substantivizes them linguistically, they are neuter."[49]

Ebner uses as proof for this assertion the fact that etymologically both the Gothic and Nordic words for God—*guth* and *gudh, godh,* are neutral. His conclusion is that: "The spiritual is neither man nor woman, is 'none of both,' neutrum."[50] This same theme is developed at considerable length in an earlier fragment (fragment 14) where Ebner asserts that the God that men addressed as well as those creatures whom He spoke to relied upon the direct and therefore nameless discourse of I and Thou.

The existential assertion of the "speaking person" of himself in the "original Word" was the self-naming of the I, although it did not yet mean a "name." . . . In the spirituality of his existence, in his immediate "personal" being, man is nameless. God originally was nameless for him (man) and only later was named with a substantive, but then, as the Being that is "called upon" as in the word "God," or as that Being toward which one points in calling, as in *deus.*[51]

For Ebner, sexuality has no place in spiritual existence; sexuality and the life in the Spirit are, in fact, polar opposites.

The more spiritual a man is, the more he suffers from his sexuality . . . as long as it has not yet been neutralized by the rebirth of his existence in the Spirit. The struggle between Spirit and sensuality is called by Swoboda the professional disease of the genius. But not only the genius suffers from it.[52]

In conjunction with this, Ebner asserts that names are associated with indirect discourse, with the third person, although this mode of discourse represents a departure, in his opinion, from authentic pneumatological discourse. In the light of previous remarks about the importance of names as against pronouns, formal as against informal discourse, it is apparent that both Buber and Ebner give the highest priority to direct, intensely personal forms of discourse. Direct discourse for Ebner is nameless discourse restricted to pronominal relationships and corresponds closely to Kierkegaard's use of maieutic or indirect discourse in his prereligious stage. Each evidently used opposite terms to describe the same kind of speech. In this context, remember also that names, rather than pronouns, embodied for Rosenstock-Huessy the key to the mystery of our multiform, multirole historical existence within a Johannine context. Recall also that Johannine, for Rosenstock-Huessy, can only be understood in conjunction with John's vision on Patmos, a vision whose ingredients will be revealed in terms of the successive ages of the Spirit. Note the sharp distinction in their respective interpretations of the meaning of Johannine, as well as especially Ebner's regard, or lack of, for both direct as well as indirect forms of grammatical discourse. Oddly enough, like Rosenstock-Huessy, Ebner's pneumatology is based on a spiritual grammar. In Ebner's essay "The Discovery of I and Thou" he not only suggests that his own efforts are a spiritual refinement upon Feuerbach's *Principles of Any Future Philosophy* but notes having read with indebtedness the work of a Viennese scholar, Adolf Stoker, *Algebra der Grammatik*, which appeared in 1898. The cleavage between Rosenstock-Huessy's and Ebner's grammatical approaches is not only decisive but reflects a consistent application of their grammatical approaches to the Johannine legacy. One explanation of their differences may be due to Rosenstock-Huessy's conviction that the Gospel of John must be read together with the John of Revelation. Many other differences in their writings could be accounted for simply by virtue of the fact that, as personalities, they are as unlike one another as day is to night. This should be apparent to anyone familiar on the one hand with Ebner's diaries and autobiographical observations, and on the other, not only with Rosenstock-Huessy's writings but with his outgoing robust constitution. If names do define our historical involvement as Rosenstock-Huessy asserts, then it is unfortunate that Ebner devotes so little attention to them. Not only are names a stumbling block to Ebner in his writings, but he never really resolved the question of his own identity—the meaning of his *name*.

NOTES

CHAPTER 6

1 John Cullberg, *Das Du und die Wirklichkeit* (Uppsala: Uppsala University, 1933), pp. 34–35.
2 Ferdinand Ebner, *Das Wort und die geistigen Realitäten: Pneumatologische Fragmente* (Innsbruck, 1921). All references to Ebner's writings are from the recently published (1963) three-volume edition edited by Franz Seyr. Cf. *Ferdinand Ebner: Schriften*, Herausgegeben von Franz Seyr (München: Kösel Verlag, 1963–64). Volume One: *Fragmente, Aufsätze, Aphorismen;* Volume Two: *Notizen, Tagebücher, Lebenserinnerungen;* Volume Three: *Briefe in Auswahl.*
3 Emil Brunner, *Truth as Encounter* (Philadelphia: Westminster, 1964), pp. 58–61. (Formerly entitled *The Divine-Human Encounter,* 1943.)
4 Emil Brunner, *Man in Revolt* (London: Lutterworth, 1947), p. 176.
5 *Ibid.,* pp. 23–24. In 1922, after reading Ebner's *Fragments,* Brunner sent Ebner a copy of his dissertation, "Erbebnis, Erkenntnis and Glaube," *Schriften,* Band II, p. 1094.
6 Maurice Friedman, *The Worlds of Existentialism* (New York: Random House, 1964), pp. 292–98.
7 Diary entries, January 6, 1917, and September 8, 1917.
8 Buber, *Die Schriften uber das dialogische Prinzip,* p. 292.
9 Ebner, *Schriften, II,* p. 1093.
10 *Ibid.,* II, p. 1096.
11 *Nachrichten* aus dem Kösel-Verlag, " 'Der Brenner'–Leben und Fortleben einer Zeitschrift," pp. 4–5.
12 Ebner, *Schriften,* II, p. 1115.
13 *Ibid.,* II, pp. 1121–24.
14 Ferdinand Ebner, *Wort und Liebe* (Regensburg: Friedrich Pustet, 1935). Hildegard Jone is also responsible for the appearance of Ebner's *Das Wort ist der Weg* (Vienna: Thomas-Morus, 1949).
15 Ebner, *Wort und Liebe,* p. 17.
16 Ebner, *Schriften,* I, p. 725.
17 *Ibid.*
18 *Ibid.*

19 *Ibid.,* p. 727.
20 Walter Lowrie, *Kierkegaard* (New York: Harper Torchbooks, 1962), Vol. II, p. 400.
21 Ebner, *Wort und Liebe,* p. 17.
22 Ebner, *Schriften,* II, pp. 1137–38.
23 *Ibid.,* III, p. 174.
24 The contents of every issue of *Der Brenner* are listed in the Kösel Press report referred to alone. (*Cf.* footnote 11.)
25 Walter Lowrie, " 'Existence' as Understood by Kierkegaard and/or Sartre," *The Sewanee Review* (July 1950), p. 5.
26 Søren Kierkegaard, *Concluding Unscientific Postscript* (Princeton: Princeton University Press, 1941), p. 84.
27 *Ibid.,* p. 74.
28 Søren Kierkegaard, *Johannes Climacus* (London: Adam & Charles Black, 1958), pp. 151–53. Reflection is the "possibility of relationship," while consciousness is the realization of relationship. Interest, from the Latin *interesse,* means "to be between" and "to be a matter of concern."
29 Ebner, *Schriften,* I, p. 81 ff.
30 Theodor Steinbüchel, *Der Umbruch des Denkens* (Regensburg: Friedrich Pustet, 1936).
31 Ebner, *Schriften,* I, p. 955.
32 *Ibid.,* pp. 650–54; pp. 402–32.
33 Ebner, *Wort und Liebe,* p. 288.
34 Ebner, *Schriften,* I, p. 952.
35 *Ibid.,* pp. 647–48.
36 *Ibid.,* p. 417.
37 *Ibid.,* pp. 417–18.
38 *Ibid.,* p. 681.
39 *Ibid.,* p. 648.
40 *Ibid.,* p. 653.
41 *Ibid.*
42 *Ibid.,* p. 460.
43 *Ibid.,* p. 655.
44 *Ibid.,* p. 648.
45 *Ibid.,* p. 680.
46 *Ibid.,* pp. 75–342; 381–642; 643–718.
47 *Ibid.,* p. 478.
48 *Ibid.,* p. 285.
49 *Ibid.*
50 *Ibid.*
51 *Ibid.,* pp. 254–55.
52 *Ibid.,* p. 285.

Evaluation, Interpretation, and Epilogue

> Rejoice: we who were born
> congenitally deaf are able to listen now to
> rank outsiders . . . since this morning
> it is with a vocabulary
> made wholesomely profane
>   That we endeavor
> each in his idiom to express the true magnolia.
>
> —W. H. Auden

Adlai Ewing Stevenson. Nationality—American; citizenship—the world. This is a portrait of a statesman—a man who demonstrated that language and the spoken word are powers in and of themselves . . . a man whose overwhelming moral force has played an important role in the shaping of domestic politics and international diplomacy.

> —Bill Scott, narrator—
> L.P. record,
> Adlai E. Stevenson

Language as the technology of human extension . . . may have been the "Tower of Babel" by which men sought to scale the highest heavens. Today computers hold out the promise of a means of instant translation of any code or language into any other code or language. The computer . . . promises by technology a Pentecostal condition of universal understanding and unity. The next logical step would seem to be, not to translate, but to by-pass languages in favor of a general cosmic consciousness . . . like the collective unconscious dreamt of by Bergson.

> —Marshall McLuhan

I believe that in the future, Church and Creed can be given a new lease on life only by services that are nameless and incognito. . . . In the third epoch, beginning today, Christians must immigrate *into* our workaday world, there to incarnate the spirit in unpredicatable forms . . . *each generation has to act differently precisely in order to represent the same thing.*

> —Eugen Rosenstock-Huessy

The Method: We are Polyphonic Creatures Requiring Binocular Vision

ATTEMPTS TO EVALUATE the preceding chapters involve a number of considerations. What is stressed as well as what is entirely omitted in such a discussion should betray the author's prejudices—the particular prescription of the eyeglasses used—in the evaluation. Therefore at the outset it would be useful to suggest to the reader one or two of the guidelines to be followed. First, an attempt will be made to indicate the merits and usefulness of the material just presented. Inevitably, this will suggest the limitations of these insights depending upon the kinds of questions and problems which each devoted his energies to. Second, it is assumed that there is merit to a consideration of these writings, but that this depends in large part not only upon one's estimate of the validity of the question which one tries to answer, but also upon one's estimate of the adequacy of the answer. Question, answer, and evaluation imply certain subjective factors which the reader will and should obviously feel free to accept, reject, or modify in terms of his own situation. Third, such an approach implies a multileveled evaluation in view of the variety of considerations and perspectives involved. This applies not only to their respective merits and limitations viewed from the perspective of the problems they faced during their own lifetimes, but also from the standpoint of the relevance of their insights to present as well as anticipated future needs and questions.

Thus, on one level a study and evaluation of this kind can be of interest to students of intellectual and cultural history as well as to those in the fields of theology, philosophy of religion, and hermeneutics. On another level those concerned with interpersonal relationships and problems of communication might gain something from this material. It may well be that in a computer and electronically oriented age the word, speech, and the Spirit can share in the fashioning of a society which fifty or even fifteen years ago few men in these disciplines could have anticipated or envisioned. The emphasis in the preceding chapters upon the potential sacredness of human speech set against a Johannine background may well signify the possibility of a new creative partnership among physical and social scientists, humanists, communications specialists, and students of religion. Perhaps men will once again realize that no man can totally divorce and isolate the spiritual or the sacred from human concerns. If man is the polyphonic creature which much of the preceding material suggests, then he must begin to focus his interest upon the harmony and integration of his multiform unity rather than upon any single role or style. Gradually, he may develop an ear for the appropriate tune and style a particular occasion requires of him. Naturally, this insight ought not be limited exclusively to those whose writings we have just discussed. While their writings may be of particular concern for theologians interested in hermeneutics and communication, certainly others have contributed significantly to an understanding of man as a linguistically polyphonic creature. The writings of Paul Tillich and Ernst Cassirer, for example, have stressed the importance of appreciating man's complexity, richness, and unity from a wide variety of approaches. Each, in his own idiom, has devoted considerable attention not only to language as a method of understanding man, but also as a force and energy which can shape reality. In 1939 Paul Tillich, for example, touched upon man's multiform nature in a discussion of the existentialist view of man. Though his emphasis is upon methodology rather than speech *per se*, the reader can easily see the connection between method and speech, since the former consists essentially of a particular linguistic style. Tillich wrote that:

Man is a unity and a totality. Therefore it is inadequate to develop several doctrines of man, a scientific and a philosophical one, a secular and a religious one, a psychological and a sociological one. Man is an indivisible unity. All the methods contribute to one and the same picture of man. There are, however, many elements and strata in human nature; and each of them demands a special approach—a special method. The unity of man does not imply that it is possible to examine him in one way only. Since man includes all elements of reality, every stratum of being, it is necessary to use all methods in order to deal with him adequately. He is the microcosmos, the description of which should not neglect any tool used in the description of the macrocosmos. Therefore it is wrong to make *one* method of approaching man the only one or to subordinate all other methods to one single approach, whether the theological method in early times or the empirical method today. On the other hand, we must avoid any atomism of methods. It must be shown that in each method elements appear which drive to the others; that the empirical approach cannot be used without elements discovered by the rationalistic method; and that this in turn presupposes certain elements furnished by theology. The methods of studying human nature should be neither exclusive nor merely atomistic and summative, but dialectical and mutually interdependent.[1]

Like Cassirer, Tillich focused more upon the symbolic qualities of language than have our speech thinkers. In an essay, "The Nature of Religious Language," Tillich spoke of words, which are "not only signs pointing to a meaning which is defined, but also symbols standing for a reality in the power of which they participate." Later on he referred to the fact that a symbol "opens up a level of reality for which nonsymbolic speaking is inadequate." Unlike signs, symbols "are born and die." The womb out of which symbols are born, according to Tillich, is the "group" or "collective unconscious."[2] More than our *speech-thinkers*, Tillich deals with language in psychoanalytic terms. He also emphasizes, more than does Buber, for example, the significance of narrational language as a creative cultural shaping force. However, unlike Rosenstock-Huessy and even Franz Rosenzweig, Tillich prefers terms like culture and eternity to time, timing, and history.

In his *An Essay on Man*, Ernst Cassirer stressed the importance of men's need for binocular vision. He wrote that "the depth of human experience . . . depends on the fact that we are able to vary our modes of seeing, that we can alternate our views of reality." He concluded this passage with the admonition that "It is characteristic of the nature of man that he is not limited to one specific and single approach to reality but can choose his point of view and so pass from one aspect of things to another."[3] Some will argue that vision and seeing as used here are distinct from speech and language. And yet was it not Hamann who coined the phrase, "Speak that I may see thee!" In *Being and Time* Heidegger made a similar link between speech and vision when he defined logos as discourse: "To make manifest what one is 'talking about' in one's discourse . . . the *logos* lets something be seen."[4] In the work just alluded to, Cassirer's development of his binocular vision theory is based upon the phenomenon of language—upon the fact that "In this human world . . . speech occupies a central place." He said that it is necessary to "understand what speech means in order to understand the 'meaning' of the universe." He warned that "If we fail to find this approach—the approach through the medium of language rather than through physical phenomena—we miss the gateway to philosophy."[5]

Buber, Ebner, and Kierkegaard

THE FIRST PART of this discussion considers differences in emphasis noted in the writings of those figures treated earlier. It will begin with a discussion of certain contrasts between Buber's and Ebner's use of personalist I-Thou terminology. One important aspect of this evaluation is devoted to an attempt to indicate not only the merits but the limits of personalist pronominal discourse as found, for example, in Martin Buber's writings. While I-Thou terminology may be well suited in the realm of interhuman relations, it is suggested that more formal types of discourse are necessary when dealing with the complexities inherent in more impersonal contexts. It is hoped that the exchange between Buber and Rosenstock-Huessy on this subject will not only clarify their differences, but will help one appreciate the kinds of situations to which each approach can address itself most meaningfully.

We have already noted certain similarities with respect to Martin Buber's and Ferdinand Ebner's use of personalist I-Thou terminology. It was suggested that Ebner's preoccupation with the intensely personal relationship between the divine Thou and the human I, between Jesus as the Divine Word and the frail creature's I, distinguished his orientation sharply from Martin Buber's. Though both spent their lives in pursuit of the Holy, Buber more often than Ebner was able to satisfy his quest by discovering the Holy in the realm of the there-in-between man and man. By contrast, Ebner's life was one spent in a seeming unrequited love for the Divine Thou. It was suggested that Ebner, unlike Buber, tended to rest his case in behalf of his own identity and life's meaning upon the degree to which Ebner found solace and direction in the Divine Word. The evidence suggests that Ebner felt unfulfilled in this quest and that as a consequence he derived little sense of fulfillment and joy during his lifetime. In many respects Ebner's life, even during his religious phase, parallels closely the futility and despair which Kierkegaard experi-

enced prior to his conversion to Christianity in 1848. Like Kierkegaard, Ebner was afflicted with a deep melancholia and sense of
despair which he never relinquished. Similarly, Ebner clung
throughout his life to maieutic or indirect discourse, which marked
the style of Kierkegaard's pseudonymous writings prior to Easter of
1848. We noted in the last chapter that Kierkegaard regarded his
maieutic or indirect style as that which best expressed the soul's
inward encounter with truth. However, unlike Kierkegaard, Ebner
not only adopted Kierkegaard's indirect style, but looked upon it as
the appropriate direct style for a believing Christian. Quite apart
from whether Kierkegaard, as he contended, ever really gave up his
preoccupation with his own despair and confession of sin after he
became a Christian, certainly Ebner could never have made a similar
claim. It should be added, however, that Ebner differed from
Kierkegaard decisively to the extent that the former never experienced a speculative or philosophical stage in his development. In this
respect Ebner's spiritual pilgrimage was more akin to that of Paul
and Luther, inasmuch as each underwent a period of *Anfechtung,* of
temptation, searching, and inward turmoil. In Luther's sense,
Ebner's life was a wrestling *coram deo*—in the presence of God.
When Kierkegaard employed the terms maieutic and indirect it was
during a stage wherein he regarded the self as the "merely human
self" as against "the theological self, the self in direct relation to
God."[6] The absence of this parallel in Ebner's development limits
the comparisons between Ebner and Kierkegaard, with respect to
terminology as well as style. Nevertheless, there exists a striking
similarity between them insofar as it affects the style which each
finally adopted as a convicted Christian, as a religious individual. I
refer here to both Kierkegaard's and Ebner's preoccupation with
the Divine at the expense of the Human Thou. Previous references to
Ebner's views on this subject might well be compared with Kierkegaard's remarks in one of his first religious essays, *The Lilies of the
Field* (1848). Note the preoccupation in this essay with first seeking
"God's Kingdom," apparently at the expense of one's concern for
the discovery of the Spirit in one's dealing with the Human Thou
over against the Human I.

   As was noted earlier in the chapter on Buber, it was precisely this
christological emphasis which distinguished Kierkegaard most significantly from Buber and, at the same time, placed Ebner more in

Kierkegaard's company than Buber's, despite both Buber's and Ebner's use of personalist I-Thou terminology. Note also in this essay Kierkegaard's stress upon *silence* and *dread* rather than talk and conversation when encountering God. Kierkegaard said that when a man prays to God he soon realizes that the more intense his desire to speak with Him the more silent he becomes. Man's desire to speak to God in prayer results in his becoming a Silent Hearer. Not speaking, but hearing, is for Kierkegaard the soul's proper relationship with God. Hearing is par excellence man's proper posture before God. Martin Heidegger developed this Kierkegaardian emphasis in his discussion of sacrifice and the place of traditional religious language when he said that "in sacrifice there is expressed that hidden *thanking* . . ." which is likened to an echo. "This echo is man's answer to the Word of the soundless voice of Being. The speechless answer of his thanking through sacrifice is the source of the human word, which is the prime source of language as the enunciation of the Word in words."[7] While some students of the life of dialogue and speech thinking may be dismayed by this emphasis upon silence and hearing when in the presence of God, others may well appreciate the importance of hearing—as a part of the openness and surrender necessary in any authentic encounter. Franz Rosenzweig, like Buber, was sensitive to this phenomenon and discussed the relationship between eternity and silence in his *Star of Redemption*. He said that:

> In eternity the spoken word fades away into the silence of perfect togetherness—for union occurs in silence only: the word unites, but those who are united fall silent. And so liturgy, the reflector which focuses the sunbeams of eternity in the small circle of the year, must introduce man to this silence.[8]

However, even here, Rosenzweig, the *speech-thinker*, saw fit to qualify this emphasis upon silence by adding that ". . . even in liturgy, shared silence can come only at the end. . . . In the stage of preparation the word still dominates the scene." Rosenzweig emphasized the fact that the "word itself must take man to the point of learning how to share silence." Man's ". . . preparation begins with learning to hear."[9] In the following rather lengthy passage from Kierkegaard's *The Lilies of the Field*, note not only the priority placed upon first seeking "God's kingdom," but also the similarities between Kierkegaard's and Rosenzweig's respect for *hearing* in God's presence.

For no doubt it is speech which distinguishes man from the beast, and hence, if one so will, distinguishes him very far from the lily. But because it is an advantage to be able to speak, it does not follow that to be able to keep silent is no art or that this is a humble art. On the contrary, just because a man is able to speak, it is an art to be able to keep silent; and just because this advantage of man so readily tempts him, it is a great art to be able to keep silent. But this we can learn from the silent teachers, the lilies and the birds.

"Seek ye first God's kingdom and his righteousness."

But what does this mean, what have I to do, or what sort of effort is it that can be said to seek or pursue the kingdom of God? Shall I try to get a job suitable to my talents and powers in order to exert an influence thereby? No, thou shalt first seek God's kingdom. Shall I then go out to proclaim this teaching in the world? No, thou shalt first seek God's kingdom. But then in a certain sense it is nothing I shall do. Yes, certainly, it is in a certain sense nothing; thou shalt in the deepest sense make thyself nothing, become nothing before God, learn to keep silent. In this silence is the beginning, which is, first to seek God's kingdom. . . .

It is man's superiority over the beast to be able to speak; but in relation to God it can easily become the ruin of man who is able to speak that he is too willing to speak. God is in heaven, man upon earth—therefore they cannot well talk together. . . . Only in much fear and trembling can a man talk with God; in much fear and trembling. But to talk in much fear and trembling is difficult for a further reason; for as a sense of dread causes the bodily voice to fail, so also does much fear and trembling render speech mute in silence. This the true man of prayer knows well, and he who was not the true man of prayer perhaps learned just this by praying. There was something that lay so close to his heart, a matter of such consequence to him, it was so important that he should make God understand him, he was afraid that in his prayer he might forget something.

Ah, and if he had forgotten it, he was afraid God might not of Himself remember it—therefore he would collect himself to pray right earnestly. And what happened then?—in case he did indeed pray right earnestly. The surprising happened to him. In proportion as he became more and more earnest in prayer he had less and less to say, and in the end he became quite silent. He became silent—indeed, what is if possible still more expressly the opposite of speaking, he became a hearer. He had supposed that to pray is to speak; he learnt that to pray is not merely to be silent but to hear. And so it is: to pray is not to hear oneself speak, but it is to be silent, and to remain silently waiting until one hears God speak.[10]

So intense was Ebner's and Kierkegaard's preoccupation with the christological relationship and its appropriate tone and style that neither was capable of ever fulfilling with the same intensity the second love commandment which figures so prominently in Buber's writings—*i.e.*, "And thou shall love thy neighbor as thyself." While it is true that in Ebner's and Kierkegaard's writings there is both implicitly and explicitly a social ethic, this, nevertheless, remained an undeveloped aspect in their own lives. In the above passage, the task of first seeking "God's kingdom" not only turned out to be Kierkegaard's all-consuming task in life, but implicit in his articulation of this mission was the assumption that this task is clearly distinguishable from the imperative to help the poor and proclaim the Gospel. Unlike our other *speech-thinkers*, both Ebner and Kierkegaard maintained, in effect, a sharp separation between the religious and the human social dimensions of life.

To point out that each at least had a social ethic, fulfilled or not, really doesn't help very much at this juncture. For each, the soul struggling in its own inwardness, driven by an all-consuming passion for honesty, established the tone for life's journey. They were incapable of breaking this pattern, and as a result, a major dimension of creative social discourse was denied them. Except in theory each lacked the Johannine or Hasidic concern for the potentially sacred character of the social dimension of life which marks the writings of, for example, Hamann, Rosenstock-Huessy, and Martin Buber. Unlike Ebner, Buber's writings indicate that there is no specifically Holy as against *profane* realm. The holy can be encountered in whatever situation or relationship man happens to be involved in while engaged in any one of the three thresholds of speech in which man may discover the Holy through that which is over against him. Buber, much more than any of those whose writings have been discussed, stressed the importance of those forms of address which men encounter in nature, through animals and objects, as well as through that which addresses us from beyond the human threshold. Thus, the mystery and sacredness of the entire Creation was one of Buber's lifelong preoccupations. The fact that Buber was a Jew, that Jews are a Holy People for whom all of life is sacred, made it

undoubtedly easier for Buber than it could have been for Ebner to
arrive at his sacramental view of reality. By contrast, Ebner, like
many Christians throughout history, emphasized spiritual conversion with its related notion of the *old* and the *new* man—he who has
"died" and is "born again in Christ." This emphasis in Christianity
upon death and rebirth, upon being *in*, yet not *of* the world, makes
it much more difficult for many Christians to have the kind of
sacramental outlook which one discerns in Buber's writings. Those,
like Ebner and Kierkegaard, who stand in the Pauline tradition
would find Buber's position much more difficult than would those
Christians who identify Christianity with the Incarnational elements
so common to the Johannine tradition. Perhaps this is due to differences of interpretation in Pauline and Johannine Christianity about
the nature of eternal life. You will recall, for example, that the
Gospel of John begins, rather than climaxes, with the fact of the
Resurrection and all its consequences upon human life. Many heirs
of the Johannine tradition assumed that this meant that all men born
subsequent to this event were born into a new milieu, into a world
wherein every thing and person were invested with the effects of
the fullness of the Resurrection and the Holy Spirit. Whether or
not this belief was due to an appropriation of Greek notions of the
immortality of the soul by many of the early Church Fathers does
not concern us here. The fact is that somehow there developed in
Christianity a split between those who were subsequently recognized as the heirs of Paul and those of John. With respect to this
division, Ebner's sympathies undoubtedly were more Pauline than
Johannine. The effect of Ebner's preoccupation with personalist
I-Thou terminology was to personalize and intensify the encounter
between the single man as sinner and Christ as his Redeemer. Thus,
Ebner's personalism falls far short of affecting every realm of life, as
is the case among Johannine Christians or those Jews who regard
Buber's sacramentalism or other forms of Jewish messianism as a
valid rendering of the nature and scope of Jewish spirituality.
Among Christian theologians, Paul Tillich came closest perhaps in
his discussion of eternal life to bridging the gap between tran-
scendentalism and immanentism. Though he infrequently employed
the personalist I-Thou style and was generally unsympathetic with
the approaches of the men being discussed, his blending of elements
from Schelling with New Testament Incarnational themes is worth
noting at this juncture. In the third volume of his *Systematic The-*

ology Tillich elaborated upon his statement that "The Christian emphasis on the 'body of the resurrection' . . . includes a strong affirmation of the eternal significance of the individual person's uniqueness." He said that

> . . . The world process means something for God. He is not a separated, self-sufficient entity who, driven by a whim, creates what he wants and saves whom he wants. Rather, the eternal act of creation is driven by a love which finds fulfillment only through the other one, who has the freedom to reject and to accept love. . . . The eternal dimension of what happens in the universe is the Divine Life itself. It is the content of the divine blessedness. . . .
>
> Participation in the eternal is not given to the separated individual. It is given to him in unity with all others, with mankind, with everything living, with everything that has being. . . . We do not hope for ourselves alone, nor for those alone who share our hope. . . . Certainly it would be a poor and selfish hope.[11]

In contrast to both Ebner and Kierkegaard, Tillich's writings provided a theological climate wherein the individual can not only develop his personal freedom and identity, but also have a sense of participation in the collective and cosmic spiritual forces which permeate all that is real and humanly meaningful. Certainly many individuals, nonbelievers as well as believers, have been spoken to by Tillich's writings with a force and impact equal, for example, to that of Buber. In view of earlier forecasts by Rosenzweig and Rosenstock-Huessy about the religious character of the third millennium—*i.e.*, the Age of the Spirit—it is quite significant that they and also Buber and Tillich have found as large, if not greater, audience for their writings outside of the mainstream of traditional religious orthodoxy. All of these men have indeed struck a chord which many today seem anxious to hear but find lacking in traditional religious confessionalism.

Martin Buber and Eugen Rosenstock-Huessy

THUS FAR OUR discussion has focused upon contrasts and comparisons on the one hand between Ebner and Kierkegaard and on the other between Buber and Ebner. Let us turn now to a consideration of Buber's dialogical principles and examine those areas where they are capable of application and also those where an extension of Buber's principles raises serious problems. As was noted earlier in the remarks by Buber and Rosenzweig about Jewish law and tradition, it was evident that Buber emphasizes the importance of presentness and the realm of the between as the point where eternity, history, and tradition manifest themselves. The ontological presence, the word which is revealed in I-Thou encounters, in the realm of the there-in-between creature and creature, is the arena in which God's fate is decided. Each encounter is an opportunity for men to exercise their freedom and sanctify the world and thereby glorify God or else to turn away from Him and impede the process of sanctification. The dynamics of this process take place within a markedly personalist milieu with pronominal discourse serving as midwife for the Spirit's entry. Some adherents of Buber's life of dialogue have attempted to emphasize the sovereignty and applicability of this approach in practically every conceivable situation, whether two persons or even two nations are involved. Many have criticized the extension of this personalist pronominal approach when dealing with political and national problems. Related to this is the concern of many that Buber's naïveté on this point is due precisely to the fact that he really doesn't take history and tradition seriously—that what he refers to as the presence of history and tradition when the present is manifest reflects more his earlier Jewish messianic mysticism than anything else. This issue came up, in one form, in an exchange initiated by Maurice Friedman between Buber and Rosenstock-Huessy about ten years ago. In their remarks their differences are sharply stated and raise for the reader the kinds of concerns which are suitable when evaluating Buber's contributions. It is evident from their remarks that Buber apparently does not accord to history and time the prominence which they receive in Rosenstock-Huessy's writings. Despite their respective high regard for the sacramental character of speech, the chasm which divides them is indeed a deep and wide one. Rosenstock-Huessy began by asserting that the "real gulf or gap" between their respective ways of thinking lay in their "approach to the historicity of man," which is intimately associated with their views on speech.[12] For Rosenstock-Huessy "any word spoken" has meaning "only if it testifies to the spiritual coexistence of three or *more* generations of men." To speak "means to live backward before one's own birth and forward beyond one's own death." Names are necessary because they not only establish a "time sequence" with these generations, but more importantly, they are our means of surviving "any physical destruction." Buber's thought, like his fascination with socialism, is single-aged, whereas Rosenstock-Huessy claims that his own is pluri-aged. He insisted that this was due to the fact that Buber does not take time, names, history, generations, and their calendars seriously. At the end of his attack Rosenstock-Huessy charged that

Buber . . . accepts the phenomenon of time in its reduction to an inarticulate, logically indefensible present. . . . Hence, our soil for speech differs fundamentally. Mine is at least three-dimensional in time; his is at best one-dimensional, but in truth *none*-dimensional.[13]

Rosenstock-Huessy cited Buber's preoccupation with pronouns to back up this charge. Rather than serving as "stand-ins" for nouns and proper names, he asserted that in Buber's thought they are omissions inasmuch as they omit names and the time spans, generations, and calendars which are an essential part of every name. Dialogical man, for Rosenstock-Huessy, is nothing but a fictitious abstraction, a creature divested of his historical innards. Man as an individual in Buber's writings is restricted to living off the sum total of his five senses. It is part of the "travesty of the democratic superstition" that the testimony and evidences of our senses are deemed sufficient and capable of holding a nation together. By contrast, Rosenstock-Huessy said that:

It is the power of a dynasty of generations—at least three or four—to pool their energies around one and the same experience. For instance, the Constitution of the United States of America is that incorporating tool through which that nation is made *at all* capable of registering certain domestic experiences over one hundred and fifty years.[14]

Again, note the sharpness of Rosenstock-Huessy's attack upon any presentation of authentic man which is not historically—*i.e.*, calendrically—name-oriented and name-conditioned. Natural man, for Rosenstock-Huessy, is the opposite of historical man. The former attempts to present man as an accomplished and self-contained individual irrespective of any consideration of those themes so central to Rosenstock-Huessy's grammatical and calendrical thinking.

Buber's placing I before Thou is another example of his single-aged thinking. As was noted in his grammatical thinking, Rosenstock-Huessy insisted that Thou is properly our first liturgical as well as our primary grammatical form. In support of these charges reflect upon the opening lines of *I and Thou:* "To man the world is twofold, in accordance with his twofold attitude"—*i.e.*, in accordance with the twofold nature of the primary words (I-Thou, I-It) which man speaks. Implicit in Rosenstock-Huessy's attack on Buber's dialogical approach is his insistence that history and the universe determine who we are just as much as we affect them. The Thous of the past, of history and tradition, as well as the Thous of the present, are determinative of the I's content and context, for the I's responses. He would probably have asked of Buber, "Just *how much* of the world can and do we actually shape through the utterance and realization of these primary words, even where a genuine meeting and authentic presentness occurs?"

With the exception of Part Three of *I and Thou*, Buber prefers the term "world" to "history." The worlds about us and the encounters which take place within them are the realms which concern Buber. Such encounters undoubtedly are ontologically effective when viewed from the perspectives of individuals and small communities. Are such encounters effective, however, in changing the larger social reality within which numerous individuals and small communities exist? Can the personalist language of Buber's life of dialogue, which works so well on one level, be equally effective at other levels? In other words, from the perspective of our larger social problems, can Buber's life of dialogue be anything more than an opiate which makes the vicissitudes of life more bearable? Ought not one distinguish perhaps between our little worlds, our spheres of being, influence, and contact, and the larger world of national, social, and political ambiguities and configurations which remains untouched and unscathed by the life of dialogue?

In his evaluation of Buber's thought Paul Tillich suggested that Buber's Jewishness is most apparent in his preoccupation with communities, which is a reflection of Buber's religious socialism. In accepting the socialist "criticism of bourgeois society" Buber also accepted "Marx's doctrine of the self-estrangement of man in modern capitalism, his becoming a 'thing,' a quantitatively calculable piece of working power."[15] Over against this, the living community where men could be treated as Thous was both a refuge and a point of departure for the realization of the final messianic community. Tillich asks whether this approach, this preoccupation with spiritual communities, is sufficient. His answer is negative:

It leaves the state, the political power, almost completely to the "demons," to an absolutized I-It relationship. Such a surrender is not warranted. Even the state has potentialities for an "I-Thou" relationship. It can be considered as one of those spiritual forms which for Buber belong to the third type of "I-Thou" relation. And there is no reason why this should not be so, if everything created is included in the divine and can be consecrated. . . . History . . . seems to show that without the shell of a state, a community cannot exist.[16]

Though a close friend and long admirer of Buber, Reinhold Niebuhr's criticism of Buber raised similar questions. In a review in the New York *Times* on March 23, 1958, Niebuhr wrote:

One has the feeling that the ambiguities of politics are quite inscrutable to Buber, though he confesses to some awareness of them in an "eschatological" passage when he says, "Only in the *polis* of God will religion and politics be blended into the life of world community in an eternity in which religion or politics will no longer exist. . . ." That is a valid insight, which savours a little of the old mysticism. In any case it can only be relevant to political judgments in a negative way, but Buber insists on trying to make the religious vision of a "whole man" living in a "redeemed community" directly relevant. It cannot be done in that way, but Buber makes some interesting abortive attempts. A philosophy which gives us the most illuminating insights into personal, or "I-Thou" relations, seems utopian when considering the relations of the "we" and "they," particularly when we and they are organized groups or nations.

For Niebuhr, the realities of social and political discourse require that we accept the fact that for a variety of reasons, the large masses of people in society will never be able to meet one another as persons with the kind of mutuality and self-giving which are so essential to Buber's life of dialogue. Hence Niebuhr's preference for directly affecting the main political and social organs in society, for passing legislation necessary for providing the best possible climate for us frail social creatures to develop in. For Neibuhr, no amount of personal commitment, without direct involvement in the impersonal political order, is able to create a truly human and viable social order.

In the case, for example, of Selma and the voter registration movement in the South, personal self-giving, commitment, and dedication were essential for the passage of the voter registration act. But without that act of Congress no amount of dialogue would ever have created for the Negro the possibility of becoming a first-class citizen in this nation. In the ordinary course of daily existence across the nation it is exceedingly doubtful that dialogue alone, without social legislation, could seriously affect our nation's progress and the realization of its highest ideals and goals. The premises behind a personalist as well as any love ethic—*i.e.*, sacrifice, trust, and responsibility for the other—for a Thou—are useful in creating a climate of rhetorical concern about the need for social change. Such approaches are utopian, however, when they assume that they are sufficient for social unity apart from the enactment of social legislation.

Put another way, isn't it true that quite often our fascination with the life of dialogue and its personalist qualities may be due precisely to the existence of another, larger world or reality essentially impersonal and life-and-speech-stifling which forces us to seek refuge in the personal—*i.e.*, in sacred moments of presentness? In addition to the worlds created by I-Thou and I-It encounters, there often remain still other worlds which frequently remain unaffected by personalist approaches. Rosenstock-Huessy argues that it is this larger speech-conditioned, calendar-shaped historical world which is the real world. Not merely our personal worlds, but the person insofar as it partakes in the shaping of mankind's destiny is Rosenstock-Huessy's concern. It must be remembered that for Rosenstock-Huessy, speech is meaningful only to the extent that it is directed toward the "creation and preservation of a truly human society." His thoughts and speech interests, unlike Buber's, are society-rather than community-oriented.

However, Buber scholars like Maurice Friedman regard this kind of criticism as a kind of caricature of Buber's thought. The issue between Buber and Niebuhr is not from their perspective a question of the "political versus the personal," but rather one of "gradations" which must view the political, social, and personal as gradations or levels in the fabric of reality. It should be remembered, for example, that the Patmos circle, that small group of "co-speakers and listeners," was in fact, a small personal community within a larger impersonal culture. The Patmos group was an island set apart which gave its inhabitants time and nourishment for speaking to the social needs which its members faced. Without retreat centers such as these, it is doubtful whether Rosenstock-Huessy or any of his confreres would have been able to survive the speech dilemma encountered in society or in the world at large. It should further be remembered that large segments in Rosenstock-Huessy's own lifetime were devoted to creating small communities of cospeakers and listeners in Silesia, where he developed his "universities in the wilderness," which consisted of university students, factory workers, and farmers, as well as in his work-service centers at Camp William James before the Second World War and in Bavaria, at Hohenstein, after the war. The ethos in these experiments had, however, an explicitly social focus, which one finds frequently only incidental to Buber's life of dialogue.

For men like Tillich and many others, the criticisms of Buber's personalist emphasis upon community rather than society, culture, and history reflect a basic difference between a Jewish and Christian orientation. There have been many other Protestant Christians, H. H. Farmer and Emil Brunner, for example, who had been much more appreciative of Buber's writings. Among Roman Catholic Christians there are many today who find in Buber's personalist I-Thou approach the only way of ultimately affecting a fundamentally impersonal technological society. The Jesuit scholar Walter J. Ong, for example, has devoted much of his energy to precisely this task. For Ong, speech in a Catholic setting is the pre-eminently personal means whereby men shall overcome their present preoccupation with mute quantifiable approaches when dealing with burning social questions. The catholicity in the Incarnation, for Ong, is such that one must proceed "through the whole"—through "the work of One to whose Person the auditory-oral notion of Word particularly belongs."[17] Cultural crises can be creatively overcome only when the parties involved recognize that the work of the Church and the Spirit takes place from one perspective, "by means of preaching—*fides exauditu*:" by means of a deep sharing of all man's time, which is cosmic, historical, personal, and redemptive. The Christian climate for Ong is always one "in the world but not of it." He must remain always "an outsider living from within."

Personal speech, for him, provides the essence and means of living in this dual capacity. For Ong, it is precisely this intensely personalist dialogical approach which contains the key to social unity. In *American Catholic Crossroads* he wrote:

> All communication, all dialogue, has this effect: It unites, and this despite the greatest difference there is, that between your person and mine, between you and me. But finally, dialogue must be between persons who are fully persons by being committed, by having taken a stand in the world of persons. Otherwise it will degenerate into the mere talk of a television commercial. *In the tension between personal commitment and love, not for humanity but for all individual men, the promise of a free society will best be realized.*[18]

In response to those charges leveled against him by Rosenstock-Huessy, Buber suggested that his adversary's preoccupation with "the historical nature of Man" embodied a way of thinking about reality which reflects an "epoch of thought beginning with Hegel and ending with Heidegger."[19] While it is important to recognize historical concreteness, and for this Buber admitted an indebtedness to Rosenstock-Huessy, it is misleading, said Buber, to exhibit historical concreteness as the "decisive reality in man." To do so, he added, would be to drink from the same cup which we have been drinking from for so long now that nothing remains for us but "the dregs." Granted "that memory and promise are mingled in language" and that they extend "beyond the birth and death of the speaker," Buber insisted that the "historical approach" still prevents us from glimpsing that which is most characteristically human—namely "the open mystery of the person," or what Gabriel Marcel calls the mystery of "human interiority" (though by that term Marcel emphasizes something quite different from Buber). Person, for Buber, refers to the underivable, to the uniquely human problematic element in man, to the "essential constitution of a single person." Though we were capable of "perfect historical knowledge," we could never explain what is meant by the words "essential constitution" which take into account the conviction of Jews that father, mother, and God partake in every child's origin as well as in the sounds and gestures which the child produces. Buber insists that those who gaze upon or address the child behold or partake in the mystery of the saying—in the unfolding of a human creature through speech. The "open mystery of the person" is revealed not in "what is said," in the "actually spoken word," but rather in "the saying," which "stands in the present, in the personal present that must at times let itself be represented in the said through the purely evocative word."[20]

Human existence, even the most silent, is speech; and speech, whether intentionally or unintentionally, directly or indirectly, along with gaining ground and forcibly penetrating, along with sucking and tasting, along with advancing over untried ways, is always address. What addresses you, not in the said but in the saying, is the underivable person, the now living new creature. The person becomes known in the I-Thou relation.[21]

With respect to his preference for pronouns, Buber stated that it is an "error" to assume that they are "stand-ins" for the name or proper noun. "They are neither here nor there; they stand only for the relation that cannot be expressed in any other way." Whereas the name and the pronoun "he," which represent one form of I-It language, are interchangeable, the Thou cannot for Buber be replaced without losing something of the presentness of address, of the saying and its link with the mystery implicit in a person's essential constitution. For Buber, names are indispensable but nevertheless "unsatisfactory symbols of personal uniqueness." In the act of saying and the relation which is established, that which shall be made known about a person is revealed. For Buber, there is no other way to this kind and degree of awareness of the other except within the realm of the interhuman established in an I-Thou relation. Buber dismisses Rosenstock-Huessy's reverence for the biographical significance of naming and the link established therein between two or more generations, as an Old Testament custom which is

already relinquished by the Gospels where the giving of the name is no longer an important biographical act and changes of name are no longer undertaken by God or the people, but by the person. . . . Next to my death there is place for no other aside from that of the man with whom I have exchanged the most genuine Thou of my life.[22]

In answer to the charge that his thought is single-aged, Buber stated that while this is not true about his thinking, it is true about his faith. Buber "believes in the hour" which occurs in the lives of individuals and the human race "where the historical bursts open and the present reveals itself." He, literally, believes in such moments of presentness because he knows that in such moments men are opened to one another and true community is established. He concluded his response to Rosenstock-Huessy's charges with the statement that his heart is with all those who "will summon with their lost strength the single-aged and all-aged present, the presence between men."[23]

Kant, Hegel, Buber, and Rosenstock-Huessy

IN SOME RESPECTS the differences between Buber and Rosenstock-Huessy are similar to those enunciated by Hegel in his attack on Kant, Fichte, and Jacobi in Hegel's *Faith and Knowledge*, written in 1802. Although Rosenstock-Huessy would disagree with Hegel's emphasis upon the rational character of *Geist* (Spirit or mind), he would strongly agree with Hegel's principal criticism of Kant's excessive preoccupation with individual man's powers to the exclusion of other important considerations. Anyone familiar with Buber's essay *What is Man?* knows of Buber's fascination with Kant's fourth question "What is Man?" as well as with his subsequent interest in dialogical anthropology. The fact that Buber's last concern was anthropology (despite his holding at one time the chair of sociology in Jerusalem) and Rosenstock-Huessy's lifetime concern with sociology and social philosophy bears upon this evaluation.

In *Faith and Knowledge* Hegel attacked Kant's excessive subjectivism. He said that Kant had withdrawn too far into the realm of the personal and the subjective while declaring at the same time that all absolute knowledge is relative to the understanding (*Verstand*). This relativism included time and space as well. Remember too, that for Kant as for Buber men are capable of living in two worlds or realms. For Kant they were the *noumenal*, the realm of free will, and the *phenomenal*, the world of determinism. Correspondingly, for Buber, "the world is twofold, in accordance with his twofold attitude," depending upon whether he "speaks" the "primary words" I-Thou or I-It. For Buber, man determines which of the realms or worlds he will live in at every moment in order to exist authentically. Especially in the first edition of *I and Thou* it was apparent that man's existence in an I-Thou relation was not conditioned by space and time, but by the presence which revealed itself in the realm of the there-in-between an I and a Thou. We have already noted, too, that Rosenstock-Huessy rejected Buber's dualistic categories. In terms of his own cross of reality they corresponded to the inner and outer of the spatial axis of his cross; or in Kant's terminology, to Kant's subject-object terminology. Rosenstock-Huessy insisted that in addition to these two dimensions the temporal axis (past and future) must be present to do justice to man's multiformity. Buber's I-Thou realm is for Rosenstock-Huessy little more than a world of mystical fantasy. For Hegel, Kant's transcendental world had the effect of making skeptics out of rational men. Thus, Hegel's remark that "Religion constructs its temple and altar in the heart of the individual" and is known through "sighing and prayer." For Hegel, the "beautiful subjectivity" of Protestantism carries within it two dangers. The first is that morality is made "relative to the rule of instinct"; the second, that subjectivity is made "absolute to the point of the deification of the self." Another difficulty which Hegel pointed out was that in Jacobi's philosophy, either "God is, and He is outside me, or I am God."[24] That there could be no third alternative caused Hegel considerable consternation. For Hegel transcendentalist philosophy was simply "a recasting of the dogmatism of being into the dogmatism of thought; the metaphysic of objectivity into the metaphysic of subjectivity."[25] What happened in Kant, and what Rosenstock-Huessy saw occurring in Buber was that human personality had become absolutized. Rosenstock-Huessy dismissed Buber's emphasis on the fact that the I exists only in relation on the grounds that Buber's point of departure throughout I and Thou and also in his essay "What is Man?" is always I rather than Thou. In Rosenstock-Huessy's writings, revelation and history constitute the matrix within which named persons exercising all their grammatical forms, Thou, I, and He, find meaning and direction in life. No single grammatical form can be viewed in isolation, either from a named person's other grammatical forms or apart from the biographical and historical factors which are represented in a person's grammatical existence.

In one sense Buber's view of sacred speech may be looked upon as a prolegomena to the kind of historically conditioned and concerned rhetoric which one gleans from Rosenstock-Huessy's writings. Many disciples of Buber might well consider this an injustice to the richness of his life and writings. I use the term prolegomena here against what, for me, amounts to a fundamental normative concern: namely, as Rosenstock-Huessy has put it, the creation and preservation of a truly human society. From a spiritual standpoint, the Johannine framework which permeates the thoughts of most of our *speech-thinkers* is offered as one vehicle for bringing this about, inasmuch as authentic speech and communication among all men are absolute conditions for any truly human society. The Johannine setting also implies that the quest and achievement of such a vision is pre-eminently a spiritual movement which embodies all of the tension, despair, frustration, and sacrifice which the faithful have traditionally associated with Jewish Messianism on the one hand and the realized eschatology of Christians on the other.

The suggestion that Buber's dialogical approach is a prolegomena to a more embracing view of sacred speech stems from the conviction that all too often the life of dialogue will make it possible for an individual to come into being as a person on one level without that person's recognizing that the we that is lived on other levels will require involvement in situations where the personalist and largely individualist emphasis upon meeting, mutuality, and encounter in the context of two real persons as I and Thou is either impossible or irrelevant. For example, it was always a rule of Buber's never to interfere in the life of another without the presentness of the meeting between two people evoking a mutual acknowledgment that the words which should be spoken from the heart are actually uttered. Very often, as was the case with a mutual close friend of ours, Buber refused to suggest a possible course of action for this friend, and preferred to view his role as a co-sufferer and co-listener until the moment should present itself when such words could be spoken in the context of full mutuality and understanding. As it happened, the moment never did present itself, and the words, which many wished our friend to hear at a meeting with Buber, remained unspoken. This is cited as one example of the way in which the life of dialogue was controlled for Buber by conditions which for most of us in our personal everyday life rarely present themselves. In terms, for example, of the civil rights movement throughout the nation, these are impossible conditions to expect. Nonviolence toward another in a civil rights setting does not mean, for example, that the words which must be sung and said depend, either for their being received or their effectiveness, upon those factors which surround the life of dialogue as presented by Buber. This is equally true for the teacher, clergyman, and analyst who on occasion are compelled out of necessity, concern, and love for the other to utter words which for the moment the other over against us either does not want to hear or perhaps even cannot understand. This quality, incidentally, marks the difference between the life of dialogue which I experienced on several occasions with Buber and the sharp exchange which accompanied, for example, the conversation between Rosenstock-Huessy and Rosenzweig on a July evening in 1913. At the same time it must be reiterated that Buber's life of dialogue has been for countless souls the vehicle for their own self-discovery as persons. To discover one's *I-ness* when addressed or listened to by a *Thou* has meant for many the discovery of the key to the mystery of life's meaning. I refer to this experience as a prolegomena in order to suggest that the times require our ability to advance to a stage beyond the strictly personal where speech grounded in sacred social and historical concern must take place although a Thou in Buber's sense may perhaps be lacking. Although Buber has used terms like "summon" in this context, the total effect of his thinking is to submit the act of calling and summoning to the presentness of the word and related conditions of mutuality which must accompany it. By contrast, the speech which others prefer has all the marks of Old Testament prophetic concern and the New Testament *kerygma*. In our day we might refer to this simply as concerned rhetoric which embraces both the spoken concern for the one over against us as well as the solitary or collective imperative directed at those individuals or forces having ears to hear, but who will not, or cannot listen. In the social arena, in the marketplace of concerned rhetoric, one seldom has the opportunity to be recognized as a Thou despite the fact that our entry into this arena often involves our preconditioning, our coming into being, as a person, as an I conscious of the power and effect of the word of speech. Thus, prolegomenatic speech—*i.e.*, Buber's life of dialogue—may serve as the gateway or arch through which one enters into the arena of concerned rhetoric —but nevertheless a gateway into an arena where the concerned rhetoric of individuals is associated with named persons rather than with Thous, Hes or I's. While the Rev. James Reeb may have functioned as a Thou in Selma, Alabama, among those clustered around Brown's Chapel on that fateful Tuesday in March of 1965, the effect of his person upon the course of the civil rights cause, upon history, can only be in terms of his being remembered not as a Thou but as the Rev. James Reeb, Unitarian minister from Boston, Massachusetts, who was attacked and subsequently died from injuries inflicted upon him on the streets of Selma, Alabama, by those opposed to the interference of "outsiders" supporting the Negroes' right to vote in Dallas County. Somehow we become conscious of the importance of our existence in an adult sense under conditions such as those where someone asks us, "You! What's your name?" History is filled with accounts of men who have known one another on an I-Thou basis until their true identities, their names, have been revealed to one another. Similarly, we know of the countless instances where our being accepted as a Thou has had the effect of suspending the deserved sentence which a name has earned. When this occurs, it happens as a reprieve, a miracle, something extraordinary. In the ordinary life of men the most serious and meaningful speech is that which takes place where our name is often at stake. This is the difference between the anonymous letter writer and the signed statement. Is it not significant that when we sense danger, when our real status as persons and creatures is threatened, that we often are faced with the decision which the apostle Peter faced—*i.e.*, whether to reveal one's name, one's true identity.

Though perhaps merely an Old Testament custom for Buber, names, rather than pronouns, decided the fate of six million Jews. The historical identity present in the name—*i.e.*, Israel—overcame all sympathy for the anguish and terror in the eyes and on the lips of those who pleaded to be treated as persons, as God's creatures. They were murdered simply because they were Jews. Though unpleasant and distasteful, the fact of the matter is that names under many circumstances are more important than pronouns. The refusal to recognize the Thou over against one, to condemn that individual to death simply because he was a Jew and had a number on his arm, was to treat him as an It—a thing. From Buber's standpoint, one basis for the crime against the Jews and humanity was that they were not treated as Thous, as God's creatures, but as Its—as objects, things. On the other hand, and from the standpoint of history and the existential crisis which each individual faced, it was the name that decided the personal fate of God's creatures. The *name* forces the issue. The announcement of the name is the key factor in such circumstances in determining initially how that person shall be received—whether as a Thou or as an It. From Buber's personalist dialogical perspective, he attempted and succeeded in a way rarely achieved by ordinary mortals to submerge the name in the person and to be open to all men as I to Thou. However, this is the rare exception rather than the rule, even among the most dedicated and devout religious believers.

In ordinary historical existence the name and the responsibilities of offices associated with the name have social and historical implications far beyond that individual's significance as a person. Real life as you and I experience it is a manifestation of the words, the statements, and the pronouncements of persons whose names are authoritative in a particular area or realm. In many instances the words and declarations uttered while in office—*i.e.*, in one's official capacity as President, Congressman, soldier, teacher, clergyman, analyst—betray greater integrity, authenticity, and a respected personal quality than those same persons betray in their personal, unofficial I-Thou relations with other persons. In such instances the measure of the man is discovered in his formal as against informal pronominal discourse. Very often an awareness of the historical and social responsibilities and implications of one's formal office and formal speech are sufficient to evoke (and often at a terrific price upon one's private life) qualities of greatness which otherwise might never be realized in an individual.

From Rosenstock-Huessy's perspective, rooted as it is in the cross of reality, the I-Thou, I-It options are utopian and too simplistic. The problematic element and "essential constitution," to use Buber's terminology, can best be appreciated by realizing that to be a person involves our speaking alternately in at least four different named capacities—*i.e.*, son, husband, father, teacher. Each role or office determines the norm and tone of discourse employed. Depending upon the timing, certain offices involve us directly, others indirectly, in the historymaking and history-shaping process. Thus, each office has its own canons and norms with respect to authenticity and appropriateness. Usually we are weak and frail in some and stronger in others. The name, however, is the bond which unites these various roles and provides the substance of our existence. Person and name in this context are interchangeable only to the extent that our personality—the various sounds we speak and roles we fulfill—is an expression of our named existence.

Once having experienced the miracle of the power of speech as a Thou and I, one must be directed to the more complicated level of named existence and all the vicissitudes which involvement in history on various levels and fronts entails. It is on the basis of named existence that we enter into the process of having our words shape our reality and also determine what shall be past for our children. Named existence as presented by Rosenstock-Huessy is the most viable means of discovering how speech is the vehicle for creating and preserving a truly human society. In the process of discovering this secret we simultaneously discover the meaning of sacred living through the power of the sacramental word.

The Prolegomenatic Character of Buber's Personalism

It is also true that Buber's dialogical approach has been appropriated by many who are directly involved in social issues and concerns. For such individuals it would be unfair, for example, to suggest that in the absence of a satisfactory answer to criticisms of the kinds raised by Rosenstock-Huessy, Paul Tillich, and Reinhold Niebuhr, that Buber's thinking has little, if any, social as against historical and political relevance. Mention need only be made of Buber's early involvement in Zionism, his correspondence with Ghandi, his position during the Eichmann trial, his correspondence with Bertrand Russell about world peace shortly before his death, together with many other instances of political activity. It is true that for the most part Buber's dialogical writings have appealed to an audience whose interests were personal to the extent that they reflected the nonpolitical, more spiritual, philosophical, and psychological concerns of sensitive individuals wrestling with affairs of the heart, soul, and spirit. While Buber's life of dialogue may not be of much help in those areas involving problems about international peace and understanding, integration, the war on poverty and disease, and the hard facts of political intrigue as they affect national and local leadership, nevertheless as a poet and man of faith deeply sensitive to the particular needs of individuals his contribution has been significant and indirectly has had considerable social relevance. His influence upon the mystical spirituality of the late Dag Hammarskjold is certainly an excellent case in point. It is precisely this quality of influence which confirms, in my opinion, my earlier characterization of Buber's contribution in the area of speech as prolegomenatic. All this is said quite apart from sophisticated discussions about his mysticism, his interpretation of Hasidism, his preoccupation with presentness and pronouns, or his attitude toward history and Judaism.

Few would deny, for example, that history and society are affected in a wide variety of ways and with varying intensities by people from every condition and social class. The effect of some is naturally greater than that of others. Who, for a moment, could declare that only those names and words which make the headlines or are repeated and revered in the home, sanctuary, classroom, or political and legislative arena, represent par excellence *the* forces of social and historical change? If the importance of personal speech, whether formal or informal, has any meaning for most of us, it should in the final analysis give each of us a confidence that somehow and in some degree our words can enable us to partake in the remaking of some portion, no matter how small, of the social fabric. For example, a major portion of Buber's writings during the last fifteen years of his life were devoted to practical social problems of particular interest to teachers, clergymen, and psychoanalysts. In this connection mention need only be made of his William Alanson White lectures, and his *Postscript* to the second edition of *I and Thou*. His thoughts in each of these areas centered on crucial problems of communication and relationship in situations where two souls are struggling with problems which affect the existence and destiny of individual souls. As such, these are matters of existential concern—of life and death, being and nonbeing—to those involved. Directly or indirectly, the consequences of these individual relationships may enable a person to participate more fully in the larger collective existential concerns which face him as a responsible member of society. For example, the possibility of something happening in the encounters between teacher and student, clergyman and layman, analyst and patient, may enable that individual to function creatively and make positive responses to the larger social questions which confront all of us today. Many of Buber's principles (though not his alone), have been successfully applied in a wide variety of social situations. They underlie, for example, the person-to-person approach of the South Bronx Neighborhood Service Centers in New York City, where the deprived in that area help one another in solving their common problems. Staffed by nonprofessionals who have been helped by others, the centers operate on the principle that in helping others, the helper is helped as much as the one being aided. Dr. Frank Riessman, one of the originators and supervisors of the project, attributes the success of these centers to an application of many of Buber's insights. His is but one of two hundred sixty-five groups, along with Synanon (for drug addicts) and Alcoholics Anonymous, which are listed in the directory, *Their Brother's Keepers*. In an article "The 'Helper' Therapy Principle" Riessman states, "while it may be uncertain that people receiving help are always benefitted, it seems more likely that the people *giving* help are profiting from their role."[26] Whether this particular point reflects more of Buber's or Rosenstock-Huessy's insights can be debated *ad nauseam*. Certainly, the latter's motto, "I respond *although* I will be changed," is as applicable here as is Buber's I-Thou principle.

On the basis of Riessman's experience it appears that an application of the helper therapy principle must accompany any proposed social service program irrespective of the sums of money or social legislation which might be made available. In such circumstances, personalist discourse is as vital and essential as is the more impersonal discourse of legislators and politicians. Not only that, but the personalist language of encounter is the only approach or tone which has proven effective in this setting. From Buber's standpoint, what Rosenstock-Huessy refers to as informal pronominal discourse is in this situation equivalent to the more formal and impersonal discourse in the political arena where one's presence as a *named* person is so essential. In situations such as these the real concern is not a matter of formal versus informal speech, but rather is a question of which rhetorical style is appropriate for the occasion. Many of the conflicts and disputes between advocates of Buber and Rosenstock-Huessy seem due, in part, to an insistence by one side or the other that their particular style is the only one appropriate for the situation. The South Bronx Neighborhood Service Center example not only illustrates the effectiveness of Buber's personalist approach, but also indicates the relevance of Rosenstock-Huessy's motto, "I respond *although* I will be changed" for this undertaking. In that particular situation, I feel certain that each man would have proceeded in the same manner, even though each would have viewed it as a reflection of his own principles rather than those of his opponent.

In conjunction with these remarks the reader is reminded that if such experiences as that of the Patmos circle meant anything to its members it confirmed their conviction that the unique style and background of each individual should be recognized for what it is and that no one should be expected to provide a mode of discourse valid for every person on every occasion. In this connection one is reminded of H. J. Paton's response to critics of *I and Thou* who found this poetic work totally lacking in systematic unity. His response was a plain one, "It is stupid to blame a man for not writing a different book from the one he has written or for not answering questions he has not chosen to ask."[27]

Throughout these chapters, both implicitly and explicitly, each speech thinker has acknowledged the validity of the doctrine of correlation, of the question and answer approach to life's ultimate concerns. The questions confronting us do so during particular periods when for one reason or another we are more preoccupied with one problem, with one aspect of our personality or society, or with one role, at the expense of others. In accordance with both Rosenzweig's and Rosenstock-Huessy's principles, *time* is the factor which determines which role and what style and tone shall be employed. Thus, it is quite possible, in fact essential, that we expect to be called upon to respond during various stages of life to different kinds of existential questions which call forth new and different responses from other sides of our personality. Another important consideration in this discussion is that due to our general temperament, or to use Buber's words, our "essential constitution," the style and quality of one man's words may speak to us more clearly than another's. Each of us has had the experience of listening to a speaker or reading a book and having a sense of instantaneous rapport. Similarly, words which spoke to us on one occasion at a particular period in life frequently lose their power at a later time under different circumstances. The word, the times, and the places give us our cue;

each response is a unique one. Hopefully, against this setting, one would find it necessary to take seriously both Buber and Rosenstock-Huessy's insights into the power of speech, despite the fact that at any one time one approach might be preferred over the other. The weighing of the merits of their insights must be always relative and considered against the manner in which the thought of each has spoken to the person charged with this task. Hence, any appraisal involves autobiographical considerations over and above knowledge of the essential elements of their writings. While some degree of distance and objectivity can be obtained with respect to the structure and substance of a person's writings, the ultimate evaluation should reflect the particular response, as well as the preference of the author and reader.

If it is true that the nature of the question confronting us determines the kind of response one makes, then the appropriate response is indeed the formal or correct one. We have just noted that in many situations Buber's and others' use of informal I-Thou language is the appropriate one and therefore formally the correct one. In most instances where this is so, it is equally apparent, however, that the speech of administrators, public officials, and legislators acting in their official or public capacity as *named* persons could do much to effect social changes which could alleviate those conditions which make intensely personalist forms of dialogue necessary. Naturally, this does not apply in every situation, but only in those circumstances where changing the social climate would directly affect the individual's lot. Suffice it to say that the leaders in our nation at every level of public responsibility are becoming increasingly aware of, if not troubled by, a sense of personal responsibility for helping to create a more truly human and free society. Gradually they are recognizing that from a religious or moral standpoint their public and formal words probably have more bearing, in a Hasidic and Johannine sense, upon the life of the Spirit than do their private utterances as fathers, or even as pillars of their local religious institutions. If public life is at least as important as private from a religious perspective, then indeed during most of our public life our names give meaning to our words. The test, in many cases, of sincerity is whether or not what was said, promised, or agreed upon privately and informally will, if necessary for its completion, be affirmed publicly and formally by an officeholder. Anyone familiar with politics at any level knows this to be true. In such circumstances the pronouns I and Thou lack the stature and force inherent in public pronouncements by a named official. And when one speaks publicly it usually means that we are identified by name as well as by role or office. This is equally true when we simply stand up in a PTA meeting, for example, and identify ourselves as I, so-and-so, father of so-and-so, a student in that school. The point here is that names normally link a person with some institution or person, in this last instance, for example, with another generation. Names are one of our most precious links with history. No matter what kind of informal speech may occur, it becomes formal, and in a real sense public, whether we speak as son, husband, father, or teacher, or as Congressman or President of the United States of America. Pronominal I-Thou discourse inevitably takes place within some context in which we not only participate as I or Thou but also as father, teacher, counselor, friend. In most instances one or more of our publicly identifiable roles provides the context and climate for whatever we say, whether formally or informally. Naturally, what we say to ourselves privately is conditioned by what has been said to us in one of our public roles. Not even death alters the fact that when a man dies his name is still a part of many people, and many institutions and organizations. Though the soul may be extinguished and the *I* no longer speak, the *name* still speaks and becomes a remembered portion of history.

In the light of Rosenstock-Huessy's differences with Buber, I suggest that informal pronominal speech does justice to but one limited dimension of named existence—namely, the personal. If this is so, then those concerned with the life of dialogue owe it to themselves to determine whether Buber's ontological sense of history does justice to historical named existence as developed by Rosenstock-Huessy. Their respective preferences for the personal as against the historical, for pronominal as against named speech and grammar, illustrate the truly deep and fundamental differences in their approaches to these problems. These are differences, however, which should concern not only students and disciples of these men, but all of those concerned with the nature of man, existentialism, hermeneutics, and certainly, social ethics. Whatever one's evaluation of this discussion, one negative conclusion is certain. Eugen Rosenstock-Huessy's thinking, though containing much which on first

reading sounds like Buber's I-Thou philosophy (or for those familiar with his writings, Martin Heidegger's), is hardly, in the final
analysis, to be identified with philosophical or religious existentialism.

Sacred Speech as the Shaper of History

MY OWN PREFERENCE for Rosenstock-Huessy's position in this discussion stems from a number of factors, many of which are purely
personal and would have little bearing upon this evaluation were
they enumerated. What is worth mentioning reflects a conviction
that men of faith everywhere must concern themselves more and
more with what I choose to call the rhetoric of history, and all that
this symbolizes for those who, like David and Jeremiah, accept the
fact which Rosenstock-Huessy put so well when he said that God
"is the power which makes us speak. He puts words of life on our
lips." The danger in identifying sacred speech with the purely personal is borne out in the self-centered lives of both Kierkegaard and
Ebner. This is a danger which is inherent in the very concept of the
religious life and also of religious institutions. It stems, in part, from
the fear of secular contamination, which is viewed as a threat by
those preoccupied with purity of heart, mind, soul, speech, and
Spirit. Individuals and institutions so oriented are never quite fully
able to look upon our diverse everyday modes of discourse as a form
of sacred witness.

The danger inherent in the writings of both Ebner and Kierkegaard was that they identified the sacred too exclusively with their
own personal *Anfechtung* at the expense of other forms of sacred
rhetorical concern. The only meaningful I for each man was the I of
faith. They were unable to recognize that the I of faith is multiform, rather than uniform. By that I mean that they identified their
names with a single posture, a single role, a single religious style. In
effect, they reduced and denigrated the spiritual life by their confusion of the pronoun I with the significance of their names.

Names, as was noted previously in Rosenstock-Huessy's discussion, are a blending of the sum total of at least four relationships, not
just one. As noted earlier, to be a person historically meant that

one wore many masks, played many roles, whether on the stage or in real life. For the term religion to have any positive meaning it would have to represent the harmony and unity which can be discovered when the entire grammar of our name is examined. This means that authentic spirituality encompasses more and is greater than the intensity, earnestness, and dedication with which one role is lived. Our names encompass more than a single role, posture, or a single rhetorical style tone. The metaphor, the name's grammar, is simply a way of doing justice to this fact. By virtue of our various roles we are social and historical creatures—*i.e.*, more than simply I's or Thous. Equally significantly, speech is the name's link with each of these dimensions of existence. With respect to this last point, the term speech as used here should not be viewed simply as that style and tone which we employ in each of our roles as if to suggest that we had complete control over our words. Rather I wish to convey the conviction that in many of our roles we are the instruments rather than the masters of speech. Certain roles demand that the personal I be subordinated—that personal volition and desire occasionally be set aside. When a teacher, judge, or legislator speaks, he does not represent only himself. Rather, a segment of society and a portion of history are being combined with his own personal judgment. In such circumstances the words actually spoken, if they do justice to the role, must reflect the fact that speech is not always entirely personal. Even that portion of a judgment which we refer to as ours (within the latitude possible on any given occasion) and which we regard as having some wisdom to it, usually reflects the insights of a number of our roles rather than just a single one, as well as an appropriation of our social and historical legacies.

Undoubtedly, the ambiguity and relativism which seemingly shrouds the notion of sacred discourse set within a Johannine context is too nebulous and ambiguous a setting for those accustomed to the assurances of doctrinal theological and moral absolutes. The absolute relativism occasioned by the rhetoric of history is still too great a leap for those accustomed to traditional forms of religious discourses. For such souls, religion and all that the term implies serves as a haven and refuge rather than as a tool for social and historical reconstruction. When history and society are of concern for such individuals they are frequently viewed as fields for religious witness and missionary endeavor. It was precisely this frame of mind which caused Dietrich Bonhoeffer to urge upon us that we discard the "religious *a priori*" wherein God is pictured as the *deus ex machina*. Unfortunately, most of us in the West have a religious mind-set, a mental and spiritual block which makes it difficult, if not impossible, for us to appreciate the fact that the Spirit, as Paul wrote to the Corinthians, speaks in diverse ways and tongues. We are undoubtedly approaching a time when the ostensible ultimate goals of religious concern may be best served and realized when we all cease acting and speaking either as religious people or in the name of religion. The phrase "rhetoric of history" does not contain or imply religious words or implications. It says nothing that is either for or against religion. It refers simply to a sacred appreciation and respect for speech, time, timing, and history. The context which produced this phrase is one filled, however, with appreciation for, and indebtedness to, a spiritual heritage which in most respects was as rich and traditional as one could possibly imagine. The implications of this concern for speech and history stem from a twofold but related conviction. The first assumption is that all that which we associate with the term religion will eventually be outmoded and obsolete in the interest of the Spirit. The second assumption reflects an acceptance of Bonhoeffer's reference to our time as a world come of age, and elsewhere, as a post-Christian age. It implies, however, a preference for the term history (which implies temporal considerations) as against the term world (which does not necessarily have temporal considerations). Moreover, the term history as used here suggests that the realm of the Spirit and, therefore, the domain of speech, of concerned rhetoric, is one which knows no boundaries, one which does not accept *a priori* any sacred-profane distinctions.

A Concluding Apologia

OUR EXCURSION INTO the domain of the life of dialogue and *speech-thinking* is near an end. A few concluding comments and observations are in order at this juncture. First, my apologies to those who have not had to travel the *religious* road and thus might have been bored by constant references to distinctions between religious language and sacramental speech. The laboring of this point is for a number of people a sign of the turbulent mood which has afflicted men of faith in all walks and conditions of life. On the other hand, many readers undoubtedly incorporate in their lives the principles of *speech-thinking* without ever reflecting seriously upon matters of faith and the Spirit. For this latter group a work of this type might serve to challenge the seeming irrelevance in their lives of spiritual concern and reflection. Such individuals might well wish to re-examine their avowed "secularism" or "atheism" in the light of the foregoing presentations. In the fields of theology and academia those familiar with the writings of men like Bonhoeffer, Tillich, Cox, and Bishop Robinson are certainly aware of the direction suggested by a work such as this. If we have moved beyond the writings of these men at all it is perhaps most evident in the absence of our lack of concern for retaining the term theology or theological discourse or theological apologetics of any sort. Along this line one wonders why, for example, men like Altizer, Hamilton, and Vahanian (the death-of-God theologians) are so preoccupied with a theological rationale for a position which inevitably must turn them away from theology and force them to pay attention to the potentially sacred role of the so-called secular disciplines—*i.e.*, the physical and social sciences, the humanities, jurisprudence, and as was alluded to in our first chapter, especially the communication arts and sciences.

Although our dialogicians and *speech-thinkers* antedate most of those involved in theological hermeneutics and radical or death-of-God theology, their concerns seem particularly relevant just at the point where the interest of death-of-God and hermeneutic theologians ends. Those in the theological disciplines closest to our concerns are perhaps men like professors Joseph Fletcher, Roger Shinn, and James Luther Adams, who are preoccupied with situational ethics and with the ambiguities inherent in a phrase like objective relativism. Hopefully, those familiar with Deweyan instrumentalism and with legal realism have some notion of the possibilities implicit in taking seriously the principles of *speech-thinking*. In another area, certainly the political writings of Reinhold Niebuhr and Walter Lippmann are examples of concerned historical rhetoric. In the field of jurisprudence the writings of Karl Llewellyn, Alf Ross, Harry W. Jones, and Charles Perelman provide us with other examples of approaches close to those involved in *speech-thinking*. In academic disciplines such as those just mentioned, *speech-thinking* is perhaps most at home as a method of problem solving capable of application in almost any area affected by social value considerations. However, as a method, these principles would have little force were one to discount the concern for history, time, timing, and intonation, which are of paramount interest to those whose thoughts have just been discussed. In this respect speech thinking goes beyond the heirs of John Dewey insofar as the lessons and tones of history are taken seriously.

Some of the richest areas for application of these insights undoubtedly lie quite outside the field of academia. In every conceivable walk of life there are those who know the meaning and possible consequences of a well-timed and intoned word. For most people, words, on one or more occasions, are a matter of life and death. But all too often it is difficult, if not impossible, for those same persons to regard such occasions as having any connection with spiritual or sacramental living. Hopefully, the writings of these men have extended the tonal as well as visual horizons of sacred concern. To know that time and our words can determine the shape of reality is an awesome insight but also a great privilege and comfort. Against the background of *speech-thinking* set within a Johannine context the future must be spoken into existence, history must be told, and we finite creatures must learn to discern the proper harmony which can exist amid the various sounds and tones which our fellowmen and history will identify with our names.

Having said this, we must also bear in mind the fact that there are many climates and cultures where concerns of this kind would fall on deaf ears. In many respects the themes dealt with here are recognizable primarily to those peoples and cultures which have been affected by the legacies or influences of Judaism and Christianity. Few realize, for example, that among some American Indian tribes there is no word or its equivalent for "time," or that Arab peoples "regard anyone who tries to look into the future as slightly insane. . . . To the Arab only God knows the future, and it is presumptious even to talk about it."[28] Although the author of these lines, Edward T. Hall, was directing his remarks against a kind of naïve American ethnocentrism, he nevertheless provides many of us with an awareness of the limitations which cloak our Western Jewish-Christian vocabulary. An awareness of our linguistic limitations can only help humble us when we attempt to generalize and assume a kind of universal rapport among all men on the essentials and principles of *speech-thinking.* At the same time let us remind ourselves that the life of dialogue requires an openness and availability on our part to the Thou over against us so that communication and therefore oneness among all men may be possible.

From a quite different perspective, all of those concerned with the life of dialogue and *speech-thinking* know the dangers and pitfalls in writing a book like this. Franz Rosenzweig knew this as well as anyone. In 1906 he jotted down the following lines:

> Better write   than read,
> Better write poetry than write,
> Better live   than write poetry![29]

In this same vein, the last line of *The Star of Redemption* concludes with the words "Into Life!"[30] In 1951 I was introduced to Martin Buber's writings and the life of dialogue through my friend and teacher, Fr. Caesarius Lauer, O.S.B., monk of the German Benedictine Abbey of Maria Laach. In that year he wrote a letter to Buber pointing up many of the dangers. He said:

> The *dialogue* about dialogue is growing on all sides. That should make one glad, but it disquiets me. For—if all the signs do not deceive —the talk about dialogue takes from men the living realization that is decisive, since it is working reality that means—Life. Now, the word certainly belongs to this realization, as Ebner has well shown. But just the word not words, not talk, logicizing dialectic. . . . It is just the *spiritual* man of today who suffers in a frightful fashion the old temptation of the human spirit, that is to say, that of objectifying the living accomplishment. . . . These *dialogical* dialecticians do not seem to notice that the dialogic is essentially a way. However, "the way is there that one may walk on it," as you once said.[31]

For men like Father Caesarius the life of dialogue is incompatible with any climate such as that found in the academic world, where third person or expository language is employed. More than anyone I know, he has attempted to pitch his ear, constantly waiting for the eternal Thou of address and encounter. When I left Maria Laach in the summer of 1952, Father Caesarius gave me a small photo of himself on the back of which he had written a well-known phrase of Cardinal Newman. These words seem equally appropriate and timely just now: "Heart speaks to heart; the heart of the Church is the Church of hearts." For many frail mortals this may also be the essence, in the very best and richest sense, of being truly a *Mensch!*

NOTES

CHAPTER 7

1 Paul Tillich, "The Conception of man in Existential Philosophy," *The Journal of Religion*, XIX (July 1939), p. 201.
2 Paul Tillich, *Theology of Culture*, (New York: Oxford University Press, 1959), pp. 56, 58.
3 Ernst Cassirer, *An Essay On Man* (New Haven: Yale University Press, 1944), p. 170.
4 Martin Heidegger, *Being and Time* (New York: Harper & Row, 1962), p. 56.
5 Cassirer, *op. cit.*, p. 111.
6 Walter Lowrie, *Søren Kierkegaard*, Volume II (New York: Harper & Row, 1962), p. 399.
7 Thomas Langan, *The Meaning of Heidegger* (New York: Columbia University Press, 1959), p. 101.
8 Nahum Glatzer, *Franz Rosenzweig*, p. 307.
9 *Ibid.*
10 Lowrie, *op. cit.*, Volume II, pp. 420–22.
11 Paul Tillich, *Systematic Theology*, Volume III (Chicago: University of Chicago Press, 1963), pp. 406–23.
12 Sydney and Beatrice Rome (editors), *Philosophical Interrogations* (New York: Holt, Rinehart and Winston, 1964), pp. 31–35.
13 *Ibid.*
14 *Ibid.*
15 Paul Tillich, *Theology of Culture* (New York: Oxford University Press, 1959), p. 198.
16 *Ibid.*, p. 199.
17 Walter J. Ong, *The Barbarian Within*, (New York: Macmillan, 1962), p. 178.
18 Walter J. Ong, *American Catholic Crossroads* (New York: Macmillan, 1959), p. 45.
19 Sydney and Beatrice Rome, *op. cit.*, p. 33.
20 *Ibid.*, pp. 33–34.
21 *Ibid.*, p. 34.

22 *Ibid.*, p. 35.
23 *Ibid.*
24 Carl Michalson, "The Boundary Between Faith and Reason: A Study of Hegel's *Glauben und Wissen*," *The Drew University Bulletin*, XXXIX, 4 (December 1951), pp. 7–8.
25 *Ibid.*, p. 9.
26 Frank Riessman, "The 'Helper' Therapy Principle," *Social Work* 10, 2 (April 1965).
27 H. J. Paton, *The Modern Predicament* (London: George Allen & Unwin, 1955), p. 172.
28 Edward T. Hall, *The Silent Language* (Greenwich: Premier Book, 1959), p. 11.
29 Franz Rosenzweig, Letter dated October 8, 1906. Cited in Glatzer, *op. cit.*, p. 14.
30 Franz Rosenzweig, *Der Stern der Erlösung*, (Heidelberg: Lambert Schneider, 1954), III, p. 211.
31 Maurice Friedman, *Martin Buber: The Life of Dialogue*, (New York: Harper & Brothers, 1955), pp. 271–72.

A Selective Bibliography

General Works on Language, Hermeneutics, and Related Themes

Auerbach, Eric. *Mimesis*. Garden City, N.Y., Doubleday, 1957.
Barr, James. *The Semantics of Biblical Language*. London, Oxford, 1961.
Boman, Thorleif. *Hebrew Thought Compared with Greek*. Philadelphia, Westminster, 1960.
Bowra, C. M. *Primitive Song*. New York, Mentor, 1963.
Bultmann, Rudolf. *Primitive Christianity*. New York, Living Age, 1956.
——. *Kerygma and Myth*. London, S.P.C.K., 1953.
Cassirer, Ernst. *Essay on Man*. New Haven, Yale, 1951.
——. *Theory of Symbolic Forms*, Volume One: *Language*. New Haven, Yale, 1953.
Clarke, M. L. *Rhetoric at Rome*. New York, Barnes & Noble, 1953.
Diamond, A. S. *The History and Origin of Language*. London, Methuen, 1959.
Dodds, C. R. *The Greeks and the Irrational*. Boston, Beacon Press, 1957.
Ebeling, Gerhard. *Word and Faith*. Philadelphia, Fortress Press, 1964.
Frankfort, Henri. *Before Philosophy*. Middlesex, Penguin, 1951.
Havelock, Eric. *Preface to Plato*. Cambridge, Belknap Press, 1963.
Heidegger, Martin. *Unterwegs zur Sprache*. Tübingen, H. Laupp, Jr., 1959.
Kennedy, George. *The Art of Persuasion in Greece*. Princeton, Princeton University Press, 1963.
Kraus, Karl. *Die Sprache*. München, Kösel, 1954.
Lord, Albert. *The Singer of Tales*. Cambridge, Harvard University Press, 1964.
Marrou, H. I. *A History of Education in Antiquity*. New York, Mentor, 1964.
McLuhan, Marshall. *The Gutenberg Galaxy*. Toronto, University of Toronto, 1962.
——. *Understanding Media*. New York, McGraw-Hill, 1965.

Muilenburg, James. *The Way of Israel.* New York, Harper Torchbooks, 1965.

Noack, Hermann. *Sprache und Offenbarung.* Gütersloh, Gerd Mohn, 1960.

Ong, Walter J., S.J. *In the Human Grain.* New York, Macmillan, 1967.

———. *The Barbarian Within.* New York, Macmillan, 1962.

Robinson, James M. and Cobb, John B., Jr. (Editors). *The New Hermeneutic.* New York, Harper & Row, 1964.

Wheelwright, Philip. *The Burning Fountain.* Bloomington, Indiana University, 1954.

Whitman, Cedric. *Homer and the Homeric Tradition.* Cambridge, Harvard University, 1963.

Wilder, Amos. *The Language of the Gospel.* New York, Harper & Row, 1964.

Willey, Basil. *The Seventeenth Century Background.* New York, Doubleday, 1953.

Wilson, R. A. *The Miraculous Birth of Language.* New York, Philosophical Library, 1948.

Johann Georg Hamann

Primary Sources:

Hamann, Johann Georg. *Sämtliche Werke.* 6 volumes, Historisch-kritische Ausgabe von Joseph Nadler. Vienna, Herder, 1949–53.

A complete list of primary and secondary material up to 1956 is contained in Volume One of Fritz Blanke and Lothar Schreiner (Editors), *Johann Georg Hamanns Hauptschriften Erklärt,* (Gütersloh, Carl Bertelsmann, 1956). There are six additional volumes in this series which discuss critically Hamann's writings. Those secondary works listed have been selected either for their availability and scholarly contribution or because of their appearance subsequent to 1956.

Secondary Works:

Gregor Smith, Ronald. *J. G. Hamann: A Study in Christian Existence.* London, Collins, 1960.

Hamilton, W. M. *Johann Georg Hamann: Philosophy and Faith.* The Hague, Martinus Nijhoff, 1966.

———. "J. G. Hamann: Metacritic of Kant." *Journal of the History of Ideas,* XXVII, (Jan.–March 1966).

Knoll, Renate. *Johann Georg Hamann und Friedrich Heinrich Jacobi.* Heidelberg, Carl Winter, 1963.

Leibrecht, Walter. *God and Man in the Thought of Hamann.* Philadelphia, Fortress, 1966.

Lowrie, Walter. *Johann Georg Hamann: An Existentialist.* Princeton, Princeton University, 1950.

Merlan, Philip. "From Hume to Hamann." *The Personalist*, XXXII, 1 (Winter 1951).

O'Flaherty, James. *Unity and Language: A Study in the Philosophy of Johann Georg Hamann.* Chapel Hill, University of North Carolina, 1952.

Pascal, Roy. *The German Sturm und Drang.* Manchester, Manchester University, 1959.

Eugen Rosenstock-Huessy

Primary Sources:

A complete bibliography of Rosenstock-Huessy's writings between 1910 and 1958 is contained in Eugen Rosenstock-Huessy, *Bibliography/Biography* (New York, Four Wells, 1959). The following is a partial list of his principal works which are currently available, as well as his publications subsequent to 1958.

Rosenstock-Huessy, Eugen. "Rückblick auf 'die Kreatur.'" *Deutsche Beiträge*, Arnold Bergstrasser (Editor). Chicago, University of Chicago, 1947.

———. *The Multiformity of Man.* Norwich, Vermont, Beachhead, 1949.

———. *The Driving Power of Western Civilization.* Boston, Beacon, 1950.

———. *Soziologie*, Volumes I & II. Stuttgart, Kohlhammer, 1956–57.

———. *Zurück in das Wagnis der Sprache.* Berlin, Käthe Vogt, 1957.

———. *Das Geheimnis der Universität.* Stuttgart, Kohlhammer, 1958.

———. *Die Sprache des Menschengeschlects*, Volumes I & II. Heidelberg, Lambert Schneider, 1963–64.

———. *Out of Revolution.* New York, Four Wells, 1964.

———. *The Christian Future or The Modern Mind Outrun.* New York, Harper Torchbook, 1966.

———. *Judaism Despite Christianity.* (To be published by the University of Alabama Press in 1968.) This work will contain the 1916 correspondence between Rosenstock-Huessy and Franz Rosenzweig on "Judaism and Christianity," as well as several related essays by Rosenstock-Huessy.

Secondary Works:

Leibholz, Sabine. "Eugen Rosenstock-Huessy and Dietrich Bonhoffer— Two Witnesses to the Change in our Time." *Universitas*, Volume 8, 3 (1966).

Müller, Georg. "Von der Bedeutung der Philosophie für die Weltorientierung der Theologen." *Evangelische Theologie*, Heft 9 (März 1953).

———. "Der Sprachdenker Eugen Rosenstock-Huessy." *Evangelische Theologie*, Heft 7/8 (July–August 1954).

———. "Vom Stern der Erlösung zum Kreuz der Wirklichkeit." *Junge Kirche: Protestantische Monatshefte* (1956).

———. "Zum Problem der Sprache." *Kerygma und Dogma*, 2 Jahrgang, Heft 2 (April 1956).

———. "Religionsphilosophie und Heilsgeschichte." *Zeitwende: die neue Furche*, 28 Jahrgang, Heft 10 (Oktober 1957).

———. "Eugen Rosenstock-Huessy und Nikolai Berdjaev." *Kyrios*, Neue Folge, VI, Heft 3 (1966).

Müller-Ganghoff, Erich. "Ein drittes Volk Gottes?" *Quatember: Evangelische Jahresbrief* (1956).

Smith, Page. *The Historian and History*. New York, Alfred Knopf, 1964.

von der Gablentz, Von Ottoheinz. "Die Krisis der Säkularen Religionen." *Kosmos und Ekklesia*. Kassel, Johannes Stauda, 1953.

Franz Rosenzweig

Primary Sources:

Rosenzweig, Franz. *The Star of Redemption*. New York, Holt, Rinehart and Winston. Scheduled to appear sometime in 1968. Original German edition (Frankfurt am Main: J. Kauffmann, 1921).

———. *Briefe*. Berlin, Schocken, 1935.

———. *Kleinere Schriften*. Berlin, Schocken, 1937.

———. *Understanding the Sick and the Healthy*. New York, Noonday, 1953.

———. *On Jewish Learning*. New York, Schocken, 1965.

———. "The Way Through Time: Christian History." David W. McKain (Editor), *Christianity: Some Non-Christian Appraisals*. New York, McGraw-Hill, 1964.

Secondary Works:

Glatzer, Nahum. *Franz Rosenzweig: His Life and Thought*. New York, Schocken, 1953. (This is the best introduction to Rosenzweig's thought by way of excerpts from his writings. The work also contains a complete bibliography of his writings, together with a selected bibliography of secondary material.)

Agus, Jacob. "The Life and Influence of Franz Rosenzweig." *Modern Philosophies of Judaism*. New York, Behrman's, 1941.

Altmann, Alexander. "Franz Rosenzweig on History." Altmann

(Editor), *Between East and West*. London, East and West Library, 1958.

Bergman, Samuel Hugo. *Faith and Reason: An Introduction to Modern Jewish Thought*. New York, Schocken, 1961.

Cohen, Arthur A. *The Natural and the Supernatural Jew*. New York, Pantheon, 1962.

Cohen, Carl. "Franz Rosenzweig." *Conservative Judaism*, III, 1 (1951).

Efros, Israel. "Rosenzweig's Star of Redemption." *Jewish Quarterly Review*, XXVII, 1 (1936).

Freund, Else. *Die Existenzphilosophie Franz Rosenzweigs*. Hamburg, Felix Meiner, 1959.

Glatzer, Nahum. "Franz Rosenzweig." *Yivo Annual of Jewish Social Science*, 1 (1946).

Herberg, Will. "Rosenzweig's Judaism of Personal Existence." *Commentary*, X (1950).

Horwitz, Rivka. "Franz Rosenzweig on Language." *Judaism*, 13, 4 (Fall 1964).

Lichtigfeld, A. "Franz Rosenzweig." *Philosophy and Revelation*. London, M. L. Cailingold, 1937.

Löwith, Karl. "Martin Heidegger and Franz Rosenzweig or Temporality and Eternity." *Philosophy and Phenomenological Research*, III, 1 (1942).

Maybaum, Ignaz. "Franz Rosenzweig's Life and Work." The Chief Rabbi's Festival Volume, London, 1944.

Franz Rosenzweig and Eugen Rosenstock-Huessy: Their Correspondence on Judaism and Christianity

Rosenstock-Huessy, Eugen. *Judaism Despite Christianity*. Alabama, University of Alabama, 1968.

Rosenzweig, Franz. *Briefe*. Berlin, Schocken, 1935, pp. 637–720.

Altmann, Alexander. "Franz Rosenzweig and Eugen Rosenstock-Huessy: An Introduction to their Letters on Judaism and Christianity." *The Journal of Religion*, XXIV, 4 (October 1944).

Altmann, Alexander. "Franz Rosenzweig on History." Altmann (Editor), *Between East and West*. London, East and West Library, 1958.

Emmett, Dorothy. "The Letters of Franz Rosenzweig and Eugen Rosenstock-Huessy." *The Journal of Religion*, XXV, 4 (October 1945).

Horwitz, Rivka. "Franz Rosenzweig on Language." *Judaism*, 13, 4 (Fall 1964).

Schwarzschild, Steven S. "Rosenzweig on Judaism and Christianity." *Conservative Judaism*, XI (1956).

Martin Buber

Primary Sources:

Buber, Martin. *Tales of the Hasidim*, 2 Volumes. New York, Schocken, 1947–48.
——. *Israel and the World*. New York, Schocken, 1948.
——. *Good and Evil*. New York, Scribner's, 1953.
——. *Eclipse of God*. New York, Harper Torchbook, 1957.
——. *Pointing the Way*. New York, Harper Torchbook, 1957.
——. *I and Thou*, Second Edition. New York, Scribner's, 1958.
——. *Two Types of Faith*. New York, Harper Torchbook, 1961.
——. *Between Man and Man*. New York, Macmillan, 1965.
——. *Daniel*. New York, McGraw-Hill (Paperback), 1965.
——. *Hasidism and Modern Man*. New York, Harper Torchbook, 1966.
——. *Origin and Meaning of Hasidism*. New York, Harper Torchbook, 1966.
——. *The Prophetic Faith*. New York, Harper Torchbook, 1966.
——. *The Knowledge of Man*. New York, Harper Torchbook, 1966.
Buber, Martin and Rosenzweig, Franz. *Die Schrift und ihre Verdeutschung*. Berlin, Schocken, 1936.
Glatzer, Nahum (Editor). *The Way of Response: Martin Buber; Selections from his Writings*. New York, Schocken, 1966.
Herberg, Will (Editor). *The Writings of Martin Buber*. New York, Meridian, 1956.

Secondary Works:

The following works contain nearly complete bibliographies of Buber's writings. No complete bibliography of secondary material published since 1960 is available. Exhaustive references to Buber's writings and works about Buber prior to 1960 are contained in Maurice Friedman's *Martin Buber: The Life of Dialogue* (New York, Harper Torchbook, 1960). Cf. also:

Kohn, Hans. *Martin Buber: Sein Werk und seine Zeit—Ein Beitrag zur geistesgeschichte Mitteleuropas* 1880–1930. Nachtwort: 1930–60 Robert Weltsch. Köln, Joseph Melzer, 1961.
Schlipp, Paul Arthur and Friedman, Maurice (Editors). *The Philosophy of Martin Buber*. Volume of *The Library of the Living Philosophers*. LaSalle, Illinois, Open Court, 1967.

The following selected works in English treat various aspects of Buber's thought:

Cohen, Arthur A. *Martin Buber.* New York, Hillary House, 1957.
Diamond, Malcolm M. *Martin Buber: Jewish Existentialist.* New York, Oxford, 1960.
Pfeutze, Paul. *Self, Society, Existence.* New York, Harper Torchbook, 1961.
Rome, Sydney and Beatrice (Editors). *Philosophical Interrogations.* New York, Holt, Rinehart and Winston, 1964.
von Balthasar, Hans Urs. *Martin Buber and Christianity.* New York, Macmillan, 1960.

Ferdinand Ebner

Primary Sources:

Ebner, Ferdinand. *Schriften.* 3 volumes, edited by Franz Seyr. München, Kösel-Verlag, 1963–64.
    Volume One— *Fragmente, Aufsätze, Aphorismen*
    Volume Two—*Notizen, Tagebücher, Lebenserinnerungen*
    Volume Three—*Briefe*
——. *Wort und Liebe.* Regensburg, Friedrich Pustet, 1935.
——. *Das Wort ist der Weg.* Edited and with an Introduction by Hildegard Jone. Vienna, Thomas-Morus, 1949.

Secondary Works:

Brunner, Emil. *Man in Revolt.* London, Lutterworth, 1947.
Buber, Martin. *Between Man and Man.* New York, Macmillan, 1965.
    (Note the "Afterword" by Martin Buber.)
Cullberg, John. *Das Du und die Wirklichkeit.* Uppsala, Uppsala University, 1933.
Friedman, Maurice (Editor). *The Worlds of Existentialism.* New York, Random House, 1964.
Langemeyer, Bernhard. *Der dialogische Personalismus.* Paderborn, Bonifacius, 1963.
Nachrichten aus dem Kösel-Verlag, " 'Der Brenner'—Leben und Fortleben einer Zeitschrift." München, Kösel-Verlag, 1965.
Sandmann, Peter. *Das Weltproblem bei Ferdinand Ebner.* Freisung, Kyrios, 1962.
Schleiermacher, Theodor. *Das Heil des Menschen und sein Traum vom Geist.* Berlin, Alfred Töpelmann, 1962.
Steinbüchel, Theodor. *Der Umbruch des Denkens.* Regensburg, Friedrich Pustet, 1936.

Index

Index

Index

303